Classic Readings in Cultural Anthropology

SECOND EDITION

GARY FERRARO
The University of North Carolina at Charlotte

D0770232

WADSWORTH
CENGAGE Learning

Australia • Brazil • Japan • Korea • Mexico • Singapore • Spain • United Kingdom • United States

WADSWORTH
CENGAGE Learning

Classic Readings in Cultural Anthropology, Second Edition

Gary Ferraro

Anthropology Editor: Lin Marshall Gaylord

Editorial Assistant: Paige Leeds

Marketing Manager: Meghan Pease

Marketing Assistant: Mary Anne Payumo

Marketing Communications Manager: Tami Strang

Project Manager, Editorial Production: Jerilyn Emori

Creative Director: Rob Hugel

Art Director: Caryl Gorska

Print Buyer: Linda Hsu

Permissions Editor: Scott Bragg

Production Service: Smitha Pillai, Newgen

Cover Designer: Bartay Studio

Cover Image: © Leong Ka Tai

Compositor: Newgen

For product information and technology assistance, contact us at **Cengage Learning Customer & Sales Support, 1-800-354-9706.**

For permission to use material from this text or product, submit all requests online at **cengage.com/permissions.** Further permissions questions can be e-mailed to **permissionrequest@cengage.com.**

Library of Congress Control Number: 2007943305

ISBN-13: 978-0-495-50736-9

ISBN-10: 0-495-50736-9

Cengage Learning is a leading provider of customized learning solutions with office locations around the globe, including Singapore, the United Kingdom, Australia, Mexico, Brazil, and Japan. Locate your local office at **international.cengage.com/region.**

Cengage Learning products are represented in Canada by Nelson Education, Ltd.

For your course and learning solutions, visit **academic.cengage.com.**

Purchase any of our products at your local college store or at our preferred online store **www.ichapters.com.**

Printed in Canada
2 3 4 5 6 7 12 11 10 09

Contents

Preface

Cultural anthropologists have estimated that there are more than five thousand different cultures in the world today that speak mutually unintelligible languages. With such enormous linguistic and cultural variability in the world, it is virtually impossible to become conversant with *all* of the details of *all* of these different cultures. Thus, by necessity, the study of cultural anthropology at the introductory level needs to take a more conceptual approach. Beginning students, in other words, are exposed typically to certain core ideas, which provide a conceptual framework for studying comparative cultures. Introductory textbooks, for example, are organized around such chapters as marriage and family, which, in turn, cover such key concepts as polygyny, levirate, arranged marriages, sororate, cross-cousin marriage, and bridewealth. These central concepts are defined and illustrated with ethnographic data from around the world.

Admittedly introductory textbooks in cultural anthropology take a broad-brush approach to a vast subject matter. The emphasis, by necessity, is to expose beginning students to the enormity of cultural variability, while at the same time allowing them to see universal similarities among the cultures of the world. This general approach to studying other cultures, however, can be enhanced by supplemental readings, which permit the student to explore some areas of the subject matter in greater depth. It is with this idea of "post holing" in mind that *Classic Readings in Cultural Anthropology* was conceived.

This reader was carefully designed to include those articles and segments from books that best represent the discipline over the course of the past century. These readings were not selected because they represent the most recent research and cutting-edge thinking of twenty-first-century scholars. Rather, they represent writings that have been assigned to introductory students by their professors for the past sixty-plus years. While being eminently relevant for cultural anthropology today, these selections have endured the decades to become classics in the field. As one anthropologist has put it, these readings are the "gold standard" for modern cultural anthropology.

The readings found in *Classic Readings in Cultural Anthropology* were selected after consulting with a number of cultural anthropologists, including some leading authors of introductory textbooks. Included are pieces dating back as early as 1937 (Evans-Pritchard's study of witchcraft among the Azande) and as recently as 2005 (McFate's piece on anthropology and counterinsurgency). It should be pointed out that selections were not excluded because they contain terminology that is considered politically incorrect today. In some of the earlier writings, for example, we will see such terms as *man* used to refer generically to humans or the use of the term *Eskimo* instead of the more current term *Inuit*. Nevertheless, the use of these outdated terms (which were not politically incorrect at the time they were written) does not invalidate the relevance of these writings for contemporary cultural anthropology.

Classic Readings in Cultural Anthropology is organized according to the major categories found in most introductory courses of cultural anthropology. These include perspectives on culture, language and communication, economics and ecology, marriage and family, gender, politics and social control, supernatural belief systems, and issues of culture change. The timeless "Body Ritual Among the Nacirema" is as relevant today as it was when it was written by Horace Miner more than a half century ago, for it forces us to confront our own ethnocentrism. George Gmelch reminds us that despite the fact that Americans view themselves as highly rational, scientific, and objective, they often rely on supernatural forces (such as rituals, taboos, and fetishes) to bring about desired outcomes. And Lauriston Sharp's piece on the Yir Yoront remains today (more than five decades after it was written) a vivid example of the principle of the functional interconnectedness of the parts of culture.

There are five new selections in this second edition of *Classic Readings*. In order to remind us of the importance of nonverbal communication, an article by Edward and Mildred Hall, titled "The Sounds of Silence," deals with the many ways that humans in all cultures send and receive messages without using words. Gerald Murray's description of his applied work as the head of a reforestation project in Haiti during the 1980s serves as an excellent example of the relevance of applied anthropology. Cultural anthropologist Serena Nanda's selection is a very personal account of how she not only overcame her initial skepticism of arranged marriages in India, but actually found herself helping some of her Indian friends arrange marriages for their adult children. Montgomery McFate explores the curious (and controversial) relationship between cultural anthropology and the military/national-security establishment over the course of the past hundred years, and makes a strong plea for more anthropological input into the conduct of the military/political struggles in contemporary Iraq and Afghanistan. And finally, Angelique Haugerud argues convincingly that, when viewed from the perspective of cultural anthropology, the writings of *New York Times* columnist Thomas Friedman, a major pundit on globalization, are overly simplistic and ideologically distorted.

The reader contains a number of pedagogical features designed to help the beginning student learn the content of cultural anthropology more efficiently. First, each reading is preceded by a brief introduction, which helps the reader better understand both the article's relevance and context. Second, a series of "Discussion Questions" at the end of each piece serves not only as a check on understanding, but also as a means to stimulate lively class discussions and encourage the reader to make connections to their everyday lives. Third, a "Resources on the Internet" section follows the discussion questions and enables students to access recent information related to each article.

The purpose of this reader is to provide beginning students of cultural anthropology with a set of readings that have stood the test of time. To ensure that this selection of readings meets your needs as both students and instructors, I encourage you to send me your thoughts on how we can improve upon this volume. Please send your comments to me at gpferrar@uncc.edu.

Gary Ferraro
The University of North Carolina at Charlotte

Introduction

In a recent article in the *Anthropology Newsletter*, anthropologists Elizabeth Bird and Carolena Von Trapp report on a nonscientific survey they conducted among one hundred undergraduates who had never taken a course in anthropology. Many of the common stereotypes about anthropology were confirmed. The majority of respondents associated the discipline with stones and bones exclusively; very few could cite the name of a real anthropologist other than the fictional Indiana Jones; and the image of the anthropologist that emerged was a person who was drab, eccentric, elderly, bookish, unbusiness-like, disheveled, wears shabby clothes, and has very little to do with anything outside of academia. All of these impressions are misleading stereotypes, which do nothing but obscure the nature of the discipline and its relevance beyond academia.

Of all of the social sciences, anthropology is the most broadly defined. Some anthropologists do, in fact, deal primarily with stones and bones. One branch of anthropology *(archaeology)* searches for artifacts and other cultural remains of people who lived in the distant past. The subfield of *physical anthropology* unearths fossil remains for the purpose of reconstructing the human evolutionary record. Yet, there are other anthropologists *(cultural anthropologists* and *linguists)* whose focus is on live, warm bodies (i.e., living cultures). Even though these different branches of anthropology have different research agendas, they are all directed at a single purpose: the scientific study of humans, both biologically and culturally, wherever and whenever they may be found. This volume deals only with cultural anthropology, defined most simply as the comparative study of contemporary peoples throughout the world.

Even cultural anthropology, when contrasted with other social sciences, tends to be a wide-ranging discipline. Political scientists focus on power relationships among a group of people. Economists confine their studies to how people produce, distribute, and consume goods and services. Sociologists concentrate on social interaction as their major theoretical construct. Cultural anthropologists, on the other hand, do not limit themselves to a single domain of activity.

Rather, by focusing on the concept of culture, cultural anthropologists look at *all* aspects of behavior, attitudes, beliefs, and material possessions. This comprehensive perspective on the study of human behavior makes cultural anthropology particularly effective at helping us better understand people different from ourselves.

What do we mean by the term *culture?* Although we all think we know what culture is, anthropologists have a considerably different definition than the one popularly held. In everyday usage, the term *culture* refers to the finer things in life, such refinements as symphonies, great works of art, and fine wines. In other words, the so-called cultured person prefers Bach to Britney Spears, spends time at art openings rather than at the NASCAR track, and drinks expensive French champagne rather than Bud Light. Cultural anthropologists, however, define the term *culture* much more broadly to include the total life ways of a group of people. This anthropological definition of culture involves much more than playing cello in a string quartet or eating pheasant under glass. For the anthropologist, a culture encompasses all aspects of a group's behavior, attitudes, beliefs, and material possessions—both the artistic and the mundane. Shaking hands, brushing one's teeth, visiting Aunt Maude, or eating a hot dog are all part of the widely defined anthropological definition of the term *culture.*

But what is it that enables the discipline of cultural anthropology to so effectively reveal human nature? To be certain, cultural anthropologists over the past century have adhered to certain guiding principles, which have distinguished them from other social scientists. First, anthropologists take a highly comparative approach by examining cultural similarities and differences throughout the world. Such an approach serves as a valuable corrective against the pitfall of explaining all human behavior in terms of one's own culture. A case in point is the revision of a prominent psychological theory in the early twentieth century in light of comparative, cross-cultural data from Melanesia. Bronislaw Malinowski, one of the founders of modern anthropology, spent four years of uninterrupted fieldwork among the Trobriand Islanders of the Pacific between 1914 and 1918. At the time, a widely held theory of psychotherapy was the Oedipus Complex, in which Sigmund Freud explained the social/psychological tension between fathers and sons as the result of sexual jealousy over the mother. Freud reasoned that, since all males have an innate desire to have sexual relations with their mother, they are jealous of their fathers, who, in fact, do have such sexual relations.

However, Malinowski's research among the matrilineal Trobrianders revealed no social or psychological tension between a man and his biological father, as was common in western Europe where Freud made his observations. The Trobriand Islanders made the distinction between a man's *biological* father (who actually impregnated the mother) and his *social* father (who is actually the man's maternal uncle). Malinowski found that in Trobriand society there was considerable tension with the social father (the man actually responsible for his upbringing) and little or no tension with the biological father, who was more like an older brother. Clearly everyone understood that it was the biological father who slept with the mother to produce the child. Malinowski concluded that the tension between fathers and sons observed by Freud in Europe was in fact the result of authority rather than sexual jealousy, and as a result, the so-called Oedipus Complex was a culture-bound explanation of human behavior. Here, then, is an example of how the broad, comparative approach of cultural anthropology served as a check against an oversimplified explanation of human behavior based solely on evidence from one's own culture.

A second principle that has guided cultural anthropology over the past hundred years has been firsthand observation and inquiry. Many social scientists rely primarily on secondary data such as census data or survey information collected from respondents with whom the scientists never have any face-to-face contact. Cultural anthropologists, by way of contrast, rely on participant observation to a greater extent than any other single data-gathering technique. As its name implies, participant observation involves living in the culture under study while at the same time making systematic observations about it. By engaging in participant observation, cultural anthropologists share in the everyday activities of the local people while making detailed observations of people working, playing, eating, talking, trading, educating, or any other cultural activity. The methodological advantages of hands-on research should be obvious. Since most people appreciate any attempt from outsiders to at least try to live according to their culture, participant observation will, in most cases, improve both rapport and the quality of the data received. Moreover, firsthand research allows the anthropologist to distinguish between what people actually do and what they say they do. Participant-observers, in other words, have the advantage of observing actual behavior rather than relying on hearsay.

Perhaps the single-most important feature that cultural anthropologists bring to the study of other cultures is the insistence upon viewing a foreign cultural object within its proper *cultural context*. Whenever people encounter a foreign cultural item (such as an idea, a material object, or a behavior pattern), the usual tendency is to make sense of it in terms of their own cultural assumptions. They generally ask themselves the question: how does this foreign idea or thing fit into my culture? Of course, since it is not part of their culture, there is absolutely no reason why it should fit in. There is, in other words, nothing in their own culture that would tend to support that particular cultural item. If you really want to understand why this particular idea or thing is part of that foreign culture, it must be examined in terms of that culture, rather than your own.

Perhaps an example would help. Most middle-class North Americans, men and women alike, see no sense in the practice of polygyny (a man having more than one wife at a time). They see it as nonsensical, or worse yet, downright immoral and illegal. And, viewed from the perspective of their own cultural assumptions, they would be right. There is very little in our culture that would support or reinforce the practice of polygyny. In fact, there are many parts of our culture that would be in direct conflict with polygyny, such as our legal system and the norms of Christian churches. Even our economic system is at odds with polygyny, because, in a cash economy such as our own, it makes no economic sense whatsoever to have large numbers of wives and large numbers of children.

However, if we view polygyny from its original cultural context—let us say from the cultural perspective of an East African mixed farming community—it makes a good deal of sense. In fact, given all of the other parts of *that* culture, polygyny is the most logical form of marriage imaginable. First, there is nothing illegal about having more than one wife at a time in East Africa. Second, their traditional agricultural system encourages men to take more than one wife to maximize the size of the family. Unlike in the United States where large families are economically irrational, in East Africa the more family members there are to cultivate crops, the better off the entire group will be. Third, the system of social prestige in East Africa is based on the number of wives and overall family size, not material wealth as is the case in our own society. Even women in traditional African societies, wanting to be part of a high-status household, supported their husbands' efforts to take additional wives. And, finally, the practice of polygyny is supported in many East African societies by the traditional religious practice of ancestor worship. Since men are often elevated to the status of ancestor-god upon death, it is only logical that men would want to have large families so they will have large numbers of people worshiping them after they die. A man with one wife and one child would have only a "congregation" of two people!

Thus, cultural anthropology teaches us that if we view a foreign cultural item through our own cultural lens, it is not likely to make much sense. When polygyny is wrenched from its original cultural context in East Africa, there is no way that it can seem rational. The best way to truly understand an item from another culture is to view it from within its proper cultural content. No one is asking you to practice a foreign cultural norm (such as polygyny). In fact, you are not even required to like it. But, if you want to understand the inherent logic of why people in another culture think and behave the way they do (which is the primary objective of the discipline of cultural anthropology), then it is imperative that you follow the lead of cultural anthropology, which from its beginnings has insisted on analyzing the parts of different cultures within their original contexts.

1

Body Ritual among the Nacirema

HORACE MINER

Since the early decades of the twentieth century, Western anthropologists have concentrated their research on small-scale, technologically simple societies outside of Europe and North America. In that same tradition, Horace Miner, a former professor of sociology and anthropology at the University of Michigan, wrote a piece for the American Anthropologist, in 1956 about an exotic people called the Nacirema, whose central belief is that their susceptibility to disease and ill health can only be averted by engaging in a wide range of rituals and magical practices. Miner's elegant description of this highly ritualistic culture provides what at first glance would be a classic example of an exotic non-Western culture. But as you get further into this article—which is probably the most widely reproduced article in twentieth-century anthropology—you get the feeling that it sounds a little too familiar.

Unlike Miner himself, the editor of this reader will not try to obscure the true identity of the Nacirema, who, Miner tells us, "live between the Canadian Cree, the Yaqui and Tarahumare of Mexico, and the Carib and Arawak of the Antilles." The Nacirema, of course, are us—middle-class residents of the United States. The name Nacirema is American spelled backwards.

The significance of this first selection, and no doubt the reasons for its enormous popularity among anthropologists, is that it forces us to confront our own ethnocentrism. That is, we tend to view other, non-Western societies as filled with ritual, while automatically assuming that our own behavior is based totally on rational thought. The reason that first-time American readers fail to recognize themselves as Nacirema is because they have never applied such terms as ritual or superstition to their own, everyday, mundane behavior. Their ethnocentrism, in other words, prevents them from seeing their own culture as anything other than normal and natural. But Miner's article, now nearly a half century old, forces us to confront our biases when trying to understand our own culture in relation to others.

The anthropologist has become so familiar with the diversity of ways in which different peoples behave in similar situations that he is not apt to be surprised by even the most exotic customs. In fact, if all of the logically possible combinations of behavior have not been found somewhere in the world, he is apt to suspect that they must be present in some yet undescribed tribe. This point has, in

SOURCE: From "Body Ritual among the Nacirema" by Horace Miner in the *American Anthropologist*, 58(3): 503–507, 1956. Reprinted with permission from the American Anthropological Association.

fact, been expressed with respect to clan organization by Murdock (1949: 71). In this light, the magical beliefs and practices of the Nacirema present such unusual aspects that it seems desirable to describe them as an example of the extremes to which human behavior can go.

Professor Linton first brought the ritual of the Nacirema to the attention of anthropologists twenty years ago (1936: 326), but the culture of this people is still very poorly understood. They are a North American group living in the territory between the Canadian Cree, the Yaqui and Tarahumare of Mexico, and the Carib and Arawak of the Antilles. Little is known of their origin, though tradition states that they came from the east. According to Nacirema mythology, their nation was originated by a culture hero, Notgnishaw, who is otherwise known for two great feats of strength—the throwing of a piece of wampum across the river Pa-To-Mac and the chopping down of a cherry tree in which the Spirit of Truth resided.

Nacirema culture is characterized by a highly developed market economy which has evolved in a rich natural habitat. While much of the people's time is devoted to economic pursuits, a large part of the fruits of these labors and a considerable portion of the day are spent in ritual activity. The focus of this activity is the human body, the appearance and health of which loom as a dominant concern in the ethos of the people. While such a concern is certainly not unusual, its ceremonial aspects and associated philosophy are unique.

The fundamental belief underlying the whole system appears to be that the human body is ugly and that its natural tendency is to debility and disease. Incarcerated in such a body, man's only hope is to avert these characteristics through the use of the powerful influences of ritual and ceremony. Every household has one or more shrines devoted to this purpose. The more powerful individuals in the society have several shrines in their houses and, in fact, the opulence of a house is often referred to in terms of the number of such ritual centers it possesses. Most houses are of wattle and daub construction, but the shrine rooms of the more wealthy are walled with stone. Poorer families imitate the rich by applying pottery plaques to their shrine walls.

While each family has at least one such shrine, the rituals associated with it are not family ceremonies but are private and secret. The rites are normally only discussed with children, and then only during the period when they are being initiated into these mysteries. I was able, however, to establish sufficient rapport with the natives to examine these shrines and to have the rituals described to me.

The focal point of the shrine is a box or chest which is built into the wall. In this chest are kept the many charms and magical potions without which no native believes he could live. These preparations are secured from a variety of specialized practitioners. The most powerful of these are the medicine men, whose assistance must be rewarded with substantial gifts. However, the medicine men do not provide the curative potions for their clients, but decide what the ingredients should be and then write them down in an ancient and secret language. This writing is understood only by the medicine men and by the herbalists who, for another gift, provide the required charm.

The charm is not disposed of after it has served its purpose, but is placed in the charm-box of the household shrine. As these magical materials are specific for certain ills, and the real or imagined maladies of the people are many, the charm-box is usually full to overflowing. The magical packets are so numerous that people forget what their purposes were and fear to use them again. While the natives are very vague on this point, we can only assume that the idea in retaining all the old magical materials is that their presence in the charm-box, before which the body rituals are conducted, will in some way protect the worshipper.

Beneath the charm-box is a small font. Each day every member of the family, in succession, enters the shrine room, bows his head before the charm-box, mingles different sorts of holy water in the font, and proceeds with a brief rite of ablution. The holy waters are secured from the Water Temple of the community, where the priests conduct elaborate ceremonies to make the liquid ritually pure.

In the hierarchy of magical practitioners, and below the medicine men in prestige, are specialists whose designation is best translated "holy-mouth-men." The Nacirema have an almost pathological horror and fascination with the mouth, the condition of which is believed to have a supernatural influence on all social relationships. Were it not for the rituals of the mouth, they believe that their teeth would fall out, their gums bleed, their jaws shrink, their friends desert them, and their lovers reject them. (They also believe that a strong relationship exists between oral and moral characteristics. For example, there is a ritual ablution of the mouth for children, which is supposed to improve their moral fiber.)

The daily body ritual performed by everyone includes a mouth-rite. Despite the fact that these people are so punctilious about care of the mouth, this rite involves a practice which strikes the uninitiated stranger as revolting. It was reported to me that the ritual consists of inserting a small bundle of hog hairs into the mouth, along with certain magical powders, and then moving the bundle in a highly formalized series of gestures.

In addition to the private mouth-rite, the people seek out a holy-mouth-man once or twice a year. These practitioners have an impressive set of paraphernalia, consisting of a variety of augers, awls, probes, and prods. The use of these objects in the exorcism of the evils of the mouth involves almost unbelievable ritual torture of the client. The holy-mouth-man opens the client's mouth and, using the above mentioned tools, enlarges any holes which decay may have created in the teeth. Magical materials are put into these holes. If there are no naturally occurring holes in the teeth, large sections of one or more teeth are gouged out so that the supernatural substance can be applied. In the client's view, the purpose of these ministrations is to arrest decay and to draw friends. The extremely sacred and traditional character of the rite is evident in the fact that the natives return to the holy-mouth-men year after year, despite the fact that their teeth continue to decay.

It is to be hoped that, when a thorough study of the Nacirema is made, there will be a careful inquiry into the personality structure of these people. One has

but to watch the gleam in the eye of a holy-mouth-man, as he jabs an awl into an exposed nerve, to suspect that a certain amount of sadism is involved. If this can be established, a very interesting pattern emerges, for most of the population shows definite masochistic tendencies. It was to these that Professor Linton referred in discussing a distinctive part of the daily body ritual which is performed only by men. This part of the rite involves scraping and lacerating the surface of the face with a sharp instrument. Special women's rites are performed only four times during each lunar month, but what they lack in frequency is made up in barbarity. As part of this ceremony, women bake their heads in small ovens for about an hour. The theoretically interesting point is that what seems to be a preponderantly masochistic people have developed sadistic specialists.

The medicine men have an imposing temple, or *latipso*, in every community of any size. The more elaborate ceremonies required to treat very sick patients can only be performed at this temple. These ceremonies involve not only the thaumaturge but a permanent group of vestal maidens who move sedately about the temple chambers in distinctive costume and headdress.

The *latipso* ceremonies are so harsh that it is phenomenal that a fair proportion of the really sick natives who enter the temple ever recover. Small children whose indoctrination is still incomplete have been known to resist attempts to take them to the temple because "that is where you go to die." Despite this fact, sick adults are not only willing but eager to undergo the protracted ritual purification, if they can afford to do so. No matter how ill the supplicant or how grave the emergency, the guardians of many temples will not admit a client if he cannot give a rich gift to the custodian. Even after one has gained admission and survived the ceremonies, the guardians will not permit the neophyte to leave until he makes still another gift.

The supplicant entering the temple is first stripped of all his or her clothes. In every-day life the Nacirema avoids exposure of his body and its natural functions. Bathing and excretory acts are performed only in the secrecy of the household shrine, where they are ritualized as part of the body-rites. Psychological shock results from the fact that body secrecy is suddenly lost upon entry into the *latipso*. A man, whose own wife has never seen him in an excretory act, suddenly finds himself naked and assisted by a vestal maiden while he performs his natural functions into a sacred vessel. This sort of ceremonial treatment is necessitated by the fact that the excreta are used by a diviner to ascertain the course and nature of the client's sickness. Female clients, on the other hand, find their naked bodies are subjected to the scrutiny, manipulation and prodding of the medicine men.

Few supplicants in the temple are well enough to do anything but lie on their hard beds. The daily ceremonies, like the rites of the holy-mouth-men, involve discomfort and torture. With ritual precision, the vestals awaken their miserable charges each dawn and roll them about on their beds of pain while performing ablutions, in the formal movements of which the maidens are highly trained. At other times they insert magic wands in the supplicant's mouth or force him to eat substances which are supposed to be healing. From time to time the medicine men come to their clients and jab magically treated needles into their flesh. The fact that these temple ceremonies may not cure, and may even kill the neophyte, in no way decreases the people's faith in the medicine men.

There remains one other kind of practitioner, known as a "listener." This witch-doctor has the power to exorcise the devils that lodge in the heads of people who have been bewitched. The Nacirema believe that parents bewitch their own children. Mothers are particularly suspected of putting a curse on children while teaching them the secret body rituals. The counter-magic of the witch-doctor is unusual in its lack of ritual. The patient simply tells the "listener" all his troubles and fears, beginning with the earliest difficulties he can remember. The memory displayed by the Nacirema in these exorcism sessions is truly remarkable. It is not uncommon for the patient to bemoan the rejection he felt upon being weaned as a babe, and a few individuals even see their troubles going back to the traumatic effects of their own birth.

In conclusion, mention must be made of certain practices which have their base in native esthetics but which depend upon the pervasive aversion to the natural body and its functions. There are ritual fasts to make fat people thin and ceremonial feasts to make thin people fat. Still other rites are used to make women's breasts large if they are small, and smaller if they are large. General dissatisfaction with breast shape is symbolized in the fact that the ideal form is virtually outside the range of human variation. A few women afflicted with almost inhuman hypermammary development are so idolized that they make a handsome living by simply going from village to village and permitting the natives to stare at them for a fee.

Reference has already been made to the fact that excretory functions are ritualized, routinized, and relegated to secrecy. Natural reproductive functions are similarly distorted. Intercourse is taboo as a topic and scheduled as an act. Efforts are made to avoid pregnancy by the use of magical materials or by limiting intercourse to certain phases of the moon. Conception is actually very infrequent. When pregnant, women dress so as to hide their condition. Parturition takes place in secret, without friends or relatives to assist, and the majority of women do not nurse their infants.

Our review of the ritual life of the Nacirema has certainly shown them to be a magic-ridden people. It is hard to understand how they have managed to exist so long under the burdens which they have imposed upon themselves. But even such exotic customs as these take on real meaning when they are viewed with the insight provided by Malinowski when he wrote (1948: 70):

> Looking from far and above, from our high places of safety in the developed civilization, it is easy to see all the crudity and irrelevance of magic. But without its power and guidance early man could not have mastered his practical difficulties as he has done, nor could man have advanced to the higher stages of civilization.

REFERENCES

Linton, Ralph. 1936. *The Study of Man*. New York: D. Appleton-Century Co.

Malinowski, Bronislaw. 1948. *Magic, Science, and Religion*. Glencoe, IL.: The Free Press.

Murdock, George P. 1949. *Social Structure*. New York: The Macmillan Co.

DISCUSSION QUESTIONS

1. What does Miner's piece tell us about the difficulty of describing another culture?

2. What other areas of U.S. culture could you write about in a fashion similar to this reading? It might be interesting to write an "outsider" description of the "American VUS."

3. How effective are the potions and magical cures found in the Nacirema charm boxes? Is this an important question for cultural anthropologists to answer?

RESOURCES ON THE INTERNET

 InfoTrac College Edition

infotrac-college.com

You can find further relevant readings by searching *InfoTrac College Edition*, an online library with access to thousands of scholarly and popular periodicals. Below are suggested search terms for this article:

- ritual
- ceremony
- superstition

Anthropology Online: Wadsworth's Anthropology Resource Center

academic.cengage.com/anthropology

The Wadsworth Anthropology Resource Center contains a wealth of information and useful tools for students including information on careers in anthropology.

2

Queer Customs

CLYDE KLUCKHOHN

In this selection, written more than half a century ago, Clyde Kluckhohn explains the anthropological concept of culture in a way that is eminently understandable for the beginning student of comparative cultures. Referring to culture as a "design for living," Kluckhohn, who for much of his career was the leading authority on the Navajo, used the anthropological perspective to explain what most non-anthropologists at the time considered to be "queer customs." He examined culture by showing how it is different from biological influences on our behavior, how culture influences biological processes, how it is learned rather than being genetically transmitted, and how it functions to help people adapt to their environment. Even though some of his references are today politically incorrect (for example, the use of such terms as primitive and heathen), Kluckhohn's piece serves as a valuable reminder that the study of other cultures allows us to better understand our own culture.

Why do the Chinese dislike milk and milk products? Why would the Japanese die willingly in a Banzai charge that seemed senseless to Americans? Why do some nations trace descent through the father, others through the mother, still others through both parents? Not because different peoples have different instincts, not because they were destined by God or Fate to different habits, not because the weather is different in China and Japan and the United States. Sometimes shrewd common sense has an answer that is close to that of the anthropologist: "because they were brought up that way." By "culture" anthropology means the total life way of a people, the social legacy the individual acquires from his group. Or culture can be regarded as that part of the environment that is the creation of man.

This technical term has a wider meaning than the "culture" of history and literature. A humble cooking pot is as much a cultural product as is a Beethoven sonata. In ordinary speech a man of culture is a man who can speak languages other than his own, who is familiar with history, literature, philosophy, or the fine arts. In some cliques that definition is still narrower. The cultured person is one who can talk about James Joyce, Scarlatti, and Picasso. To the anthropologist, however, to be human is to be cultured. There is culture in general, and then there are the specific cultures such as Russian, American, British, Hottentot, Inca. The general abstract notion services to remind us that we cannot explain acts solely in terms of the biological properties of the people concerned, their individual past experience, and the immediate situation. The past experience of other men in the form of culture enters into almost every event. Each specific culture constitutes a kind of blueprint for all of life's activities.

One of the interesting things about human beings is that they try to understand themselves

SOURCE: From *Mirror for Man: Anthropology and Modern Life* by Clyde Kluckhohn, p. 17–27. Used with permission.

and their own behavior. While this has been particularly true of Europeans in recent times, there is no group which has not developed a scheme or schemes to explain man's actions. To the insistent human query "why?" the most exciting illumination anthropology has to offer is that of the concept of culture. Its explanatory importance is comparable to categories such as evolution in biology, gravity in physics, disease in medicine. A good deal of human behavior can be understood, and indeed predicted, if we know a people's design for living. Many acts are neither accidental nor due to personal peculiarities nor caused by supernatural forces nor simply mysterious. Even those of us who pride ourselves on our individualism follow most of the time a pattern not of our own making. We brush our teeth on arising. We put on pants—not a loincloth or a grass skirt. We eat three meals a day—not four or five or two. We sleep in a bed—not in a hammock or on a sheep pelt. I do not have to know the individual and his life history to be able to predict these and countless other regularities, including many in the thinking process, of all Americans who are not incarcerated in jails or hospitals for the insane.

To the American woman a system of plural wives seems "instinctively" abhorrent. She cannot understand how any woman can fail to be jealous and uncomfortable if she must share her husband with other women. She feels it "unnatural" to accept such a situation. On the other hand, a Koryak woman of Siberia, for example, would find it hard to understand how a woman could be so selfish and so undesirous of feminine companionship in the home as to wish to restrict her husband to one mate.

Some years ago I met in New York City a young man who did not speak a word of English and was obviously bewildered by American ways. By "blood" he was as American as you or I, for his parents had gone from Indiana to China as missionaries. Orphaned in infancy, he was reared by a Chinese family in a remote village. All who met him found him more Chinese than American. The facts of his blue eyes and light hair were less impressive than a Chinese style of gait, Chinese arm

and hand movements, Chinese facial expression, and Chinese modes of thought. The biological heritage was American, but the cultural training had been Chinese. He returned to China.

Another example of another kind: I once knew a trader's wife in Arizona who took a somewhat devilish interest in producing a cultural reaction. Guests who came her way were often served delicious sandwiches filled with a meat that seemed to be neither chicken nor tuna fish yet was reminiscent of both. To queries she gave no reply until each had eaten his fill. She then explained that what they had eaten was not chicken, not tuna fish, but the rich, white flesh of freshly killed rattlesnakes. The response was instantaneous—vomiting, often violent vomiting. A biological process is caught in a cultural web.

A highly intelligent teacher with long and successful experience in the public schools of Chicago was finishing her first year in an Indian school. When asked how her Navaho pupils compared in intelligence with Chicago youngsters, she replied, "Well, I just don't know. Sometimes the Indians seem just as bright. At other times they just act like dumb animals. The other night we had a dance in the high school. I saw a boy who is one of the best students in my English class standing off by himself. So I took him over to a pretty girl and told them to dance. But they just stood there with their heads down. They wouldn't even say anything." I inquired if she knew whether or not they were members of the same clan. "What difference would that make?"

"How would you feel about getting into bed with your brother?" The teacher walked off in a huff, but, actually, the two cases were quite comparable in principle. To the Indian the type of bodily contact involved in our social dancing has a directly sexual connotation. The incest taboos between members of the same clan are as severe as between true brothers and sisters. The shame of the Indians at the suggestion that a clan brother and sister should dance and the indignation of the white teacher at the idea that she should share a bed with an adult brother represent equally nonrational responses, culturally standardized unreason.

All this does not mean that there is no such thing as raw human nature. The very fact that certain of the same institutions are found in all known societies indicates that at bottom all human beings are very much alike. The files of the Cross-Cultural Survey at Yale University are organized according to categories such as "marriage ceremonies," "life crisis rites," "incest taboos." At least seventy-five of these categories are represented in every single one of the hundreds of cultures analyzed. This is hardly surprising. The members of all human groups have about the same biological equipment. All men undergo the same poignant life experiences such as birth, helplessness, illness, old age, and death. The biological potentialities of the species are the blocks with which cultures are built. Some patterns of every culture crystallize around focuses provided by the inevitables of biology: the difference between the sexes, the presence of persons of different ages, the varying physical strength and skill of individuals. The facts of nature also limit culture forms. No culture provides patterns for jumping over trees or for eating iron ore.

There is thus no "either-or" between nature and that special form of nurture called culture. Culture determinism is as one-sided as biological determinism. The two factors are interdependent. Culture arises out of human nature, and its forms are restricted both by man's biology and by natural laws. It is equally true that culture channels biological processes—vomiting, weeping, fainting, sneezing, the daily habits of food intake and waste elimination. When a man eats, he is reacting to an internal "drive," namely, hunger contractions consequent upon the lowering of blood sugar, but his precise reaction to these internal stimuli cannot be predicted by physiological knowledge alone. Whether a healthy adult feels hungry twice, three times, or four times a day and the hours at which this feeling recurs is a question of culture. *What* he eats is of course limited by availability, but is also partly regulated by culture. It is a biological fact that some types of berries are poisonous; it is a cultural fact that, a few generations ago, most Americans considered tomatoes to be poisonous and refused to eat them. Such selective, discriminative use of the environment is characteristically cultural. In a still more general sense, too, the process of eating is channeled by culture. Whether a man eats to live, lives to eat, or merely eats and lives is only in part an individual matter, for there are also cultural trends. Emotions are physiological events. Certain situations will evoke fear in people from any culture. But sensations of pleasure, anger, and lust may be stimulated by cultural cues that would leave unmoved someone who has been reared in a different social tradition.

Except in the case of newborn babies and of individuals born with clear-cut structural or functional abnormalities we can observe innate endowments only as modified by cultural training. In a hospital in New Mexico where Zuñi Indian, Navaho Indian, and white American babies are born, it is possible to classify the newly arrived infants as unusually active, average, and quiet. Some babies from each "racial" group will fall into each category, though a higher proportion of the white babies will fall into the unusually active class. But if a Navaho baby, a Zuñi baby, and a white baby—all classified as unusually active at birth—are again observed at the age of two years, the Zuñi baby will no longer seem given to quick and restless activity—*as compared with the white child*—though he may seem so as compared with the other Zuñis of the same age. The Navaho child is likely to fall in between as contrasted with the Zuñi and the white, though he will probably still seem more active than the average Navaho youngster.

It was remarked by many observers in the Japanese relocation centers that Japanese who were born and brought up in this country, especially those who were reared apart from any large colony of Japanese, resemble in behavior their white neighbors much more closely than they do their own parents who were educated in Japan.

I have said "culture channels biological processes." It is more accurate to say "the biological functioning of individuals is modified if they have been trained in certain ways and not in others." Culture is not a disembodied force. It is created and transmitted by people. However, culture, like well-known concepts of the physical sciences, is a convenient abstraction. One never sees gravity. One sees bodies falling in regular ways. One never sees an electromagnetic field. Yet certain happenings that can be seen may be given a neat abstract formulation by assuming that the electromagnetic field exists. Similarly, one never sees culture as such. What is seen are regularities in the behavior or artifacts of a group that has adhered to a common tradition. The regularities in style and technique of ancient Inca tapestries or stone axes from Melanesian islands are due to the existence of mental blueprints for the group.

Culture is a *way* of thinking, feeling, believing. It is the group's knowledge stored up (in memories of men; in books and objects) for future use. We study the products of this "mental" activity: the overt behavior, the speech and gestures and activities of people, and the tangible results of these things such as tools, houses, cornfields, and what not. It has been customary in lists of "culture traits" to include such things as watches or law books. This is a convenient way of thinking about them, but in the solution of any important problem we must remember that they, in themselves, are nothing but metals, paper, and ink. What is important is that some men know how to make them, others set a value on them, are unhappy without them, direct their activities in relation to them, or disregard them.

It is only a helpful shorthand when we say "The cultural patterns of the Zulu were resistant to Christianization." In the directly observable world of course, it was individual Zulus who resisted. Nevertheless, if we do not forget that we are speaking at a high level of abstraction, it is justifiable to speak of culture as a cause. One may compare the practice of saying "syphilis caused the extinction of the native population of the island." Was it "syphilis" or "syphilis germs" or "human beings who were carriers of syphilis?"

"Culture," then, is "a theory." But if a theory is not contradicted by any relevant fact and if it helps us to understand a mass of otherwise chaotic facts, it is useful. Darwin's contribution was much less the accumulation of new knowledge than the creation of a theory which put in order data already

known. An accumulation of facts, however large, is no more a science than a pile of bricks is a house. Anthropology's demonstration that the most weird set of customs has a consistency and an order is comparable to modern psychiatry's showing that there is meaning and purpose in the apparently incoherent talk of the insane. In fact, the inability of the older psychologies and philosophies to account for the strange behavior of madmen and heathens was the principal factor that forced psychiatry and anthropology to develop theories of the unconscious and of culture.

Since culture is an abstraction, it is important not to confuse culture with society. A "society" refers to a group of people who interact more with each other than they do with other individuals—who cooperate with each other for the attainment of certain ends. You can see and indeed count the individuals who make up a society. A "culture" refers to the distinctive ways of life of such a group of people. Not all social events are culturally patterned. New types of circumstances arise for which no cultural solutions have as yet been devised.

A culture constitutes a storehouse of the pooled learning of the group. A rabbit starts life with some innate responses. He can learn from his own experience and perhaps from observing other rabbits. A human infant is born with fewer instincts and greater plasticity. His main task is to learn the answers that persons he will never see, persons long dead, have worked out. Once he has learned the formulas supplied by the culture of his group, most of his behavior becomes almost as automatic and unthinking as if it were instinctive. There is a tremendous amount of intelligence behind the making of a radio, but not much is required to learn to turn it on.

The members of all human societies face some of the same unavoidable dilemmas, posed by biology and other facts of the human situation. This is why the basic categories of all cultures are so similar. Human culture without language is unthinkable. No culture fails to provide for aesthetic expression and aesthetic delight. Every culture supplies standardized orientations toward the deeper problems, such as death. Every culture is designed to perpetuate the group and its solidarity, to meet the demands of individuals for an orderly way of life and for satisfaction of biological needs.

However, the variations on these basic themes are numberless. Some languages are built up out of twenty basic sounds, others out of forty. Nose plugs were considered beautiful by the predynastic Egyptians but are not by the modern French. Puberty is a biological fact. But one culture ignores it, another prescribes informal instructions about sex but no ceremony, a third has impressive rites for girls only, a fourth for boys and girls. In this culture, the first menstruation is welcomed as a happy, natural event; in that culture the atmosphere is full of dread and supernatural threat. Each culture dissects nature according to its own system of categories. The Navaho Indians apply the same word to the color of a robin's egg and to that of grass. A psychologist once assumed that this meant a difference in the sense organs, that Navahos didn't have the physiological equipment to distinguish "green" from "blue." However, when he showed them objects of the two colors and asked them if they were exactly the same colors, they looked at him with astonishment. His dream of discovering a new type of color blindness was shattered.

Every culture must deal with the sexual instinct. Some, however, seek to deny all sexual expression before marriage, whereas a Polynesian adolescent who was not promiscuous would be distinctly abnormal. Some cultures enforce lifelong monogamy, others, like our own, tolerate serial monogamy; in still other cultures, two or more women may be joined to one man or several men to a single woman. Homosexuality has been a permitted pattern in the Greco-Roman world, in parts of Islam, and in various primitive tribes. Large portions of the population of Tibet, and of Christendom at some places and periods, have practiced completely celibacy. To us marriage is first and foremost an arrangement between two individuals. In many more societies marriage is merely one facet of a complicated set of reciprocities, economic and otherwise, between two families or two clans.

The essence of the cultural process is selectivity. The selection is only exceptionally conscious and rational. Cultures are like Topsy. They just grew. Once, however, a way of handling a situation becomes institutionalized, there is ordinarily great resistance to change or deviation. When we speak of "our sacred beliefs," we mean of course that they are beyond criticism and that the person who suggests modification or abandonment must be punished. No person is emotionally indifferent to his culture. Certain cultural premises may become totally out of accord with a new factual situation. Leaders may recognize this and reject the old ways in theory. Yet their emotional loyalty continues in the face of reason because of the intimate conditionings of early childhood.

A culture is learned by individuals as the result of belonging to some particular group, and it constitutes that part of learned behavior which is shared with others. It is our social legacy, as contrasted with our organic heredity. It is one of the important factors which permits us to live together in an organized society, giving us ready-made solutions to our problems, helping us to predict the behavior of others, and permitting others to know what to expect of us.

Culture regulates our lives at every turn. From the moment we are born until we die there is, whether we are conscious of it or not, constant pressure upon us to follow certain types of behavior that other men have created for us. Some paths we follow willingly, others we follow because we know no other way, still others we deviate from or go back to most unwillingly. Mothers of small children know how unnaturally most of this comes to us—how little regard we have, until we are "culturalized," for the "proper" place, time, and manner for certain acts such as eating, excreting, sleeping, getting dirty, and making loud noises. But by more or less adhering to a system of related designs for carrying out all the acts of living, a group of men and women feel themselves linked together by a powerful chain of sentiments. Ruth Benedict gave an almost complete definition of the concept when she said, "Culture is that which binds men together."

It is true any culture is a set of techniques for adjusting both to the external environment and to other men. However, cultures create problems as well as solve them. If the lore of a people states that frogs are dangerous creatures, or that it is not safe to go about at night because of witches or ghosts, threats are posed which do not arise out of the inexorable facts of the external world. Cultures produce needs as well as provide a means of fulfilling them. There exists for every group culturally defined, acquired drives that may be more powerful in ordinary daily life than the biologically inborn drives. Many Americans, for example, will work harder for "success" than they will for sexual satisfaction.

Most groups elaborate certain aspects of their culture far beyond maximum utility or survival value. In other words, not all culture promotes physical survival. At times, indeed, it does exactly the opposite. Aspects of culture which once were adaptive may persist long after they have ceased to be useful. An analysis of any culture will disclose many features which cannot possibly be construed as adaptations to the total environment in which the group now finds itself. However, it is altogether likely that these apparently useless features represent survivals, with modifications through time, of cultural forms which were adaptive in one or another previous situation.

Any cultural practice must be functional or it will disappear before long. That is, it must somehow contribute to the survival of the society or to the adjustment of the individual. However, many cultural functions are not manifest but latent. A cowboy will walk three miles to catch a horse which he then rides one mile to the store. From the point of view of manifest function this is positively irrational. But the act has the latent function of maintaining the cowboy's prestige in the terms of his own subculture. One can instance the buttons on the sleeve of a man's coat, our absurd English spelling, the use of capital letters, and a host of other apparently nonfunctional customs. They serve mainly the latent function of assisting individuals to maintain their security by preserving continuity with the past and by making certain sectors of life familiar and predictable.

Every culture is a precipitate of history. In more than one sense history is a sieve. Each culture embraces those aspects of the past which, usually in altered form and with altered meanings, live on in the present. Discoveries and inventions, both material and ideological, are constantly being made available to a group through its historical contacts with other peoples or being created by its own members. However, only those that fit the total immediate situation in meeting the group's needs for survival or in promoting the psychological adjustment of individuals will become part of the culture. The process of culture building may be regarded as an addition to man's innate biological capacities, an addition providing instruments which enlarge, or may even substitute for, biological functions, and to a degree compensating for biological limitations—as in ensuring that death does not always result in the loss to humanity of what the deceased has learned.

Culture is like a map. Just as a map isn't the territory but an abstract representation of a particular area, so also a culture is an abstract description of trends toward uniformity in the words, deeds, and artifacts of a human group. If a map is accurate and you can read it, you won't get lost; if you know a culture, you will know your way around in the life of a society. Many educated people have the notion that culture applies only to exotic ways of life or to societies where relative simplicity and relative homogeneity prevail. Some sophisticated missionaries, for example, will use the anthropological conception in discussing the special modes of living of South Sea Islanders, but seem amazed at the idea that it could be applied equally to inhabitants of New York City. And social workers in Boston will talk about the culture of a colorful and well-knit immigrant group but boggle at applying it to the behavior of staff members in the social-service agency itself.

In the primitive society the correspondence between the habits of individuals and the customs of the community is ordinarily greater. There is probably some truth in what an old Indian once said, "In the old days there was no law; everybody did what was right." The primitive tends to find happiness in the fulfillment of intricately involuted cultural patterns; the modern more often tends to feel the pattern as repressive to his individuality. It is also true that in a complex stratified society there are numerous exceptions to generalizations made about the culture as a whole. It is necessary to study regional, class, and occupational subcultures. Primitive cultures have greater stability than modern cultures; they change—but less rapidly.

DISCUSSION QUESTIONS

1. What does Kluckhohn mean when he says that "culture channels biological processes"?

2. Can you think of any contemporary examples of this principle?

3. What is meant by the nature-nurture debate?

4. The title of the book from which this selection is taken is *Mirror for Man*. What is the meaning of this title?

 **RESOURCES ON THE INTERNET**

 InfoTrac College Edition

infotrac-college.com
You can find further relevant readings by searching *InfoTrac College Edition*, an online library with access to thousands of scholarly and popular

However, modern men also are creators and carriers of culture. Only in some respects are they influenced differently from primitives by culture. Moreover, there are such wide variations in primitive cultures that any black-and-white contrast between the primitive and the civilized is altogether fictitious. The distinction which is most generally true lies in the field of conscious philosophy.

periodicals. Below are suggested search terms for this article:

- custom
- trait
- environment

Anthropology Online: Wadsworth's Anthropology Resource Center

academic.cengage.com/anthropology
The Wadsworth Anthropology Resource Center contains a wealth of information and useful tools for students including information on careers in anthropology.

3

Rapport-talk and Report-talk

DEBORAH TANNEN

In the selection, Deborah Tannen, a professor of sociolinguistics at Georgetown University, explores the very real differences in linguistic style between men and women in the United States. Women feel that men never express their feelings, are critical, and tend to operate in "lecture mode." Men, on the other hand, feel that their wives nag them and never get to the point. Often women and men walk away from a conversation with totally different impressions of what has just transpired. In many respects, Tannen suggests that discourse between men and women takes on some of the difficulties of cross-cultural communication.

Tannen distinguishes between the female mode of "rapport-talk" and the male mode of "report-talk." Women, according to Tannen, use talk for the purpose of building rapport with others. This rapport-talk involves a good deal of emotional self-disclosure and emphasizes matching experiences and showing empathy and understanding. Report-talk, on the other hand, the prominent linguistic style of men, uses talk to establish and maintain status and power. Personal disclosures are avoided because they can make the highly combative male appear vulnerable. For men discourse is competitive, information-oriented, and geared to solving problems and accomplishing goals. Men feel more comfortable engaging in public speaking while women operate more effectively in the private domain.

It is no coincidence that the book from which this selection is taken stayed on the New York Times best-seller list for nearly four years. Tannen combines a keen eye for observation with the power of original analysis to provide an excellent description of gender discourse in the United States. But Tannen's work is also relevant to applied anthropology because of its usefulness for helping us better understand and improve our discourse with members of the opposite sex.

I was sitting in a suburban living room, speaking to a women's group that had invited men to join them for the occasion of my talk about communication between women and men. During the discussion, one man was particularly talkative, full of lengthy comments and explanations. When I made the observation that women often complain that their husbands don't talk to them enough, this man volunteered that he heartily agreed. He gestured toward his wife, who had sat silently beside him on the couch throughout the evening, and said, "She's the talker in our family."

Everyone in the room burst into laughter. The man looked puzzled and hurt. "It's true," he explained. "When I come home from work, I usually have nothing to say, but she never runs out. If it weren't for her, we'd spend the whole evening in silence." Another woman expressed a similar paradox about her husband: "When we go out, he's the life of the party. If I happen to be in another room, I can always hear his voice above the others. But when we're home, he doesn't have that much to say. I do most of the talking."

Who talks more, women or men? According to the stereotype, women talk too much. Linguist Jennifer Coates notes some proverbs:

A woman's tongue wags like a lamb's tail.

Foxes are all tail and women are all tongue.

The North Sea will sooner be found wanting in water than a woman be at a loss for a word.

Throughout history, women have been punished for talking too much or in the wrong way. Linguist Connie Eble lists a variety of physical punishments used in Colonial America: Women were strapped to dunking stools and held underwater until they nearly drowned, put into the stocks with signs pinned to them, gagged, and silenced by a cleft stick applied to their tongues.

Though such institutionalized corporal punishments have given way to informal, often psychological ones, modern stereotypes are not much different from those expressed in the old proverbs. Women are believed to talk too much. Yet study after study finds that it is men who talk more—at meetings, in mixed-group discussions, and in classrooms where girls or young women sit next to boys or young men. For example, communications researchers Barbara and Gene Eakins tape-recorded and studied seven university faculty meetings. They found that, with one exception, men spoke more often and, without exception, spoke for a longer time. The men's turns ranged from 10.66 to 17.07 seconds, while the women's turns ranged from 3 to 10 seconds. In other words, the women's longest turns were still shorter than the men's shortest turns.

When a public lecture is followed by questions from the floor, or a talk show host opens the phones, the first voice to be heard asking a question is almost always a man's. And when they ask questions or offer comments from the audience, men tend to talk longer. Linguist Marjorie Swacker recorded question-and-answer sessions at academic conferences. Women were highly visible as speakers at the conferences studied; they presented 40.7 percent of the papers at the conferences studied and made up 42 percent of the audiences. But when it came to volunteering and being called on to ask questions, women contributed only 27.4 percent. Furthermore, the women's questions, on the average, took less than half as much time as the men's. (The mean was 23.1 seconds for women, 52.7 for men.) This happened, Swacker shows, because men (but not women) tended to preface their questions with statements, ask more than one question, and follow up the speaker's answer with another question or comment.

I have observed this pattern at my own lectures, which concern issues of direct relevance to women. Regardless of the proportion of women and men in the audience, men almost invariably ask the first question, more questions, and longer questions. In these situations, women often feel that men are talking too much. I recall one discussion period following a lecture I gave to a group assembled in a bookstore. The group was composed mostly of women, but most of the discussion was being conducted by men in the audience. At one point, a man sitting in the middle was talking at such great length that several women in the front rows began shifting in their seats and rolling their eyes at me. Ironically, what he was going on about was how frustrated he feels when he has to listen to women going on and on about topics he finds boring and unimportant.

RAPPORT-TALK
AND REPORT-TALK

Who talks more, then, women or men? The seemingly contradictory evidence is reconciled by the difference between what I call *public* and *private speaking*. More men feel comfortable doing "public speaking," while more women feel comfortable doing "private" speaking. Another way of capturing these differences is by using the terms *report-talk* and *rapport-talk*.

For most women, the language of conversation is primarily a language of rapport: a way of establishing connections and negotiating relationships. Emphasis is placed on displaying similarities and matching experiences. From childhood, girls criticize peers who try to stand out or appear better than others. People feel their closest connections at home, or in settings where they *feel* at home—with one or a few people they feel close to and comfortable with—in other words, during private speaking. But even the most public situations can be approached like private speaking.

For most men, talk is primarily a means to preserve independence and negotiate and maintain status in a hierarchical social order. This is done by exhibiting knowledge and skill, and by holding center stage through verbal performance such as storytelling, joking, or imparting information. From childhood, men learn to use talking as a way to get and keep attention. So they are more comfortable speaking in larger groups made up of people they know less well—in the broadest sense, "public speaking." But even the most private situations can be approached like public speaking, more like giving a report than establishing rapport.

PRIVATE SPEAKING: THE WORDY WOMAN AND THE MUTE MAN

What is the source of the stereotype that women talk a lot? Dale Spender suggests that most people feel instinctively (if not consciously) that women, like children, should be seen and not heard, so any amount of talk from them seems like too much. Studies have shown that if women and men talk equally in a group, people think the women talked more. So there is truth to Spender's view. But another explanation is that men think women talk a lot because they hear women talking in situations where men would not: on the telephone; or in social situations with friends, when they are not discussing topics that men find inherently interesting; or, like the couple at the women's group, at home alone—in other words, in private speaking.

Home is the setting for an American icon that features the silent man and the talkative woman. And this icon, which grows out of the different goals and habits I have been describing, explains why the complaint most often voiced by women about the men with whom they are intimate is "He doesn't talk to me"—and the second most frequent is "He doesn't listen to me."

A woman who wrote to Ann Landers is typical:

My husband never speaks to me when he comes home from work. When I ask, "How did everything go today?" he says, "Rough..." or "It's a jungle out there." (We live in Jersey and he works in New York City.)

It's a different story when we have guests or go visiting. Paul is the gabbiest guy in the crowd—a real spellbinder. He comes up with the most interesting stories. People hang on every word. I think to myself, "Why doesn't he ever tell *me* these things?"

This has been going on for 38 years. Paul started to go quiet on me after 10 years of marriage. I could never figure out why. Can you solve the mystery?
—*The Invisible Woman*

Ann Landers suggests that the husband may not want to talk because he is tired when he comes home from work. Yet women who work come home tired too, and they are nonetheless eager to tell their partners or friends everything that happened to them during the day and what these fleeting, daily dramas made them think and feel.

Sources as lofty as studies conducted by psychologists, as down to earth as letters written to advice columnists, and as sophisticated as movies and plays come up with the same insight: Men's silence at home is a disappointment to women. Again and again, women complain, "He seems to have everything to say to everyone else, and nothing to say to me."

The film *Divorce American Style* opens with a conversation in which Debbie Reynolds is claiming that she and Dick Van Dyke don't communicate, and he is protesting that he tells her everything that's on his mind. The doorbell interrupts their quarrel, and husband and wife compose themselves before opening the door to greet their guests with cheerful smiles.

Behind closed doors, many couples are having conversations like this. Like the character played by Debbie Reynolds, women feel men don't communicate. Like the husband played by Dick Van Dyke, men feel wrongly accused. How can she be convinced that he doesn't tell her anything, while he is equally convinced he tells her everything that's on his mind? How can women and men have such different ideas about the same conversations?

When something goes wrong, people look around for a source to blame: either the person they are trying to communicate with ("You're demanding, stubborn, self-centered") or the group that the other person belongs to ("All women are demanding"; "All men are self-centered"). Some generous-minded people blame the relationship ("We just can't communicate"). But underneath, or overlaid on these types of blame cast outward, most people believe that something is wrong with them.

If individual people or particular relationships were to blame, there wouldn't be so many different people having the same problems. The real problem is conversational style. Women and men have different ways of talking. Even with the best intentions, trying to settle the problem through talk can only make things worse if it is ways of talking that are causing trouble in the first place.

BEST FRIENDS

Once again, the seeds of women's and men's styles are sown in the ways they learn to use language while growing up. In our culture, most people, but especially women, look to their closest relationships as havens in a hostile world. The center of a little girl's social life is her best friend. Girls' friendships are made and maintained by telling secrets. For grown women too, the essence of friendship is talk, telling each other what they're thinking and feeling, and what happened that day: who was at the bus stop, who called, what they said,

how that made them feel. When asked who their best friends are, most women name other women they talk to regularly. When asked the same question, most men will say it's their wives. After that, many men name other men with whom they do things such as play tennis or baseball (but never just sit and talk) or a chum from high school whom they haven't spoken to in a year.

When Debbie Reynolds complained that Dick Van Dyke didn't tell her anything, and he protested that he did, both were right. She felt he didn't tell her anything because he didn't tell her the fleeting thoughts and feelings he experienced throughout the day—the kind of talk she would have with her best friend. He didn't tell her these things because to him they didn't seem like anything to tell. He told her anything that seemed important—anything he would tell his friends.

Men and women often have very different ideas of what's important—and at what point "important" topics should be raised. A woman told me, with lingering incredulity, of a conversation with her boyfriend. Knowing he had seen his friend Oliver, she asked, "What's new with Oliver?" He replied, "Nothing." But later in the conversation it came out that Oliver and his girlfriend had decided to get married. "That's nothing?" the woman gasped in frustration and disbelief.

For men, "Nothing" may be a ritual response at the start of a conversation. A college woman missed her brother but rarely called him because she found it difficult to get talk going. A typical conversation began with her asking, "What's up with you?" and his replying, "Nothing." Hearing his "Nothing" as meaning "There is nothing personal I want to talk about," she supplied talk by filling him in on her news and eventually hung up in frustration. But when she thought back, she remembered that later in the conversation he had mumbled, "Christie and I got into another fight." This came so late and so low that she didn't pick up on it. And he was probably equally frustrated that she didn't.

Many men honestly do not know what women want, and women honestly do not know why men find what they want so hard to comprehend and deliver.

DISCUSSION QUESTIONS

1. How would you summarize Tannen's characterization of gender differences in linguistic styles found in the United States?
2. Have you seen any of these gender differences in linguistic style operating in your own conversations with members of the opposite gender? Be specific.
3. Based on Tannen's description of female and male communication styles, what practical suggestions would you make to men and women in the United States to help them improve their cross-gender communication?

 **RESOURCES ON THE INTERNET**

 **InfoTrac College Edition**

infotrac-college.com
You can find further relevant readings by searching InfoTrac College Edition, an online library with access to thousands of scholarly and popular periodicals. Below are suggested search terms for this article:

- linguistics
- cross-cultural communication
- Genderlects

Anthropology Online: Wadsworth's Anthropology Resource Center

academic.cengage.com/anthropology
The Wadsworth Anthropology Resource Center contains a wealth of information and useful tools for students including information on careers in anthropology.

4

The Sounds of Silence

EDWARD T. HALL AND MILDRED REED HALL

When we think of human communication, it is usually language that first comes to mind. As important as language is to the communications process, humans also send and receive an enormous numbers of messages without ever uttering words. Humans communicate nonverbally in a number of different ways. We communicate through "body language," such as gestures, facial expressions, posture, gait, body movement, and eye contact. We communicate by touching others, or by withholding physical contact. Certain physical qualities of our bodies (such as body type, height, weight, skin color, and body odor, among others) also convey different meanings in different parts of the world. We communicate by the artifacts we put on our bodies, such as clothing, make-up, perfumes, jewelry, and eyeglasses. We communicate by using time when we keep people waiting or arrive early to a party. And, as the Halls point out in this selection, spatial distancing, such as conversational distances and seating arrangements, also send various messages in different cultures.

In this article, written nearly 40 years ago, the Halls remind us that people from all cultures communicate without words, there are many different modes of nonverbal communication (such as facial expressions, hand gestures, eye contact, posture, and touching, among others), and the actual details of nonverbal communication varies enormously from culture to culture. Mastering the realm of nonverbal communication becomes even more challenging when we realize that there are some cultures that tend to emphasize nonverbal communication over language. U.S. culture, for example, places greater importance upon the spoken word, while many eastern cultures, the Japanese in particular, look to nonverbal messages as the primary conveyer of meaning. North Americans, therefore, are likely to underestimate the importance of nonverbal cues in a cross-cultural setting. As important as language is in all human communication, it is imperative that, if we are to become globally savvy in the 21st Century, we need to learn to "hear" the silent messages and "read" the invisible words of nonverbal communication wherever we may encounter them.

Bob leaves his apartment at 8:15 a.m. and stops at the corner drug-store for breakfast. Before he can speak, the counterman says, "The usual?" Bob nods yes. While he savors his Danish, a fat man pushes onto the adjoining stool and overflows into his space. Bob scowls and the man pulls himself in as much as he can. Bob has sent two messages without speaking a syllable.

Henry has an appointment to meet Arthur at 11 o'clock; he arrives at 11:30. Their conversation is friendly, but Arthur retains a lingering hostility. Henry has unconsciously communicated that he doesn't think the appointment is very important or that Arthur is a person who needs to be treated with respect.

George is talking to Charley's wife at a party. Their conversation is entirely trivial, yet Charley glares at them suspiciously. Their physical proximity and the movements of their eyes reveal that they are powerfully attracted to each other.

José Ybarra and Sir Edmund Jones are at the same party and it is important for them to establish a cordial relationship for business reasons. Each is trying to be warm and friendly, yet they will part with mutual distrust and their business transaction will probably fall through. José, in Latin fashion, moved closer and closer to Sir Edmund as they spoke, and this movement was miscommunicated as pushiness to Sir Edmund, who kept backing away from this intimacy, and this was miscommunicated to José as coldness. The silent languages of Latin and English cultures are more difficult to learn than their spoken languages.

In each of these cases, we see the subtle power of nonverbal communication. The only language used throughout most of the history of humanity (in evolutionary terms, vocal communication is relatively recent), it is the first form of communication you learn. You use this preverbal language, consciously and unconsciously, every day to tell other people how you feel about yourself and them. This language includes your posture, gestures, facial expressions, costume, the way you walk, even your treatment of time and space and material things. All people communicate on several different levels at the same time but are usually aware of only the verbal dialog and don't realize that they respond to nonverbal messages. But when a person says one thing and really believes something else, the discrepancy between the two can usually be sensed. Nonverbal-communication systems are much less subject to the conscious deception that often occurs in verbal systems. When we find ourselves thinking, "I don't know what it is about him, but he doesn't seem sincere," it's usually this lack of congruity between a person's words and his behavior that makes us anxious and uncomfortable.

Few of us realize how much we all depend on body movement in our conversation or are aware of the hidden rules that govern listening behavior. But we know instantly whether or not the person we're talking to is "tuned in" and we're very sensitive to any breach in listening etiquette. In white middle-class American culture, when someone wants to show he is listening to someone else, he looks either at the other person's face or, specifically, at his eyes, shifting his gaze from one eye to the other.

If you observe a person conversing, you'll notice that he indicates he's listening by nodding his head. He also makes little "Hmm" noises. If he agrees with what's being said, he may give a vigorous nod. To show pleasure or affirmation, he smiles; if he has some reservations, he looks skeptical by raising an eyebrow or pulling down the corners of his mouth. If a participant wants to terminate the conversation, he may start shifting his body position, stretching his legs, crossing or uncrossing them, bobbing his foot, or diverting his gaze from the speaker. The more he fidgets, the more the speaker becomes aware that he has lost his audience. As a last measure, the listener may look at his watch to indicate the imminent end of the conversation.

Talking and listening are so intricately intertwined that a person cannot do one without the other. Even when one is alone and talking to oneself, there is part of the brain that speaks while another part listens. In all conversations, the listener is positively or negatively reinforcing the speaker all the time. He may even guide the conversation without knowing it, by laughing or frowning or dismissing the argument with a wave of his hand.

The language of the eyes—another age-old way of exchanging feelings—is both subtle and complex. Not only do men and women use their eyes differently but there are class, generation, regional, ethnic, and national cultural differences. Americans often complain about the way foreigners stare at people or hold a glance too long. Most Americans look away from someone who is using his eyes in an unfamiliar way because it makes them self-conscious. If a man looks at another man's wife in a certain way, he's asking for trouble, as indicated earlier. But he might not be ill-mannered or seeking to challenge the husband. He might be a European in this country who hasn't learned our visual mores. Many American women visiting France or Italy are acutely embarrassed because, for the first time in their lives, men really look at them—their eyes, hair, nose, lips, breasts, hips, legs, thighs, knees, ankles, feet, clothes, hairdo, even their walk. These same women, once they have become used to being looked at, often return to the United States and are overcome with the feeling that "No one ever really looks at me anymore."

Analyzing the mass of data on the eyes, it is possible to sort out at least three ways in which the eyes are used to communicate: dominance vs. submission, involvement vs. detachment and positive vs. negative attitude. In addition there are three levels of consciousness and control, which can be categorized as follows: (1) conscious use of the eye to communicate, such as the flirting blink and the intimate nose-wrinkling squint; (2) the very extensive category of unconscious but learned behavior governing where the eyes are directed and when (this unwritten set of rules dictates how and under what circumstances the sexes, as well as people of all status categories, look at each other); and (3) the response of the eye itself, which is completely outside both awareness and control— changes in that cast (the sparkle) of the eye and the pupillary reflex.

The eye is unlike any other organ of the body, for it is an extension of the brain. The unconscious pupillary reflex and the cast of the eye have been known by people of Middle Eastern origin for years—although most are unaware of their knowledge. Depending on the context Arabs and others look either directly at the eye or deeply *into* the eyes of their interlocutor. We became aware of this in the Middle East several years ago while looking at jewelry. The merchant suddenly started to push a particular bracelet at a customer and said, "You buy this one." What interested us was that the bracelet was not the one that had been con-

sciously selected by the purchaser. But the merchant, watching the pupils of the eyes knew what the purchaser really wanted to buy. Whether he specifically knew *how* he knew is debatable.

A psychologist at the University of Chicago, Eckhard Hess, was the first to conduct systematic studies of the pupillary reflex. His wife remarked one evening, while watching him reading in bed, that he must be very interested in the text because his pupils were dilated. Following up on this, Hess slipped some pictures of nudes into a stack of photographs that he gave to his male assistant. Not looking at the photographs but watching his assistant's pupils, Hess was able to tell precisely when the assistant came to the nudes. In further experiments, Hess retouched the eyes in a photograph of a woman. In one print, he made the pupils small, in another, large; nothing else was changed. Subjects who were given the photographs found the woman with the dilated pupils much more attractive. Any man who has had the experience of seeing a woman look at him as her pupils widen with reflex speed knows that she's flashing him a message.

The eye-sparkle phenomenon frequently turns up in our interviews of couples in love. It's apparently one of the first reliable clues in the other person that love is genuine. To date, there is no scientific date to explain eye sparkle; no investigation of the pupil, the cornea or even the white sclera of the eye shows how the sparkle originates. Yet we all know it when we see it.

One common situation for most people involves the use of the eyes in the street and in public. Although eye behavior follows a definite set of rules, the rules vary according to the place, the needs and feelings of the people, and their ethnic background. For urban whites, once they're within definite recognition distance (16-32 feet for people with average eye-sight), there is mutual avoidance of eye contact—unless they want something specific; a pickup, a handout or information of some kind. In the West and in small towns generally however, people are much more likely to look at and greet one another, even if they're strangers.

It's permissible to look at people if they're beyond recognition distance; but once inside this sacred zone, you can only steal a glance at strangers. You *must* greet friends, however; to fail to do so is insulting. Yet, to stare too fixedly at them is considered rude and hostile. Of course, all of these rules are variable.

A great many blacks, for example, greet each other in public even if they don't know each other. To blacks, most eye behavior of whites has the effect of giving the impression that they aren't there, but this is due to white avoidance of eye contact with *anyone* in the street.

Another very basic difference between people of different ethnic backgrounds is their sense of territoriality and how they handle space. This is the silent communication, or miscommunication, that caused friction between Mr. Ybarra and Sir Edmund Jones in our earlier example. We know from research that everyone has around himself an invisible bubble of space that contracts and expands depending on several factors: his emotional state, the activity he's performing at the time and his cultural background. This bubble is a kind of mobile territory that he will defend against intrusion. If he is accustomed to close personal distance between himself and others, his bubble will be smaller than that of someone who's accustomed to greater personal distance. People of North European heritage—English, Scandinavian, Swiss, and German—tend to avoid contact. Those whose heritage is Italian, French, Spanish, Russian, Latin American, or Middle Eastern like close personal contact.

People are very sensitive to any intrusion into their spatial bubble. If someone stands too close to you, your first instinct is to back up. If that's not possible, you lean away and pull yourself in, tensing your muscles. If the intruder doesn't respond to these body signals, you may then try to protect yourself, using a briefcase, umbrella or raincoat. Women—especially when traveling alone—often plant their pocketbook in such a way that no one gets very close to them. As a last resort, you may move to another spot and position yourself behind a desk or a chair that provides screening. Everyone tries to adjust the space around himself in a way that's comfortable for him; most often, he does this unconsciously.

Emotions also have a direct effect on the size of a person's territory. When you're angry or under stress, your bubble expands and you require more space. New York psychiatrist Augustus Kinzel found a difference in what he calls Body-Buffer Zones between violent and nonviolent prison inmates. Dr. Kinzel conducted experiments in which a prisoner was placed in the center of a small room and then Dr. Kinzel slowly walked toward him. Nonviolent prisoners allowed him to come quite close, while prisoners with a history of violent behavior couldn't tolerate his proximity and reacted with some vehemence.

Apparently, people under stress experience other people as looming larger and closer than they actually are. Studies of schizophrenic patients have indicated that they sometimes have a distorted perception of space, and several psychiatrists have reported patients who experience their boundaries as filling up an entire room. For these patients, anyone who comes into the room is actually inside their body, and such an intrusion may trigger a violent outburst.

Unfortunately, there is little detailed information about normal people who live in highly congested urban areas. We do know, of course, that the noise, pollution, dirt, crowding, and confusion of our cities induce feelings of stress in more of us, and stress leads to a need for greater space. The man who's packed into a subway, jostled in the street, crowded into an elevator and forced to work all day in a bull pen or in a small office without auditory or visual privacy is going to be very stressed at the end of his day. He needs places that provide relief from constant overstimulation of his nervous system. Stress from overcrowding is cumulative and people can tolerate more crowding early in the day than later; note the increased bad temper during the evening rush hour as compared with the morning melee. Certainly one factor in people's desire to commute by car is the need for privacy and relief from crowding (except, often, from other cars); it may be the only time of the day when nobody can intrude.

In crowded public places, we tense our muscles and hold ourselves stiff, and thereby communicate to others our desire, not to intrude on their space and, above all, not to touch them. We also avoid eye contact, and the total effect is that of someone who has "tuned out." Walking along the street, our bubble expands slightly as we move in a stream of strangers, taking care not to bump into them. In the office, at meetings, in restaurants, our bubble keeps changing as it adjusts to the activity at hand.

Most white middle-class Americans use four main distances in their business and social relations: intimate, personal, social, and public. Each of these distances has a near and a far phase and is accompanied by changes in the volume of the voice. Intimate distance varies from direct physical contact with another person to a distance of six to eighteen inches and is used for our most private activities—caressing another person or making love. At this distance, you are overwhelmed by sensory inputs from the other person—heat from the body, tactile stimulation from the skin, the fragrance of perfume, even the sound of breathing—all of which literally envelop you. Even at the far phase, you're still within easy touching distance. In general, the use of intimate distance in public between adults is frowned on. It's also much too close for strangers, except under conditions of extreme crowding.

In the second zone—personal distance—the close phase is one and a half to two and a half feet; it's at this distance that wives usually stand from their husbands in public. If another woman moves into this zone, the wife will most likely be disturbed. The far phase—two and a half to four feet—is the distance used to "keep someone at arm's length" and is the most common spacing used by people in conversation.

The third zone—social distance—is employed during business transactions or exchanges with a clerk or repairman. People who work together tend to use close social distance—four to seven feet. This is also the distance for conversation at social gatherings. To stand up at this distance from someone who is seated has a dominating effect (e.g., teacher to pupil, boss to secretary). The far phase of the third zone—seven to twelve feet—is

where people stand when someone says, "Stand back so I can look at you." This distance lends a formal tone to business or social discourse. In an executive office, the desk serves to keep people at this distance.

The fourth zone—public distance—is used by teachers in classrooms or speakers at public gatherings. At its farthest phase—25 feet and beyond—it is used for important public figures. Violations of this distance can lead to serious complications. During his 1970 U.S. visit, the president of France, Georges Pompidou, was harassed by pickets in Chicago, who were permitted to get within touching distance. Since pickets in France are kept behind barricades a block or more away, the president was outraged by his insult to his person, and President Nixon was obliged to communicate his concern as well as offer his personal apologies.

It is interesting to note how American pitchmen and panhandlers exploit the unwritten, unspoken conventions of eye and distance. Both take advantage of the fact that once explicit eye contact is established, it is rude to look away, because to do so means to brusquely dismiss the other person and his needs. Once having caught the eye of his mark, the panhandler then locks on, not letting go until he moves through the public zone, the social zone, the personal zone and, finally, into the intimate sphere, where people are most vulnerable.

Touch also is an important part of the constant stream of communication that takes place between people. A light touch, a firm touch, a blow, a caress are all communications. In an effort to break down barriers among people, there's been a recent upsurge in group-encounter activities, in which strangers are encouraged to touch one another. In special situations such as these, the rules for not touching are broken with group approval and people gradually lose some of their inhibitions.

Although most people don't realize it, space is perceived and distances are set not by vision alone but with all the senses. Auditory space is perceived with the ears, thermal space with the skin, kinesthetic space with the muscles of the body and olfactory space with the nose. And, once again, it's one's culture that determines how his senses are programmed—which sensory information ranks highest and lowest. The important thing to remember is that culture is very persistent. In this country, we've noted the existence of culture patterns that determine distance between people in the third and fourth generations of some families, despite their prolonged contact with people of very different cultural heritages.

Whenever there is great cultural distance between two people, there are bound to be problems arising from difference in behavior and expectations. An example is the American couple who consulted a psychiatrist about their marital problems. The husband was from New England and had been brought up by reserved parents who taught him to control his emotions and to respect the need for privacy. His wife was from an Italian family and had been brought up in close contact with all the members of her large family, who were extremely warm, volatile and demonstrative.

When the husband came home after a hard day at the office, dragging his feet and longing for peace and quiet, his wife would rush to him and smother him. Clasping his hands, rubbing his brow, crooning over his weary head, she never left him alone. But when the wife was upset or anxious about her day, the husband's response was to withdraw completely and leave her alone. No comforting, no affectionate embrace, no attention—just solitude. The woman became convinced her husband didn't love her, and, in desperation, she consulted a psychiatrist. Their problem wasn't basically psychological but cultural.

Why has man developed all these different ways of communicating messages without words? One reason is that people don't like to spell out certain kinds of messages. We prefer to find other ways of showing our feelings. This is especially true in relationships as sensitive as courtship. Men don't like to be rejected and most women don't want to turn a man down bluntly. Instead, we work out subtle ways of encouraging or discouraging each other that save face and avoid confrontations.

How a person handles space in dating others is an obvious and very sensitive indicator of how he or she feels about the other person. On a first date,

if a woman sits or stands so close to a man that he is acutely conscious of her physical presence—inside the intimate-distance zone—the man usually construes it to mean that she is encouraging him. However, before the man starts moving in on the woman, he should be sure what message she's really sending; otherwise, he risks bruising his ego. What is close to someone of North European background may be neutral or distant to someone of Italian heritage. Also, women sometimes use space as a way of misleading a man and there are few things that put men off more than women who communicate contradictory messages—such as women who cuddle up and then act insulted when a man takes the next step.

How does a woman communicate interest in a man? In addition to such familiar gambits as smiling at him, she may glance shyly at him, blush, and then look away. Or she may give him a real come-on look and move in very close when he approaches. She may touch his arm and ask for a light. As she leans forward to light her cigarette, she may brush him lightly, enveloping him in her perfume, She'll probably continue to smile at him and she may use what ethologists call preening gestures—touching the back of her hair, thrusting her breasts forward, tilting her hips as she stands or crossing her legs if she's seated, perhaps even exposing one thigh or putting a hand on her thigh and stroking it. She may also stroke her wrists as she converses or show the palm of her hand as a way of gaining his attention. Her skin may be unusually flushed or quite pale, her eyes brighter, the pupils larger.

If a man sees a woman whom he wants to attract, he tries to present himself by his posture and stance as someone who is self-assured. He moves briskly and confidently. When he catches the eye of the woman, he may hold her glance a little longer than normal. If he gets an encouraging smile, he'll move in close and engage her in small talk. As they converse, his glance shifts over her face and body. He, too, may make preening gestures—straightening his tie, smoothing his hair or shooting his cuffs.

How do people learn body language? The same way they learn spoken language—by observing and imitating people around them as they're growing up. Little girls imitate their mothers or an older female. Little boys imitate their fathers or a respected uncle or a character in television. In this way, they learn the gender signals appropriate for their sex. Regional, class, and ethnic patterns of body behavior are also learned in childhood and persist throughout life.

Such patterns of masculine and feminine body behavior vary widely from one culture to another. In America, for example, women stand with their thighs together. Many walk with their pelvis tipped slightly forward and their upper arms close to their body. When they sit, they cross their ankles. American men hold their arms away from their body, often swinging them as they walk. They stand with their legs apart (an extreme example is the cowboy, with legs apart and thumbs tucked into his belt). When they sit, they put their feet on the floor with legs apart and, in some parts of the country, they cross their legs by putting one ankle on the other knee.

Leg behavior indicates sex, status, and personality. It so indicates whether or not one is at ease or is showing respect or disrespect for the other person. Young Latin-American males avoid crossing their legs. In their world of *machismo*, the preferred position for young males when with one another (if there is no older dominant male present to whom they must show respect) is to sit on the base of their spine with their leg muscles relaxed and their feet wide apart. Their respect position is like our military equivalent; spine straight, heels and ankles together—almost identical to that displayed by properly brought up young women in New England in the early part of this century.

American women who sit with their legs spread apart in the presence of males are *not* normally signaling a come-on—they are simply (and often unconsciously) sitting like men. Middle-class women in the presence of other women to whom they are very close may on occasion throw themselves down on a soft chair or sofa and let themselves go. This is a signal that nothing serious will be taken up. Males, on the other hand, lean back and prop their legs up on the nearest object.

The way we walk, similarly, indicates status, respect, mood, and ethnic or cultural affiliation. The many variants of the female walk are too well known to go into here, except to say that a man would have to be blind not to be turned on by the way some women walk—a fact that made Mae West rich before scientists ever studied these matters. To white Americans, some French middle-class males walk in a way that is both humorous and suspect. There is a bounce and looseness to the French walk, as though the parts of the body were somehow unrelated. Jacques Tati, the French movie actor, walks this way; so does the great mime, Marcel Marceau.

Blacks and whites in America—with the exception of middle- and upper-middle-class professionals of both groups—move and walk very differently from each other. To the blacks, whites often seem incredibly stiff, almost mechanical in their movements. Black males, on the other hand, have a looseness and coordination that frequently makes whites a little uneasy; it's too different, too integrated, too alive, too male. Norman Mailer has said that squares walk from the shoulders, like bears, but blacks and hippies walk from the hips, like cats.

All over the world, people walk not only in their own characteristic way but have walks that communicate the nature of their involvement with whatever it is they're doing. The purposeful walk of North Europeans is an important component of proper behavior on the job. Any male who has been in the military knows how essential it is to walk properly (which makes for a continuing source of tension between blacks and whites in the Service). The quick shuffle of servants in the Far East in the old days was a show of respect. On the island of Truk, when we last visited, the inhabitants even had a name for the respectful walk that one used when in the presence of a chief or when walking past a chief's house. The term was *sufan*, which meant to be humble and respectful.

The notion that people communicate volumes by their gestures, facial expressions, posture and walk is not new; actors, dancers, writers and psychiatrists have long been aware of it. Only in recent years, however, have scientists begun to make systematic observations of body motions. Ray L. Birdwhistell of the University of Pennsylvania is one of the pioneers in body-motion research and coined the term kinesics to describe this field. He developed an elaborate notation system to record both facial and body movements, using an approach similar to that of the linguist, who studies the basic elements of speech. Birdwhistell and other kinesicists such as Albert Sheflen, Adam Kendon and William Condon take movies of people interacting. They run the film over and over again, often at reduced speed for frame-by-frame analysis, so that they can observe even the slightest body movements not perceptible at normal interaction speeds. These movements are then recorded in notebooks for later analysis.

To appreciate the importance of nonverbal-communication systems, consider the unskilled inner-city black looking for a job. His handling of time and space alone is sufficiently different from the white middle-class pattern to create great misunderstandings on both sides. The black is told to appear for a job interview at a certain time. He arrives late. The white interviewer concludes from his tardy arrival that the black is irresponsible and not really interested in the job. What the interviewer doesn't know is that the black time system (often referred to by blacks as C.P.T.—colored people's time) isn't the same as that of whites. In the words of a black student who had been told to make an appointment to see his professor: "Man, you *must* be putting me on. I never had an appointment in my life."

The black job applicant, having arrived late for his interview, may further antagonize the white interviewer by his posture and his eye behavior. Perhaps he slouches and avoids looking at the interviewer; to him this is playing it cool. To the interviewer, however, he may well look shifty and sound uninterested.

The interviewer has failed to notice the actual signs of interest and eagerness in the black's behavior, such as the subtle shift in the quality of the voice—a gentle and tentative excitement—an almost imperceptible change in the cast of the eyes and a relaxing of the jaw muscles.

Moreover, correct reading of black-white behavior is continually complicated by the fact that both groups are comprised of individuals—some of whom try to accommodate and some of whom make it a point of pride *not* to accommodate. At present, this means that many Americans, when thrown into contact with one another, are in the precarious position of not knowing which pattern applies. Once identified and analyzed, nonverbal-communication systems can be taught, like a foreign language. Without this training, we respond to nonverbal communications in terms of our own culture; we read everyone's behavior as if it were our own, and thus we often misunderstand it.

Several years ago in New York City, there was a program for sending children from predominantly black and Puerto Rican low-income neighborhoods to summer school in a white upper-class neighborhood on the East Side. One morning, a group of young black and Puerto Rican boys raced down the street, shouting and screaming and overturning garbage cans on their way to school. A doorman from an apartment building nearby chased them and cornered one of them inside a building. The boy drew a knife and attacked the doorman. This tragedy would not have occurred if the doorman had been familiar with the behavior of boys from low-income neighborhoods, where such antics are routine and socially acceptable and where pursuit would be expected to invite a violent response.

The language of behavior is extremely complex. Most of us are lucky to have under control one subcultural system—the one that reflects our sex, class, generation, and geographic region within the United States. Because of its complexity, efforts to isolate bits of nonverbal communication and generalize from them are in vain; you don't become an instant expert on people's behavior by watching them at cocktail parties. Body language isn't something that's independent of the person, something that can be donned and doffed like a suit of clothes.

Our research and that of our colleagues has shown that, far from being a superficial form of communication that can be consciously manipulated, nonverbal-communication systems are interwoven into the fabric of the personality and, as sociologist Erving Goffman had demonstrated, into society itself. They are the warp and wool of daily interactions with others and they influence how one expresses oneself, how one experiences oneself as a man or a woman.

Nonverbal communications signal to members of your own group what kind of person you are, how you feel about others, how you'll fit into and work in a group, whether you're assured or anxious, the degree to which you feel comfortable with the standards of your own culture, as well as deeply significant feelings about the self including the state of your own psyche. For most of us it's difficult to accept the reality of another's behavioral system. And, of course, none of us will ever become fully knowledgeable of the importance of every nonverbal signal. But as long as each of us realizes the power of these signals, this society's diversity can be a source of great strength rather than a further —and subtly powerful—source of division.

DISCUSSION QUESTIONS

1. How many modes of human nonverbal communication can you identify?

2. How does nonverbal communication function in regulating human interaction?

3. In U.S. culture, how can you tell (from nonverbal forms of communication) whether or not someone is listening to you?

RESOURCES ON THE INTERNET

InfoTrac College Edition

infotrac-college.com

You can find further relevant readings by searching *InfoTrac College Edition*, an online library with access to thousands of scholarly and popular periodicals. Below are suggested search terms for this article:

- nonverbal communication
- hand gestures
- kinesics

Anthropology Online: Wadsworth's Anthropology Resource Center

academic.cengage.com/anthropology

The Wadsworth Anthropology Resource Center contains a wealth of information and useful tools for students including information on careers in anthropology.

5

Eating Christmas in the Kalahari

RICHARD BORSHAY LEE

In this selection, cultural anthropologist Richard Lee recounts his experience while conducting fieldwork among the !Kung (today referred to as the Ju/'hoansi) of southwest Africa. Much to Lee's dismay, his attempt to give the local !Kung the largest and fattest oxen to slaughter and share as a Christmas feast was met with ridicule.

This is a classic example of cross-cultural misunderstanding. Lee's confusion and hurt feelings stemmed from a common mistake made by people (even anthropologists!) operating in a culturally unfamiliar environment—that is, they try to understand other peoples' behavior in terms of the assumptions of their own culture. To Lee, his gift to the community of the fattest oxen he could find was no more than a generous expression of his gratitude for their assistance and hospitality. Yet the group taunted Lee with insults about the inadequacy of the gift. Did the !Kung truly not appreciate the gift, or was there another explanation for their negative reaction?

The !Kung Bushmen's knowledge of Christmas is third-hand. The London Missionary Society brought the holiday to the southern Tswana tribes in the early nineteenth century. Later, native catechists spread the idea far and wide among the Bantu-speaking pastoralists, even in the remotest corners of the Kalahari Desert. The Bushmen's idea of the Christmas story, stripped to its essentials, is "praise the birth of white man's god-chief"; what keeps their interest in the holiday high is the Tswana-Herero custom of slaughtering an ox for his Bushmen neighbors as an annual goodwill gesture. Since the 1930s, part of the Bushmen's annual round of activities has included a December congregation at the cattle posts for trading, marriage brokering, and several days of trance-dance feasting at which the local Tswana headman is host.

As a social anthropologist working with !Kung Bushmen, I found that the Christmas ox custom suited my purposes. I had come to the Kalahari to study the hunting and gathering subsistence economy of the !Kung, and to accomplish this it was essential not to provide them with food, share my own food, or interfere in any way with their food-gathering activities. While liberal handouts of tobacco and medical supplies were appreciated, they were scarcely adequate to erase the glaring disparity in wealth between the anthropologist, who maintained a two-month inventory of canned goods, and the Bushmen, who rarely had a day's

Editor's note: The !Kung and other Bushmen speak click languages. In the story, three different clicks are used:

1. The dental click (/), as in /ai/ai, /ontah, and /gaugo. The click is sometimes written in English as tsk-tsk.
2. The alveopalatal click (!), as in Ben!a and !Kung.
3. The lateral click (//), as in //gom. Clicks junction as consonants; a word may have more than one, as in /n!au.
SOURCE: Reprinted from *Natural History*, December 1969. Copyright © 1969 Natural History Magazine, Inc., 1969.

supply of food on hand. My approach, while paying off in terms of data, left me open to frequent accusations of stinginess and hard-heartedness. By their lights, I was a miser.

The Christmas ox was to be my way of saying thank you for the cooperation of the past year; and since it was to be our last Christmas in the field, I determined to slaughter the largest, meatiest ox that money could buy, insuring that the feast and trance dance would be a success.

Through December I kept my eyes open at the wells as the cattle were brought down for watering. Several animals were offered, but none had quite the grossness that I had in mind. Then, ten days before the holiday, a Herero friend led an ox of astonishing size and mass up to our camp. It was solid black, stood five feet high at the shoulder, had a five-foot span of horns, and must have weighed 1,200 pounds on the hoof. Food consumption calculations are my specialty, and I quickly figured that bones and viscera aside, there was enough meat—at least four pounds—for every man, woman, and child of the 150 Bushmen in the vicinity of /ai/ai who were expected at the feast.

Having found the right animal at last, I paid the Herero £20 ($56) and asked him to keep the beast with his herd until Christmas day. The next morning word spread among the people that the big solid black one was the ox chosen by /ontah (my Bushman name; it means, roughly, "whitey") for the Christmas feast. That afternoon I received the first delegation. Ben!a, an outspoken sixty-year-old mother of five, came to the point slowly.

"Where were you planning to eat Christmas?"

"Right here at /ai/ai," I replied.

"Alone or with others?"

"I expect to invite all the people to eat Christmas with me."

"Eat what?"

"I have purchased Yehave's black ox, and I am going to slaughter and cook it."

"That's what we were told at the well but refused to believe it until we heard it from yourself."

"Well, it's the black one," I replied expansively, although wondering what she was driving at.

"Oh, no!" Ben!a groaned, turning to her group. "They were right." Turning back to me she asked, "Do you expect us to eat that bag of bones?"

"Bag of bones! It's the biggest ox at /ai/ai."

"Big, yes, but old. And thin. Everybody knows there's no meat on that old ox. What did you expect us to eat off it, the horns?"

Everybody chuckled at Ben!a's one-liner as they walked away, but all I could manage was a weak grin.

That evening it was the turn of the young men. They came to sit at our evening fire. /gaugo, about my age, spoke to me man-to-man. "/ontah, you have always been square with us," he lied. "What has happened to change your heart? That sack of guts and bones of Yehave's will hardly feed one camp, let alone all the Bushmen around /ai/ai." And he proceeded to enumerate the seven camps in the /ai/ai vicinity, family by family. "Perhaps you have forgotten that we are not few, but many. Or are you too blind to tell the difference between a proper cow and an old wreck? That ox is thin to the point of death."

"Look, you guys," I retorted, "that is a beautiful animal, and I'm sure you will eat it with pleasure at Christmas."

"Of course we will eat it; it's food. But it won't fill us up to the point where we will have enough strength to dance. We will eat and go home to bed with stomachs rumbling."

That night as we turned in, I asked my wife Nancy: "What did you think of the black ox?"

"It looked enormous to me. Why?"

"Well, about eight different people have told me I got gypped; that the ox is nothing but bones."

"What's the angle?" Nancy asked. "Did they have a better one to sell?"

"No, they just said that it was going to be a grim Christmas because there won't be enough meat to go around. Maybe I'll get an independent judge to look at the beast in the morning."

Bright and early, Halingisi, a Tswana cattle owner, appeared at our camp. But before I could ask him to give me his opinion on Yehave's black ox, he gave me the eye signal that indicated a confidential chat. We left the camp and sat down.

"/ontah, I'm surprised at you; you've lived here for three years and still haven't learned anything about cattle."

"But what else can a person do but choose the biggest, strongest animal one can find?" I retorted.

"Look, just because an animal is big doesn't mean that it has plenty of meat on it. The black one was a beauty when it was younger, but now it is thin to the point of death."

"Well, I've already bought it. What can I do at this stage?"

"Bought it already? I thought you were just considering it. Well, you'll have to kill it and serve it, I suppose. But don't expect much of a dance to follow."

My spirits dropped rapidly. I could believe that Ben!a and /gaugo just might be putting me on about the black ox, but Halingisi seemed to be an impartial critic. I went around that day feeling as though I had bought a lemon of a used car.

In the afternoon it was Tomazo's turn. Tomazo is a fine hunter, a top trance performer, and one of most reliable informants. He approached the subject of the Christmas cow as part of my continuing Bushman education.

"My friend, the way it is with us Bushmen," he began, "is that we love meat. And even more than that, we love fat. When we hunt we always search for the fat ones, the ones dripping with layers of white fat: fat that turns into a clear, thick oil in the cooking pot, fat that slides down your gullet, fills your stomach and gives you a roaring diarrhea," he rhapsodized.

"So, feeling as we do," he continued, "it gives us pain to be served such a scrawny thing as Yehave's black ox. It is big, yes, and no doubt its giant bones are good for soup, but fat is what we really crave and so we will eat Christmas this year with a heavy heart."

The prospect of a gloomy Christmas now had me worried, so I asked Tomazo what I could do about it.

"Look for a fat one, a young one … smaller, but fat. Fat enough to make us / /gom ('evacuate the bowels'), then we will be happy."

My suspicions were aroused when Tomazo said that he happened to know of a young, fat, barren cow that the owner was willing to part with. Was Toma working on commission, I wondered? But I dispelled this unworthy thought when we approached the Herero owner of the cow in question and found that he had decided not to sell.

The scrawny wreck of a Christmas ox now became the talk of the /ai/ai water hole and was the first news told to the outlying groups as they began to come in from the bush for the feast. What finally convinced me that real trouble might be brewing was the visit from u!au, an old conservative with a reputation for fierceness. His nickname meant spear and referred to an incident thirty years ago in which he had speared a man to death. He had an intense manner; fixing me with his eyes, he said in clipped tones:

"I have only just heard about the black ox today, or else I would have come here earlier. /ontah, do you honestly think you can serve meat like that to people and avoid a fight?" He paused, letting the implications sink in. "I don't mean fight you, /ontah; you are a white man. I mean a fight between Bushmen. There are many fierce ones here, and with such a small quantity of meat to distribute, how can you give everybody a fair share? Someone is sure to accuse another of taking too much or hogging all the choice pieces. Then you will see what happens when some go hungry while others eat."

The possibility of at least a serious argument struck me as all too real. I had witnessed the tension that surrounds the distribution of meat from a kudu or gemsbok kill, and had documented many arguments that sprang up from a real or imagined slight in meat distribution. The owners of a kill may spend up to two hours arranging and rearranging the piles of meat under the gaze of a circle of recipients before handing them out. And I also knew that the Christmas feast at /ai/ai would be bringing together groups that had feuded in the past.

Convinced now of the gravity of the situation, I went in earnest to search for a second cow; but all my inquiries failed to turn one up.

The Christmas feast was evidently going to be a disaster, and the incessant complaints about the meagerness of the ox had already taken the fun out of it for me. Moreover, I was getting bored with the wisecracks, and after losing my temper a few times, I resolved to serve the beast anyway. If the meat fell short, the hell with it. In the Bushmen idiom, I announced to all who would listen:

"I am a poor man and blind. If I have chosen one that is too old and too thin, we will eat it anyway and see if there is enough meat there to quiet the rumbling of our stomachs."

On hearing this speech, Ben!a offered me a rare word of comfort. "It's thin," she said philosophically, "but the bones will make a good soup."

At dawn Christmas morning, instinct told me to turn over the butchering and cooking to a friend and take off with Nancy to spend Christmas alone in the bush. But curiosity kept me from retreating. I wanted to see what such a scrawny ox looked like on butchering, and if there *was* going to be a fight, I wanted to catch every word of it. Anthropologists are incurable that way.

The great beast was driven up to our dancing ground, and a shot in the forehead dropped it in its tracks. Then, freshly cut branches were heaped around the fallen carcass to receive the meat. Ten men volunteered to help with the cutting. I asked /gaugo to make the breast bone cut. This cut, which begins the butchering process for most large game, offers easy access for removal of the viscera. But it also allows the hunter to spot check the amount of fat on the animal. A fat game animal carries a white layer up to an inch thick on the chest, while in a thin one, the knife will quickly cut to bone. All eyes fixed on his hand as /gaugo, dwarfed by the great carcass, knelt to the breast. The first cut opened a pool of solid white in the black skin. The second and third cut widened and deepened the creamy white. Still no bone. It was pure fat; it must have been two inches thick.

"Hey /gau," I burst out, "that ox is loaded with fat. What's this about the ox being too thin to bother eating? Are you out of your mind?"

"Fat?" /gau shot back, "You call that fat? This wreck is thin, sick, dead!" And he broke out laughing. So did everyone else. They rolled on the ground, paralyzed with laughter. Everybody laughed except me; I was thinking.

I ran back to the tent and burst in just as Nancy was getting up. "Hey, the black ox. It's fat as hell! They were kidding about it being too thin to eat. It was a joke or something. A put-on. Everyone is really delighted with it!"

"Some joke," my wife replied. "It was so funny that you were ready to pack up and leave /ai/ai."

If it had indeed been a joke, it had been an extraordinarily convincing one, and tinged, I thought, with more than a touch of malice as many jokes are. Nevertheless, that it was a joke lifted my spirits considerably, and I returned to the butchering site where the shape of the ox was rapidly disappearing under the axes and knives of the butchers. The atmosphere had become festive. Grinning broadly, their arms covered with blood well past the elbow, men packed chunks of meat into the big cast-iron cooking pots, fifty pounds to the load, and muttered and chuckled all the while about the thinness and worthlessness of the animal and /ontah's poor judgment.

We danced and ate that ox two days and two nights; we cooked and distributed fourteen potfuls of meat and no one went home hungry and no fights broke out.

But the "joke" stayed in my mind. I had a growing feeling that something important had happened in my relationship with the Bushmen and that the clue lay in the meaning of the joke. Several days later, when most of the people had dispersed back to the bush camps, I raised the question with Hakekgose, a Tswana man who had grown up among the !Kung, married a !Kung girl, and who probably knew their culture better than any other non-Bushman.

"With us whites," I began, "Christmas is supposed to be the day of friendship and brotherly love. What I can't figure out is why the Bushmen went to such lengths to criticize and belittle the ox I had bought for the feast. The animal was perfectly good and their jokes and wisecracks practically ruined the holiday for me."

"So it really did bother you," said Hakekgose. "Well, that's the way they always talk. When I take my rifle and go hunting with them, if I miss, they laugh at me for the rest of the day. But even if I hit and bring one down, it's no better. To them, the kill is always too small or too old or too thin; and as we sit down on the kill site to cook and eat the liver, they keep grumbling, even with their mouths full of meat. They say things like, 'Oh this is awful! What a worthless animal! Whatever made me think that this Tswana rascal could hunt!'"

"Is this the way outsiders are treated?" I asked.

"No, it is their custom; they talk that way to each other too. Go and ask them."

/gaugo had been one of the most enthusiastic in making me feel bad about the merit of the Christmas ox. I sought him out first.

"Why did you tell me the black ox was worthless, when you could see that it was loaded with fat and meat?

"It is our way," he said smiling. "We always like to fool people about that. Say there is a Bushman who has been hunting. He must not come home and announce like a braggart, 'I have killed a big one in the bush!' He must first sit down in silence until I or someone else comes up to his fire and asks, 'What did you see today?' He replies quietly, 'Ah, I'm no good for hunting. I saw nothing at all [pause] just a little tiny one.' Then I smile to myself," /gaugo continued, "because I know he has killed something big.

"In the morning we make up a party of four or five people to cut up and carry the meat back to the camp. When we arrive at the kill we examine it and cry out, 'You mean to say you have dragged us all the way out here in order to make us cart home your pile of bones? Oh, if I had known it was this

thin I wouldn't have come.' Another one pipes up, 'People, to think I gave up a nice day in the shade for this. At home we may be hungry but at least we have nice cool water to drink.' If the horns are big, someone says, 'Did you think that somehow you were going to boil down the horns for soup?'

"To all this you must respond in kind. 'I agree,' you say, 'this one is not worth the effort; let's just cook the liver for strength and leave the rest for the hyenas. It is not too late to hunt today and even a duiker or a steenbok would be better than this mess.'

"Then you set to work nevertheless; butcher the animal, carry the meat back to the camp and everyone eats," /gaugo concluded.

Things were beginning to make sense. Next, I went to Tomazo. He corroborated /gaugo's story of the obligatory insults over a kill and added a few details of his own.

"But," I asked, "why insult a man after he has gone to all that trouble to track and kill an animal and when he is going to share the meat with you so that your children will have something to eat?"

"Arrogance," was his cryptic answer.

"Arrogance?"

"Yes, when a young man kills much meat he comes to think of himself as a chief or a big man, and he thinks of the rest of us as his servants or inferiors. We can't accept this. We refuse one who boasts, for someday his pride will make him kill somebody. So we always speak of his meat as worthless. This way we cool his heart and make him gentle. "But why didn't you tell me this before?" I asked Tomazo with some heat.

"Because you never asked me," said Tomazo, echoing the refrain that has come to haunt every field ethnographer.

The pieces now fell into place. I had known for a long time that in situations of social conflict with Bushmen I held all the cards. I was the only source of tobacco in a thousand square miles, and I was not incapable of cutting an individual off for non-cooperation. Though my boycott never lasted longer than a few days, it was an indication of my strength. People resented my presence at the water hole, yet simultaneously dreaded my leaving. In short I was a perfect target for the charge of arrogance and for the Bushmen tactic of enforcing humility.

I had been taught an object lesson by the Bushmen; it had come from an unexpected corner and had hurt me in a vulnerable area. For the big black ox was to be the one totally generous, unstinting act of my year at /ai/ai, and I was quite unprepared for the reaction I received.

As I read it, their message was this: There are no totally generous acts. All "acts" have an element of calculation. One black ox slaughtered at Christmas does not wipe out a year of careful manipulation of gifts given to serve your own ends. After all, to kill an animal and share the meat

with people is really no more than Bushmen do for each other every day and with far less fanfare.

In the end, I had to admire how the Bushmen had played out the farce—collectively straight-faced to the end. Curiously, the episode reminded me of the *Good Soldier Schweik* and his marvelous encounters with authority. Like Schweik, the Bushmen had retained a thoroughgoing skepticism of good intentions. Was it this independence of spirit, I wondered, that had kept them culturally viable in the face of generations of contact with more powerful societies, both black and white? The thought that the Bushmen were alive and well in the Kalahari was strangely comforting. Perhaps, armed with that independence and with their superb knowledge of their environment, they might yet survive the future.

DISCUSSION QUESTIONS

1. How would you explain the misunderstanding that occurred between Lee and the !Kung concerning the gift of the oxen?

2. Why was Lee a particularly good candidate for charges of arrogance?

3. What general principle about cross-cultural understanding does this story exemplify?

 **RESOURCES ON THE INTERNET**

 InfoTrac College Edition

infotrac-college.com
You can find further relevant readings by searching *InfoTrac College Edition*, an online library with

access to thousands of scholarly and popular periodicals. Below are suggested search terms for this article:

- arrogance
- humility
- farce

Anthropology Online: Wadsworth's Anthropology Resource Center

academic.cengage.com/anthropology
The Wadsworth Anthropology Resource Center contains a wealth of information and useful tools for students including information on careers in anthropology.

6

The Domestication of Wood in Haiti

A Case Study in Applied Evolution

GERALD F. MURRAY

During the 1980s Haiti, like many other developing countries, faced a major problem of deforestation. Owing to market demands for lumber and charcoal, some 50 million trees per year were being harvested, posing the dual problem of denuding the country of trees and lowering farm productivity through soil erosion. Prior attempts to stem the tide of deforestation took a conservationist approach, rewarding people for planting and penalizing them for cutting trees down. Anthropologist Gerald Murray, hired by USAID to direct the reforestation efforts in Haiti, took a different, and quite unorthodox, approach to the problem. Wanting to capitalize on the strong tradition of cash-cropping among Haiti small farmers, he suggested that local farmers be given seedlings to plant as a cash crop. Wood trees, in Murray's view, should be planted, harvested, and sold in the same way as corn or beans.

This project in applied anthropology drew heavily not only on past ethnographic studies of Haitian farmers, but also on evolutionary theory. Cultural evolutionists remind us that humans were foragers for approximately 99.8% of their time on earth, and as such ran the risk of wiping out their food supply if they became too efficient. Thus, foragers had built-in limits to the amount of food they could procure, and consequently, the size of their populations. It wasn't until humans began to domesticate plants and animals around 10,000 years ago that the world's food supply expanded exponentially. In other words, the age-old problem of food shortages was not solved by a conservationist approach, but rather by encouraging human populations to increase food supplies through their own efforts. This approach to reforestation, informed by both anthropological data and theory, was enormously successful. By the end of the four-year project more than 20 million trees had been planted.

PROBLEM AND CLIENT

Expatriate tree lovers, whether tourists or developmental planners, often leave Haiti with an upset stomach. Though during precolonial times the island Arawaks had reached a compromise with the forest, their market-oriented colonial successors saw trees as something to be removed. The Spaniards specialized in exporting wood from the eastern side of the island, whereas the French on the western third found it more profitable to clear the wood and produce sugar cane, coffee, and indigo for European markets. During the nineteenth century, long after Haiti had become an

SOURCE: From *Anthropological Praxis* by Robert Wulff, pp. 223–240. Reprinted by permission of Westview Press, a member of Perseus Books Group.

independent republic, foreign lumber companies cut and exported most of the nation's precious hardwoods, leaving little for today's peasants.

The geometric increase in population since colonial times—from an earlier population of fewer than half a million former slaves to a contemporary population of more than six million—and the resulting shrinkage of average family holding size have led to the evolution of a land use system devoid of systematic fallow periods. A vicious cycle has set in—one that seems to have targeted the tree for ultimate destruction. Not only has land pressure eliminated a regenerative fallow phase in the local agricultural cycle; in addition the catastrophic declines in per hectare food yields have forced peasants into alternative income-generating strategies. Increasing numbers crowd into the capital city, Port-au-Prince, creating a market for construction wood and charcoal. Poorer sectors of the peasantry in the rural areas respond to this market by racing each other with axes and machetes to cut down the few natural tree stands remaining in remoter regions of the republic. The proverbial snowball in Hades is at less risk than a tree in Haiti.

Unable to halt the flows either of wood into the cities or of soil into the oceans, international development organizations finance studies to measure the volume of these flows (50 million trees cut per year is one of the round figures being bandied about) and to predict when the last tree will be cut from Haiti. Reforestation projects have generally been entrusted by their well-meaning but shortsighted funders to Duvalier's Ministry of Agriculture, a kiss-of-death resource channeling strategy by which the Port-au-Prince jobs created frequently outnumber the seedlings produced. And even the few seedlings produced often died in the nurseries because peasants were understandably reluctant to cover their scarce holdings with state-owned trees. Project managers had been forced to resort to "food for work" strategies to move seedlings out of nurseries onto hillsides. And peasants have endeavored where possible to plant the trees on somebody else's hillsides and to enlist their livestock as allies in the subsequent removal of this potentially dangerous vegetation.

This generalized hostility to tree projects placed the U.S. Agency for International Development (AID)/Haiti mission in a bind. After several years of absence from Haiti in the wake of expulsion by Francois Duvalier, AID had reestablished its presence under the government of his son Jean Claude. But an ambitious Integrated Agricultural Development Project funded through the Ministry of Agriculture had already given clear signs of being a multimillion-dollar farce. And an influential congressman chairing the U.S. House Ways and Means Committee—and consequently exercising strong control over AID funds worldwide—had taken a passionate interest in Haiti. In his worldwide travels this individual had become adept at detecting and exposing developmental charades. And he had been blunt in communicating his conviction that much of what he had seen in AID/Haiti's program was precisely that. He had been touched by the plight of Haiti and communicated to the highest AID authorities his conviction about the salvific power of contraceptives and trees and his determination to have AID grace Haiti with an abundant flow of both. And he would personally visit Haiti (a convenient plane ride from Washington, D.C.) to inspect for himself, threatening a worldwide funding freeze if no results were forthcoming. A chain reaction of nervous "yes sirs" speedily worked its way down from AID headquarters in Washington to a beleaguered Port-au-Prince mission.

The pills and condoms were less of a problem. Even the most cantankerous congressman was unlikely to insist on observing them in use and would probably settle for household distribution figures. Not so with the trees. He could (and did) pooh-pooh nursery production figures and ask to be taken to see the new AID forests, a most embarrassing request in a country where peasants creatively converted daytime reforestation projects into nocturnal goat forage projects. AID's reaction was twofold—first, to commission an immediate study to explain to the congressman and others why peasants refused to plant trees (for this they called down an AID economist); and second, to devise some program strategy that would achieve the apparently unachievable: to instill in cash-needy, defiant peasant charcoalmakers a love, honor, and respect for newly planted trees. For this attitudinal transformation, a task usually entrusted to the local armed forces, AID/Haiti invited an anthropologist to propose an alternative approach.

PROCESS AND PLAYERS

During these dynamics, I completed a doctoral dissertation on the manner in which Haitian peasant land tenure had evolved in response to internal population growth. The AID economist referred to above exhaustively reviewed the available literature, also focusing on the issue of Haitian peasant land tenure, and produced for the mission a well-argued monograph (Zuvekas 1978) documenting a lower rate of landlessness in Haiti than in many other Latin American settings but documenting as well the informal, extralegal character of the relationship between many peasant families and their landholdings. This latter observation was interpreted by some in the mission to mean that the principal determinant of the failure of tree planting projects was the absence among peasants of legally secure deeds over their plots. Peasants could not be expected to invest money on land improvements when at mildest the benefits could accrue to another and at worst the very improvements themselves could lead to expropriation from their land. In short, no massive tree planting could be expected, according to this model, until a nationwide cadastral reform granted plot-by-plot deeds to peasant families.

This hypothesis was reputable but programmatically paralyzing because nobody dreamed that the Duvalier regime was about to undertake a major cadastral reform for the benefit of peasants. Several AID officers in Haiti had read my dissertation on land tenure (Murray 1977), and I received an invitation to advise the mission. Was Haitian peasant land tenure compatible with tree planting? Zuvekas' study had captured the internally complex nature of Haitian peasant land tenure. But the subsequent extrapolations as to paralyzing insecurity simply did not seem to fit with the ethnographic evidence. In two reports (Murray 1978a, 1978b) I indicated that peasants in general feel secure about their ownership rights over their land. Failure to secure plot-by-plot surveyed deeds is generally a cost-saving measure. Interclass evictions did occur, but they were statistically rare; instead most land disputes were intrafamilial. A series of extralegal tenure practices had evolved—preinheritance land grants to young adult dependents, informal inheritance subdivisions witnessed by community members, fictitious sales to favored children, complex community-internal sharecropping arrangements. And though these practices produced an internally heterogeneous system with its complexities, there was strong internal order. Any chaos and insecurity tended to be more in the mind of observers external to the system than in the behavior of the peasants themselves. There was a danger that the complexities of Haitian peasant land tenure would generate an unintended smokescreen obscuring the genuine causes of failure in tree planting projects.

What then were these genuine causes? The mission, intent on devising programming strategies in this domain, invited me to explore further, under a contract aimed at identifying the "determinants of success and failure" in reforestation and soil conservation projects. My major conclusion was that the preexisting land tenure, cropping, and livestock systems in peasant Haiti were perfectly adequate for the undertaking of significant tree planting activities. Most projects had failed not because of land tenure or attitudinal barriers among peasants but because of fatal flaws in one or more key project components. Though my contract called principally for analysis of previous or existing projects, I used the recommendation section of the report to speculate on how a Haiti-wise anthropologist would program and manage reforestation activities if he or she had the authority. In verbal debriefings I jokingly challenged certain young program officers in the mission to give me a jeep and carte blanche access to a $50,000 checking account, and I would prove my anthropological assertions about peasant economic behavior and produce more trees in the ground than their current multimillion-dollar Ministry of Agriculture charade. We had a good laugh and shook hands, and I departed confident that the report would be as dutifully perused and as honorably filed and forgotten as similar reports I had done elsewhere.

To my great disbelief, as I was correcting Anthro 101 exams some two years later, one of the program officers still in Haiti called to say that an Agroforestry Outreach Project (AOP) had been approved chapter and verse as I had recommended it; and that if I was interested in placing my life where my mouth had been and would leave the ivory tower to direct the project, my project bank account would have, not $50,000, but $4 million. After several weeks of hemming and hawing and vigorous negotiating for a leave from my department, I accepted the offer and entered a new (to me) role of project director in a strange upside-down world in which the project anthropologist was not a powerless cranky voice from the bleachers but the chief of party with substantial authority over general project policy and the allocation of project resources. My elation at commanding resources to implement anthropological ideas was dampened by the nervousness of knowing exactly who would be targeted for flak and ridicule if these ideas bombed out, as most tended to do in the Haiti of Duvalier.

The basic structural design of AOP followed a tripartite conceptual framework that I proposed for analyzing projects. Within this framework a project is composed of three essential systemic elements: a technical base, a benefit flow strategy, and an institutional delivery strategy. Planning had to focus equally on all three. I argued that defects in one would sabotage the entire project.

Technical Strategy

The basic technical strategy was to make available to peasants fast-growing wood trees (*Leucaena leucocephala, Cassia siatnea, Azadirachta indica, Casuarina equisedfolia, Eucalyptus camaldulensis*) that were not only drought resistant but also rapid growing, producing possible four-year harvest rotations in

humid lowland areas (and slower rotations and lower survival rates in arid areas) and that were good for charcoal and basic construction needs. Most of the species mentioned also restore nutrients to the soil, and some of them coppice from a carefully harvested stump, producing several rotations before the need for replanting.

Of equally critical technical importance was the use of a nursery system that produced light-weight microseedlings. A project pickup truck could transport over 15,000 of these microseedlings (as opposed to 250 traditional bag seedlings), and the average peasant could easily carry over 500 transportable seedlings at one time, planting them with a fraction of the ground preparation time and labor required for bulkier bagged seedlings. The anthropological implications of this nursery system were critical. It constituted a technical breakthrough that reduced to a fraction the fossil-fuel and human energy expenditure required to transport and plant trees.

But the technical component of the project incorporated yet another element: the physical juxtaposition of trees and crops. In traditional reforestation models, the trees are planted in large unbroken monocropped stands. Such forests or woodlots presuppose local land tenure and economic arrangements not found in Haiti. For the tree to make its way as a cultivate into the economy of Haitian peasants and most other tropical cultivators, reforestation models would have to be replaced by agroforestry models that entail spatial or temporal juxtaposition of crops and trees. Guided by prior ethnographic knowledge of Haitian cropping patterns, AOP worked out with peasants various border planting and intercropping strategies to make tree planting feasible even for small holding cultivators.

Benefit Flow Strategies

With respect to the second systemic component, the programming of benefit flows to participants, earlier projects had often committed the fatal flaw of defining project trees planted as *pyebwa leta* (the state's trees). Authoritarian assertions by project staff concerning sanctions for cutting newly planted trees created fears among peasants that even trees planted on their own land would be government property. And several peasants were frank in reporting fears that the trees might eventually be used as a pretext by the government or the "Company"(the most common local lexeme used to refer to projects) for eventually expropriating the land on which peasants had planted project trees.

Such ambiguities and fears surrounding benefit flows paralyze even the technically soundest project. A major anthropological feature of AOP was a radical frontal attack on the issue of property and usufruct rights over project trees. Whereas other projects had criticized tree cutting, AOP promulgated the heretical message that trees were meant to be cut, processed, and sold. The only problem with the present system, according to project messages, was that peasants were cutting nature's trees. But once a landowner "mete fos li deyo" (expends his resources) and plants and cares for his or her own wood trees on his or her own land, the landowner has the same right to harvest and sell wood as corn or beans.

I was inevitably impressed at the impact that this blunt message had when I delivered it to groups of prospective peasant tree planters. Haitian peasants are inveterate and aggressive cash-croppers; many of the crops and livestock that they produce are destined for immediate consignment to local markets. For the first time in their lives, they were hearing a concrete proposal to make the wood tree itself one more marketable crop in their inventory.

But the message would ring true only if three barriers were smashed.

1. The first concerned the feared delay in benefits. Most wood trees with which the peasants were familiar took an impractically long time to mature. There fortunately existed in Haiti four-year-old stands of leucaena, cassia, eucalyptus, and other project trees to which we could take peasant groups to demonstrate the growth speed of these trees.

2. But could they be planted on their scanty holdings without interfering with crops? Border and row planting techniques were demonstrated,

as well as intercropping. The average peasant holding was about a hectare and a half. If a cultivator planted a field in the usual crops and then planted 500 seedlings in the same field at 2 meters by 2 meters, the seedlings would occupy only a fifth of a hectare. And they would be far enough apart to permit continued cropping for two or three cycles before shade competition became too fierce. That is, trees would be planted on only a fraction of the peasant's holdings and planted in such a way that they would be compatible with continued food growing even on the plots where they stood. We would then calculate with peasants the potential income to be derived from these 500 trees through sale as charcoal, polewood, or boards. In a best-case scenario, the gross take from the charcoal of these trees (the least lucrative use of the wood) might equal the current annual income of an average rural family. The income potential of these wood trees clearly far offset any potential loss from decreased food production. Though it had taken AID two years to decide on the project, it took about twenty minutes with any group of skeptical but economically rational peasants to generate a list of enthusiastic potential tree planters.

3. But there was yet a third barrier. All this speculation about income generation presupposed that the peasants themselves, and not the government or the project, would be the sole owners of the trees and that the peasants would have unlimited rights to the harvest of the wood whenever they wished. To deal with this issue, I presented the matter as an agreement between the cultivator and the project: We would furnish free seedlings and technical assistance; the cultivators would agree to plant 500 of these seedlings on their own land and permit project personnel to carry out periodic survival counts. We would, of course, pay no wages or "Food for Work" for this planting. But we would guarantee to the planters complete and exclusive ownership of the trees. They did not need to ask for permission from the project to harvest the trees whenever their needs might dictate, nor would there be any penalties associated with early cutting or low survival. If peasants changed their minds, they could rip out their seedlings six months

after planting. They would never get any more free seedlings from us, but they would not be subject to any penalties. There are preexisting local forestry laws, rarely enforced, concerning permissions and minor taxes for tree cutting. Peasants would have to deal with these as they had skillfully done in the past. But from our project's point of view, we relinquish all tree ownership rights to the peasants who accept and plant the trees on their property.

Cash-flow dialogues and ownership assurances such as these were a far cry from the finger-wagging ecological sermons to which many peasant groups had been subjected on the topic of trees. Our project technicians developed their own messages; but central to all was the principle of peasant ownership and usufruct of AOP trees. The goal was to capitalize on the preexisting fuel and lumber markets, to make the wood tree one more crop in the income-generating repertoire of the Haitian peasant.

Institutional Strategy

The major potential fly in the ointment was the third component, the institutional component. To whom would AID entrust its funds to carry out this project? My own research had indicated clearly that Haitian governmental involvement condemned a project to certain paralysis and possible death, and my report phrased that conclusion as diplomatically as possible. The diplomacy was required to head off possible rage, less from Haitian officials than from certain senior officers in the AID mission who were politically and philosophically wedded to an institution-building strategy. Having equated the term "institution" with "government bureaucracy," and having defined their own career success in terms, not of village-level resource flows, but of voluminous and timely bureaucracy-to-bureaucracy cash transfers, such officials were in effect marshaling U.S. resources into the service of extractive ministries with unparalleled track records of squandering and/ or pilfering expatriate donor funds.

To the regime's paradoxical credit, however, the blatant openness and arrogance of Duvalierist predation had engendered an angry willingness in much of Haiti's development community to explore other resource flow channels. Though the nongovernmental character of the proposal provoked violent reaction, the reactionaries in the Haiti mission were overridden by their superiors in Washington, and a completely nongovernmental implementing mode was adopted for this project.

The system, based on private voluntary organizations (PVOs), worked as follows.

1. AID made a macrogrant to a Washington-based PVO (the Pan American Development Foundation, PADF) to run a tree-planting project based on the principles that had emerged in my research. At the Haiti mission's urging, PADF invited me to be chief of party for the project and located an experienced accountant in Haiti to be financial administrator. PADF in addition recruited three American agroforesters who, in addition to MA-level professional training, had several years of overseas village field experience under their belts. Early in the project they were supplemented by two other expatriates, a Belgian and a French Canadian. We opened a central office in Port-au-Prince and assigned a major region of Haiti to each of the agroforesters, who lived in their field regions.

2. These agroforesters were responsible for contacting the many village-based PVOs working in their regions to explain the project, to emphasize its microeconomic focus and its difference from traditional reforestation models, to discuss the conditions of entry therein, and to make technical suggestions as to the trees that would be appropriate for the region.

3. If the PVO was interested, we drafted an agreement in which our mutual contributions and spheres of responsibility were specified. The agreements were not drafted in French (Haiti's official language) but in Creole, the only language spoken by most peasants.

4. The local PVO selected *animateurs* (village organizers) who themselves were peasants who lived and worked in the village where trees

would be planted. After receiving training from us, they contacted their neighbors and kin, generated lists of peasants interested in planting a specified number of trees, and informed us when the local rains began to fall. At the proper moment we packed the seedlings in boxes customized to the particular region and shipped them on our trucks to the farmers, who would be waiting at specified drop-off points at a specified time. The trees were to be planted within twenty-four hours of delivery.

5. The animateurs were provided with Creole language data forms by which to gather ecological, land use, and land tenure data on each plot where trees would be planted and certain bits of information on each peasant participant. These forms were used as well to follow up, at periodic intervals, the survival of the trees, the incidence of any problems (such as livestock depredation, burning, disease), and—above all—the manner in which the farmer integrated the trees into cropping and livestock patterns, to detect and head off any unintended substitution of food for wood.

RESULTS AND EVALUATION

The project was funded for four years from October 1981 through November 1985. During the writing of the project paper we were asked by an AID economist to estimate how many trees would be planted. Not knowing if the peasants would in fact plant any trees, we nervously proposed to reach two thousand peasant families with a million trees as a project goal. Fiddling with his programmed calculator, the economist informed us that that output would produce a negative internal rate of return. We would need at least two million trees to make the project worth AID's institutional while. We shrugged and told him cavalierly to up the figure and to promise three million trees on the land of six thousand peasants. (At that time I thought someone else would be directing the project.)

Numbers of Trees and Beneficiaries

Though I doubted that we could reach this higher goal, the response of the Haitian peasants to this new approach to tree planting left everyone, including myself, open mouthed. Within the first year of the project, one million trees had been planted by some 2,500 peasant households all over Haiti. My fears of peasant indifference were now transformed into nervousness that we could not supply seedlings fast enough to meet the demand triggered by our wood-as-a-cash-crop strategy. Apologetic village animateurs informed us that some cultivators who had not signed up on the first lists were actually stealing newly planted seedlings from their neighbors' fields at night. They promised to catch the scoundrels. If they did, I told them, give the scoundrels a hug. Their pilfering was dramatic proof of the bull's-eye nature of the anthropological predictions that underlie the project.

By the end of the second year (when I left the project), we had reached the four-year goal of three million seedlings and the project had geared up and decentralized its nursery capacity to produce several million seedlings per season (each year having two planting seasons). Under the new director, a fellow anthropologist, the geometric increase continued. By the end of the fourth year, the project had planted, not its originally agreed-upon three million trees, but twenty million trees. Stated more accurately, some 75,000 Haitian peasants had enthusiastically planted trees on their own land. In terms of its quantitative outreach, AOP had more than quintupled its original goals.

Wood Harvesting and Wood Banking

By the end of its fourth year the project had already received an unusual amount of professional research attention by anthropologists, economists, and foresters. In addition to AID evaluations, six studies had been released on one or another aspect of the project (Ashley 1986; Balzano 1986; Buffum and King 1985; Conway 1986; Grosenick 1985; McGowan 1986). As predicted, many peasants were harvesting trees by the end of the fourth year. The most lucrative sale of the wood was as polewood in local markets, though much charcoal was also being made from project trees.

Interestingly, however, the harvesting was proceeding much more slowly than I had predicted. Peasants were "clinging" to their trees and not engaging in the clear cutting that I hoped would occur, as a prelude to the emergence of a rotational system in which peasants would alternate crops with tree cover that they themselves had planted. This technique would have been a revival, under a "domesticated" mode, of the ancient swidden sequence that had long since disappeared from Haiti. Though such a revival would have warmed anthropological hearts, the peasants had a different agenda. Though they had long ago removed nature's tree cover, they were extremely cautious about removing the tree cover that they had planted. Their economic logic was unassailable. Crop failure is so frequent throughout most of Haiti, and the market for wood and charcoal so secure, that peasants prefer to leave the tree as a "bank" against future emergencies. This arboreal bank makes particular sense in the context of the recent disappearance from Haiti of the peasant's traditional bank, the pig. A governmentally mandated (and U.S. financed) slaughter of all pigs because of fears of African swine fever created a peasant banking gap that AOP trees have now started to fill.

Strengthening Private Institutions

Before this project, PVOs had wanted to engage in tree planting, and some ineffective ecology-cum-conservation models had been futilely attempted. AOP has now involved large numbers of PVOs in economically dynamic tree planting activities. Though some of the PVOs, many operating with religious affiliation, were originally nervous about the nonaltruistic commercial thrust of the AOP message, the astounding response of their rural clientele has demolished their objections. In fact many have sought their own sources of funding to carry out this new style of tree planting, based on

microseedlings made available in large numbers to peasants as one more marketable crop. Although these PVOs are no longer dependent on AOP, it is safe to say that they will never revert to their former way of promoting trees. AOP has effected positive and probably irreversible changes in the behavior of dozens of well-funded, dedicated local institutions. And by nudging these PVOs away from ethereal visions of the functions of trees, AOP has brought them into closer dynamic touch with, and made them more responsive to, the economic interests of their peasant clientele.

Modifying AID's Modus Operandi

AID has not only taken preliminary steps to extend AOP (some talk is heard of a ten-year extension!); it also has adapted and adopted the privatized AOP delivery model for several other important projects. The basic strategy is twofold: to work through private institutions but to do it in a way consistent with AID administrative realities. AID missions prefer to move large chunks of money with one administrative sweep. Missions are reluctant to enter into separate small contract or grant relationships with dozens of local institutions. The AOP model utilizes an "umbrella" PVO to receive and administer a conveniently large macrogrant. This PVO, not AID, then shoulders the burden of administering the minigrants given to local participating PVOs.

Though it would be premature to predict a spread effect from AOP to other AID missions in other countries, such a spread is not unlikely. What is clear, however, is that the modus operandi of the Haiti mission itself has been deeply changed. In the late 1970s we were fighting to give nongovernmental implementing goals a toehold in Haiti. In the mid-1980s, a recent mission director announced that nearly 60 percent of the mission's portfolio was now going out through nongovernmental channels.

The preceding paragraphs discuss positive results of AOP. There have also been problems and the need for midcourse corrections.

Measurement of Survival Rates

A data-gathering system was instituted by which we hoped to get 100 percent information on all trees planted. Each tree-promoting animateur was to fill out data forms on survival of trees on every single project plot. The information provided by village animateurs on survival was inconsistent and in many cases clearly inaccurate. Project staff members themselves had to undertake separate, carefully controlled measures, on a random sample basis, of tree survival and tree growth. Such precise measurement was undertaken in the final two years of the project.

Improvement of Technical Outreach

The original project hope had been for an overall survival rate of 50 percent. The rate appears lower than that. The principal cause of tree mortality has been postplanting drought. Also in the early years the project was catapulted by peasant demand into a feverish tree production and tree distribution mode that underemphasized the need for careful instruction to all participating peasants about how to plant and properly care for the trees planted. In recent years more attention has been given to the production of educational materials.

Reduction of Per Household Planting Requirements

In its earliest mode, the project required that peasants interested in participating agree to plant a minimum of 500 trees. Peasants not possessing the fifth of a hectare were permitted to enter into combinational arrangements that allowed several peasants to apply as a unit. This mechanism, however, was rarely invoked in practice, and in some regions of the country poorer peasants were reported to have been denied access to trees. In more cases, however, peasants simply gave away trees for which there was no room on their holding.

In view of the pressure that the 500-tree requirement was placing on some families and the unexpected demand that the project had triggered, the per family tree allotment was eventually lowered to 250. This reduced the number of trees available to each farmer but doubled the number of families reached.

Elimination of Incentives

I had from the outset a deep anthropological suspicion that Haitian peasants would respond enthusiastically to the theme of wood as a cash crop. But to hedge my bets I recommended that we build into the project an incentive system. Rather than linking recompense to the planting of trees, I recommended a strategy by which participating peasants would be paid a small cash recompense for each tree surviving after nine and eighteen months. Some members of the project team objected, saying that the tree itself would be sufficient recompense. I compromised by accepting an experimental arrangement: We used the incentive in some regions but made no mention of it in others.

After two seasons it became clear that the peasants in the nonincentive regions were as enthusiastic about signing up for trees as those in incentive regions and were as careful in protecting the trees. I was delighted to back down on this incentive issue: The income-generating tree itself, not an artificial incentive, was the prime engine of peasant enthusiasm. This was a spectacular and rewarding confirmation of the underlying anthropological hypothesis on which the entire project had been built.

The Anthropological Difference

Anthropological findings, methods, and theories clearly have heavily influenced this project at all stages. We are dealing, not with an ongoing project affected by anthropological input, but with a project whose very existence was rooted in anthropological research and whose very character was determined by ongoing anthropological direction and anthropologically informed managerial prodding.

My own involvement with the project spanned several phases and tasks:

1. Proposal of a theoretical and conceptual base of AOP, the concept of "wood as a cash crop."
2. Preliminary contacting of local PVOs to assess preproject interest.
3. Identification of specific program measures during project design.
4. Preparation of social soundness analysis for the AID project paper.
5. Participation as an outside expert at the meetings in AID Washington at which the fate of the project was decided.
6. Participation in the selection and in-country linguistic and cultural training of the agro-foresters who worked for the project.
7. Direction and supervision of field operations.
8. Formative evaluation of preliminary results and the identification of needed midcourse corrections.
9. Generation of several hundred thousand dollars of supplemental funding from Canadian and Swiss sources and internationalization of the project team.
10. Preparation of publications about the project. (Murray 1984, 1986)

In addition to my own participation in the AOP, four other anthropologists have been involved in long-term commitments to the project. Fred Conway did a preliminary study of firewood use in Haiti (Conway 1979). He subsequently served for two years as overall project coordinator within AID/Haiti. More recently he has carried out revealing case study research on the harvesting of project trees (Conway 1986). Glenn Smucker likewise did an early feasibility study in the northwest (Smucker 1981) and eventually joined the project as my successor in the directorship. Under his leadership many of the crucial midcourse corrections were introduced. Ira Lowenthal took over the AID coordination of the project at a critical transitional period and has been instrumental in forging plans for its institutional future. And Anthony Balzano has carried out several years of case study

fieldwork on the possible impact of the tree-planting activities on the land tenure in participating villages. All these individuals have PhDs, or are PhD candidates, in anthropology. And another anthropologist in the Haiti mission, John Lewis, succeeded in adapting the privatized umbrella agency outreach model for use in a swine repopulation project. With the possible exception of Vicos, it would be hard to imagine a project that has been as heavily influenced by anthropologists.

But how specifically has anthropology influenced the content of the project? There are at least three major levels at which anthropology has impinged on the content of AOP.

1. *The Application of Substantive Findings.* The very choice of "wood as a marketable crop" as the fundamental theme of the project stemmed from ethnographic knowledge of the cash-oriented foundations of Haitian peasant horticulture and knowledge of current conditions in the internal marketing system. Because of ethnographic knowledge I was able to avoid succumbing to the common-sense inclination to emphasize fruit trees (whose perishability and tendency to glut markets make them commercially vulnerable) and to choose instead the fast-growing wood tree. There is a feverishly escalating market for charcoal and construction wood that cannot be dampened even by the most successful project. And there are no spoilage problems with wood. The peasants can harvest it when they want. Furthermore, ethnographic knowledge of Haitian peasant land tenure—which is highly individualistic—guided me away from the community forest schemes that so many development philosophers seem to delight in but that are completely inappropriate to the social reality of Caribbean peasantries.

2. *Anthropological Methods.* The basic research that led up to the project employed participant observation along with intensive interviewing with small groups of informants to compare current cost/benefit ratios of traditional farming with projected cash yields from plots in which trees are intercropped with food on four-year rotation cycles. A critical part of the project design stage was to establish the likelihood of increased revenues from

altered land use behaviors. During project design I also applied ethnographic techniques to the behavior of institutional personnel. The application of anthropological notetaking on 3-by-5 slips, not only with peasants but also with technicians, managers, and officials, exposed the institutional roots of earlier project failures and stimulated the proposal of alternative institutional routes. Furthermore ethnoscientific elicitation of folk taxonomies led to the realization that whereas fruit trees are classified as a crop by Haitian peasants, wood trees are not so classified. This discovery exposed the need for the creation of explicit messages saying that wood can be a crop, just as coffee, manioc, and corn can. Finally, prior experience in Creole-language instrument design and computer analysis permitted me to design a baseline data-gathering system.

3. *Anthropological Theory.* My own thinking about tree planting was heavily guided by cultural-evolutionary insights into the origins of agriculture. The global tree problem is often erroneously conceptualized in a conservationist or ecological framework. Such a perspective is very short-sighted for anthropologists. We are aware of an ancient food crisis, when humans still hunted and gathered, that was solved, not by the adoption of conservationist practices, but rather by the shift into a domesticated mode of production. From hunting and gathering we turned to cropping and harvesting. I found the analogy with the present tree crisis conceptually overpowering. Trees will reemerge when and only when human beings start planting them aggressively as a harvestable crop, not when human consciousness is raised regarding their ecological importance. This anthropological insight (or bias), nourished by the aggressive creativity of the Haitian peasants among whom I had lived, swayed me toward the adoption of a dynamic "domestication" paradigm in proposing a solution to the tree problem in Haiti. This evolutionary perspective also permitted me to see that the cash-cropping of wood was in reality a small evolutionary step, not a quantum leap. The Haitian peasants already cut and sell natural stands of wood. They already plant and sell traditional food crops. It is but a small evolutionary step to join these two

unconnected streams of Haitian peasant behavior, and this linkage is the core purpose of the Agroforestry Outreach Project.

Broader anthropological theory also motivated and justified a nongovernmental implementing mode for AOP. Not only AID but also most international development agencies tend to operate on a service model of the state. This idealized model views the basic character of the state as that of a provider of services to its population. Adherence to this theoretically naive service model has led to the squandering of untold millions of dollars in the support of extractive public bureaucracies. This waste is justified under the rubric of institution building—assisting public entities to provide the services that they are supposed to be providing.

But my anthropological insights into the origins of the state as a mechanism of extraction and control led me to pose the somewhat heretical position that the predatory behavior of Duvalier's regime was in fact not misbehavior. Duvalier was merely doing openly and blatantly what other state leaders camouflage under rhetoric. AID's search of nongovernmental implementing channels for AOP, then, was not seen as a simple emergency measure to be employed under a misbehaving regime but rather as an avenue of activity that might be valid as an option under many or most regimes. There is little justification in either ethnology or anthropological theory for viewing the state as the proper recipient of developmental funds. This theoretical insight permitted us to argue for a radically nongovernmental mode of tree-planting support in AOP. In short, sensitivity to issues in anthropological theory played a profound role in the shaping of the project.

Would AOP have taken the form it did without these varied types of anthropological input? Almost certainly not. Had there been no anthropological input, a radically different scenario would almost certainly have unfolded with the following elements.

1. AID would probably have undertaken a reforestation project—congressional pressure alone would have ensured that. But the project would have been based, not on the theme of "wood as a

peasant cash-crop," but on the more traditional approach to trees as a vehicle of soil conservation. Ponderous educational programs would have been launched to teach the peasants about the value of trees. Emphasis would have been placed on educating the ignorant and on trying to induce peasants to plant commercially marginal (and nutritionally tangential) fruit trees instead of cash-generating wood trees.

2. The project would have been managed by technicians. The emphasis would probably have been on carrying out lengthy technical research concerning optimal planting strategies and the combination of trees with optimally effective bench terraces and other soil conservation devices. The outreach problem would have been given second priority. Throughout Haiti hundreds of thousands of dollars have been spent on numerous demonstration projects to create terraced, forested hillsides, but only a handful of cooperative local peasants have been induced to undertake the same activities on their own land.

3. The project would almost certainly have been run through the Haitian government. When after several hundred thousand dollars of expenditures few trees were visible, frustrated young AID program officers would have gotten finger-wagging lectures about the sovereign right of local officials to use donor money as they see fit. And the few trees planted would have been defined as *pyebwa leta* (the government's trees), and peasants would have been sternly warned against ever cutting these trees, even the ones planted on their own land. And the peasants would soon turn the problem over to their most effective ally in such matters, the free-ranging omnivorous goat, who would soon remove this alien vegetation from the peasant's land.

Because of anthropology, the Agroforestry Outreach Project has unfolded to a different scenario. It was a moving experience for me to return to the village where I had done my original fieldwork (and which I of course tried to involve in the tree-planting activities) to find several houses built using the wood from leucaena trees planted during the project's earliest phases. Poles were beginning to be sold, although the prices had not yet stabilized for these still unknown wood types. Charcoal made from project trees was being sold in local markets. For the first time in the history of this village, people were "growing" part of their house structures and their cooking fuel. I felt as though I were observing (and had been a participant in) a replay of an ancient anthropological drama, the shift from an extractive to a domesticated mode of resource procurement. Though their sources of food energy had been domesticated millennia ago, my former village neighbors had now begun replicating this transition in the domain of wood and wood-based energy. I felt a satisfaction at having chosen a discipline that could give me the privilege of participating, even marginally, in this very ancient cultural-evolutionary transition.

REFERENCES

Ashley, Marshall D. 1986. A Study of Traditional Agroforestry Systems in Haiti and Implications for the USAID/Haiti Agroforestry Outreach Project. Port-au-Prince: University of Maine Agroforestry Outreach Research Project.

Balzano, Anthony. 1986. Socioeconomic Aspects of Agroforestry in Rural Haiti. Port-au-Prince: University of Maine Agroforestry Outreach Research Project.

Buffum, William, and Wendy King. 1985. Small Farmer Decision Making and Tree Planting: Agroforestry Extension Recommendations. Port-au-Prince: Haiti Agroforestry Outreach Project.

Conway, Frederick. 1979. A Study of the Fuelwood Situation in Haiti. Port-au-Prince: USAID.

Conway, Frederick. 1986. The Decision Making Framework for Tree Planting Within the Agroforestry Outreach Project. Port-au-Prince: University of Maine Agroforestry Outreach Research Project.

Grosenick, Gerald. 1985. Economic Evaluation of the Agroforestry Outreach Project. Port-au-Prince: University of Maine Agroforestry Outreach Research Project.

McGowan, Lisa A. 1986. Potential Marketability of Charcoal, Poles, and Planks Produced by Participants in the Agroforestry Outreach Project. Port-au-Prince: University of Maine Agroforestry Outreach Research Project.

Murray, Gerald F. 1977. The Evolution of Haitian Peasant Land Tenure: A Case Study in Agrarian Adaptation to Population Growth. Ph.D. dissertation, Columbia University, New York.

Murray, Gerald F. 1978a, Hillside Units, Wage Labor, and Haitian Peasant Land Tenure: A Strategy for the Organization of Erosion Control. Port-au-Prince: USAID.

Murray, Gerald F. 1978b. Informal Subdivisions and Land Insecurity: An Analysis of Haitian Peasant Land Tenure. Port-au-Prince: USAID.

Murray, Gerald F. 1979. Terraces, Trees, and the Haitian Peasant: An Assessment of 25 Years of Erosion Control in Rural Haiti. Port-au-Prince: USAID.

Murray, Gerald F. 1984. The Wood Tree as a Peasant Cash-Crop: An Anthropological Strategy for the Domestication of Energy. In A. Valdman and R. Foster, eds., *Haiti—Today and Tomorrow; An Interdisciplinary Study*. New York: University Press of America.

Murray, Gerald F. 1986. Seeing the Forest While Planting the Trees: An Anthropological Approach to Agroforestry in Rural Haiti. In D. W. Brinkerhoff and J. C. Garcia-Zamor, eds., *Politics, Projects, and Peasants: Institutional Development in Haiti*. New York: Praeger, pp. 193–226.

Smucker, Glenn R. 1981. Trees and Charcoal in Haitian Peasant Economy: A Feasibility Study. Port-au-Prince: USAID.

Zuvekas, Clarence. 1978. Agricultural Development in Haiti: An Assessment of Sector Problems, Policies, and Prospects under Conditions of Severe Soil Erosion. Washington, D.C.: USAID.

DISCUSSION QUESTIONS

1. What were the factors that led to Haiti's problem of deforestation?

2. In what ways did an anthropologist (using anthropological insights) contribute to the huge success of the reforestation project in Haiti?

3. What barriers did Murray have to overcome in order to convince local farmers to participate in the reforestation project?

RESOURCES ON THE INTERNET

 InfoTrac College Edition

infotrac-college.com

You can find further relevant readings by searching *InfoTrac College Edition*, an online library with access to thousands of scholarly and popular periodicals. Below are suggested search terms for this article:

■ agricultural anthropology

■ reforestation

■ Agroforestry Outreach Project

Anthropology Online: Wadsworth's Anthropology Resource Center

academic.cengage.com/anthropology

The Wadsworth Anthropology Resource Center contains a wealth of information and useful tools for students including information on careers in anthropology.

7

Arranging a Marriage in India

SERENA NANDA

When viewed from a comparative perspective, middle-class North Americans tend to be fiercely independent. Children growing up in the United States and Canada are encouraged by their parents and teachers to solve their own problems and make their own decisions. Most parents, while they might have their preferences, are not likely to force their children to attend a particular college or enter into a profession against their will. And most North Americans would be repulsed by the thought of their parents determining who they would marry.

Yet this is exactly what Serena Nanda encountered on her first fieldwork experience in India. At first, Nanda could not understand why Indian women, particularly well-educated ones, would allow this most important (and personal) decision to be made by their parents. But as she became more immersed in Indian culture through the process of fieldwork, she gained a much fuller appreciation of the role of arranged marriages in India. In fact, after a while, Nanda became a willing participant in the system by actually helping arrange the marriage of the son of one of her Indian friends.

Nanda's article, while hardly as venerable as some in this volume, is important because it demonstrates the process of understanding another cultural system. Nanda, born and raised in the United States, tried to understand the system of arranged marriages in India through the lens of her own culture. But like the good ethnographer that she is, she kept an open mind and continued to probe her female informants with more and more questions, until eventually she saw the inherent logic of this particular form of marriage.

> *Sister and doctor brother-in-law invite correspondence from North Indian professionals only, for a beautiful, talented, sophisticated, intelligent sister, 5' 3", slim, M.A. in textile design, father a senior civil officer. Would prefer immigrant doctors, between 26–29 years. Reply with full details and returnable photo.*
>
> *A well-settled uncle invites matrimonial correspondence from slim, fair, educated South Indian girl, for his nephew, 25 years, smart, M.B.A., green card holder, 5' 6". Full particulars with returnable photo appreciated.*
>
> *Matrimonial Advertisements, India Abroad*

In India, almost all marriages are arranged. Even among the educated middle classes in modern, urban India, marriage is as much a concern of the families as it is of the individuals. So customary is

SOURCE: From Serena Nanda, "Arranging a Marriage in India." In Philip De Vita (ed.). *Stumbling Toward Truth: Anthropologists at Work*, pp. 196–204. Prospect Heights, IL: Waveland, 2000. Reprinted with the permission of the author.

the practice of arranged marriage that there is a special name for a marriage which is not arranged: It is called a "love match."

On my first field trip to India, I met many young men and women whose parents were in the process of "getting them married." In many cases, the bride and groom would not meet each other before the marriage. At most they might meet for a brief conversation, and this meeting would take place only after their parents had decided that the match was suitable. Parents do not compel their children to marry a person who either marriage partner finds objectionable. But only after one match is refused will another be sought.

As a young American woman in India for the first time, I found this custom of arranged marriage oppressive. How could any intelligent young person agree to such a marriage without great reluctance? It was contrary to everything I believed about the importance of romantic love as the only basis of a happy marriage. It also clashed with my strongly held notions that the choice of such an intimate and permanent relationship could be made only by the individuals involved. Had anyone tried to arrange my marriage, I would have been defiant and rebellious!

At the first opportunity, I began, with more curiosity than tact, to question the young people I met on how they felt about this practice. Sita, one of my young informants, was a college graduate with a degree in political science. She had been waiting for over a year while her parents were arranging a match for her. I found it difficult to accept the docile manner in which this well-educated young woman awaited the outcome of a process that would result in her spending the rest of her life with a man she hardly knew, a virtual stranger, picked out by her parents.

"How can you go along with this?" I asked her, in frustration and distress. "Don't you care who you marry?"

"Of course I care," she answered. "This is why I must let my parents choose a boy for me. My marriage is too important to be arranged by such an inexperienced person as myself. In such matters, it is better to have my parents' guidance."

I had learned that young men and women in India do not date and have very little social life involving members of the opposite sex. Although I could not disagree with Sita's reasoning, I continued to pursue the subject.

"But how can you marry the first man you have ever met? Not only have you missed the fun of meeting a lot of different people, but you have not given yourself the chance to know who is the right man for you."

"Meeting with a lot of different people doesn't sound like any fun at all," Sita answered. "One hears that in America the girls are spending all their time worrying about whether they will meet a man and get married. Here we have the chance to enjoy our life and let our parents do this work and worrying for us."

She had me there. The high anxiety of the competition to "be popular" with the opposite sex certainly was the most prominent feature of life as an American teenager in the late fifties. The endless worrying about the rules that governed our behavior and about our popularity ratings sapped both our self-esteem and our enjoyment of adolescence. I reflected that absence of this competition in India most certainly may have contributed to the self-confidence and natural charm of so many of the young women I met.

And yet, the idea of marrying a perfect stranger, whom one did not know and did not "love," so offended my American ideas of individualism and romanticism, that I persisted with my objections.

"I still can't imagine it," I said. "How can you agree to marry a man you hardly know?"

"But of course he will be known. My parents would never arrange a marriage for me without knowing all about the boy's family background. Naturally we will not rely only on what the family tells us. We will check the particulars out ourselves. No one will want their daughter to marry into a family that is not good. All these things we will know beforehand."

Impatiently, I responded, "Sita, I don't mean know the family, I mean, know the man. How can you marry someone you don't know personally and don't love? How can you think of spending your life with someone you may not even like?"

"If he is a good man, why should I not like him?" she said. "With you people, you know the boy so well before you marry, where will be the fun to get married? There will be no mystery and no romance. Here we have the whole of our married life to get to know and love our husband. This way is better, is it not?"

Her response made further sense, and I began to have second thoughts on the matter. Indeed, during months of meeting many intelligent young Indian people, both male and female, who had the same ideas as Sita, I saw arranged marriages in a different light. I also saw the importance of the family in Indian life and realized that a couple who took their marriage into their own hands was taking a big risk, particularly if their families were irreconcilably opposed to the match. In a country where every important resource in life—a job, a house, a social circle—is gained through family connections, it seemed foolhardy to cut oneself off from a supportive social network and depend solely on one person for happiness and success.

———————

Six years later I returned to India to again do fieldwork, this time among the middle class in Bombay, a modern, sophisticated city. From the experience of my earlier visit, I decided to include a study of arranged marriages in my project. By this time I had met many Indian couples whose marriages had been arranged and who seemed very happy. Particularly in contrast to the fate of many of my married friends in the United States who were already in the process of divorce, the positive aspects of arranged marriages appeared to me to outweigh the negatives. In fact, I thought I might even participate in arranging a marriage myself. I had been fairly successful in the United States in "fixing up" many of my friends, and I was confident that my matchmaking skills could be easily applied to this new situation, once I learned the basic rules. "After all," I thought, "how complicated can it be? People want pretty much the same things in a marriage whether it is in India or America."

An opportunity presented itself almost immediately. A friend from my previous Indian trip was in the process of arranging for the marriage of her eldest son. In India there is a perceived shortage of "good boys," and since my friend's family was eminently respectable and the boy himself personable, well educated, and nice looking, I was sure that by the end of my year's fieldwork, we would have found a match.

The basic rule seems to be that a family's reputation is most important. It is understood that matches would be arranged only within the same caste and general social class, although some crossing of subcastes is permissible if the class positions of the bride's and groom's families are similar. Although dowry is now prohibited by law in India, extensive gift exchanges took place with every marriage. Even when the boy's family do not "make demands," every girl's family nevertheless feels the obligation to give the traditional gifts, to the girl, to the boy, and to the boy's family. Particularly when the couple would be living in the joint family—that is, with the boy's parents and his married brothers and their families, as well as with unmarried siblings—which is still very common even among the urban, upper-middle class in India, the girl's parents are anxious to establish smooth relations between their family and that of the boy. Offering the proper gifts, even when not called "dowry," is often an important factor in influencing the relationship between the bride's and groom's families and perhaps, also, the treatment of the bride in her new home.

In a society where divorce is still a scandal and where, in fact, the divorce rate is exceedingly low, an arranged marriage is the beginning of a lifetime relationship not just between the bride and groom but between their families as well. Thus, while a girl's looks are important, her character is even more so, for she is being judged as a prospective daughter-in-law as much as a prospective bride. Where she would be living in a joint family, as was the case with my friend, the girl's ability to get along harmoniously in a family is perhaps the single most important quality in assessing her suitability.

My friend is a highly esteemed wife, mother, and daughter-in-law. She is religious, soft-spoken, modest, and deferential. She rarely gossips and never quarrels, two qualities highly desirable in a woman. A family that has the reputation for gossip and conflict among its womenfolk will not find it easy to get good wives for their sons. Parents will not want to send their daughter to a house in which there is conflict.

My friend's family were originally from North India. They had lived in Bombay, where her husband owned a business, for forty years. The family had delayed in seeking a match for their eldest son because he had been an Air Force pilot for several years, stationed in such remote places that it had seemed fruitless to try to find a girl who would be willing to accompany him. In their social class, a military career, despite its economic security, has little prestige and is considered a drawback in finding a suitable bride. Many families would not allow their daughters to marry a man in an occupation so potentially dangerous and which requires so much moving around.

The son had recently left the military and joined his father's business. Since he was a college graduate, modern, and well traveled, from such a good family, and, I thought, quite handsome, it seemed to me that he, or rather his family, was in a position to pick and choose. I said as much to my friend.

While she agreed that there were many advantages on their side, she also said, "We must keep in mind that my son is both short and dark; these are drawbacks in finding the right match." While the boy's height had not escaped my notice, "dark" seemed to me inaccurate; I would have called him "wheat" colored perhaps, and in any case, I did not realize that color would be a consideration. I discovered, however, that while a boy's skin color is a less important consideration than a girl's, it is still a factor.

An important source of contacts in trying to arrange her son's marriage was my friend's social club in Bombay. Many of the women had daughters of the right age, and some had already expressed an interest in my friend's son. I was most enthusiastic about the possibilities of one particular family who had five daughters, all of whom were pretty, demure, and well educated. Their mother had told my friend, "You can have your pick for your son, whichever one of my daughters appeals to you most."

I saw a match in sight. "Surely," I said to my friend, "we will find one there. Let's go visit and make our choice." But my friend held back; she did not seem to share my enthusiasm, for reasons I could not then fathom.

When I kept pressing for an explanation of her reluctance, she admitted, "See, Serena, here is the problem. The family has so many daughters, how will they be able to provide nicely for any of them? We are not making any demands, but still, with so many daughters to marry off, one wonders whether she will even be able to make a proper wedding. Since this is our eldest son, it's best if we marry him to a girl who is the only daughter, then the wedding will truly be a gala affair." I argued that surely the quality of the girls themselves made up for any deficiency in the elaborateness of the wedding. My friend admitted this point but still seemed reluctant to proceed.

"Is there something else," I asked her, "some factor I have missed?" "Well," she finally said, "there is one other thing. They have one daughter already married and living in Bombay. The mother is always complaining to me that the girl's in-laws don't let her visit her own family often enough. So it makes me wonder, will she be that kind of mother who always wants her daughter at her own home? This will prevent the girl from adjusting to our house. It is not a good thing." And so, this family of five daughters was dropped as a possibility.

Somewhat disappointed, I nevertheless respected my friend's reasoning and geared up for the next prospect. This was also the daughter of a woman in my friend's social club. There was clear interest in this family and I could see why. The family's reputation was excellent; in fact, they came from a subcaste slightly higher than my friend's own. The girl, who was an only daughter, was pretty and well educated and had a brother studying in the United States. Yet, after expressing an interest to me in this family, all talk of them suddenly died down and the search began elsewhere.

"What happened to that girl as a prospect?" I asked one day. "You never mention her any more.

She is so pretty and so educated, what did you find wrong?"

"She is too educated. We've decided against it. My husband's father saw the girl on the bus the other day and thought her forward. A girl who 'roams about' the city by herself is not the girl for our family." My disappointment this time was even greater, as I thought the son would have liked the girl very much. But then I thought, my friend is right, a girl who is going to live in a joint family cannot be too independent or she will make life miserable for everyone. I also learned that if the family of the girl has even a slightly higher social status than the family of the boy, the bride may think herself too good for them, and this too will cause problems. Later my friend admitted to me that this had been an important factor in her decision not to pursue the match.

The next candidate was the daughter of a client of my friend's husband. When the client learned that the family was looking for a match for their son, he said, "Look no further, we have a daughter." This man then invited my friends to dinner to see the girl. He had already seen their son at the office and decided that "he liked the boy." We all went together for tea, rather than dinner—it was less of a commitment—and while we were there, the girl's mother showed us around the house. The girl was studying for her exams and was briefly introduced to us.

After we left, I was anxious to hear my friend's opinion. While her husband liked the family very much and was impressed with his client's business accomplishments and reputation, the wife didn't like the girl's looks. "She is short, no doubt, which is an important plus point, but she is also fat and wears glasses." My friend obviously thought she could do better for her son and asked her husband to make his excuses to his client by saying that they had decided to postpone the boy's marriage indefinitely.

By this time almost six months had passed and I was becoming impatient. What I had thought would be an easy matter to arrange was turning out to be quite complicated. I began to believe that between my friend's desire for a girl who was modest enough to fit into her joint family, yet attractive and educated enough to be an acceptable

partner for her son, she would not find anyone suitable. My friend laughed at my impatience: "Don't be so much in a hurry," she said. "You Americans want everything done so quickly. You get married quickly and then just as quickly get divorced. Here we take marriage more seriously. We must take all the factors into account. It is not enough for us to learn by our mistakes. This is too serious a business. If a mistake is made we have not only ruined the life of our son or daughter, but we have spoiled the reputation of our family as well. And that will make it much harder for their brothers and sisters to get married. So we must be very careful."

What she said was true and I promised myself to be more patient, though it was not easy. I had really hoped and expected that the match would be made before my year in India was up. But it was not to be. When I left India my friend seemed no further along in finding a suitable match for her son than when I had arrived.

Two years later, I returned to India and still my friend had not found a girl for her son. By this time, he was close to thirty, and I think she was a little worried. Since she knew I had friends all over India, and I was going to be there for a year, she asked me to "help her in this work" and keep an eye out for someone suitable. I was flattered that my judgment was respected, but knowing now how complicated the process was, I had lost my earlier confidence as a matchmaker. Nevertheless, I promised that I would try.

It was almost at the end of my year's stay in India that I met a family with a marriageable daughter whom I felt might be a good possibility for my friend's son. The girl's father was related to a good friend of mine and by coincidence came from the same village as my friend's husband. This new family had a successful business in a medium-sized city in central India and were from the same subcaste as my friend. The daughter was pretty and chic; in fact, she had studied fashion design in college. Her parents would not allow her to go off by herself to any of the major cities in India where she could make a career, but they had compromised with her wish to work by allowing her to run a small dressmaking boutique from their home. In spite of her desire to have a career, the daughter was both modest and home-loving and had had a traditional, sheltered upbringing. She had only one other sister, already married, and a brother who was in his father's business.

I mentioned the possibility of a match with my friend's son. The girl's parents were most interested. Although their daughter was not eager to marry just yet, the idea of living in Bombay—a sophisticated, extremely fashion-conscious city where she could continue her education in clothing design—was a great inducement. I gave the girl's father my friend's address and suggested that when they went to Bombay on some business or whatever, they look up the boy's family.

Returning to Bombay on my way to New York, I told my friend of this newly discovered possibility. She seemed to feel there was potential

but, in spite of my urging, would not make any moves herself. She rather preferred to wait for the girl's family to call upon them. I hoped something would come of this introduction, though by now I had learned to rein in my optimism.

A year later I received a letter from my friend. The family had indeed come to visit Bombay, and their daughter and my friend's daughter, who were near in age, had become very good friends. During that year, the two girls had frequently visited each other. I thought things looked promising.

Last week I received an invitation to a wedding: My friend's son and the girl were getting married. Since I had found the match, my presence was particularly requested at the wedding. I was thrilled. Success at last! As I prepared to leave for India, I began thinking, "Now, my friend's younger son, who do I know who has a nice girl for him ...?"

The previous essay was written from the point of view of a family seeking a daughter-in-law. Arranged marriage looks somewhat different from the point of view of the bride and her family. Arranged marriage continues to be preferred, even among the more educated, Westernized sections of the Indian population. Many young women from these families still go along, more or less willingly, with the practice, and also with the specific choices of their families. Young women do get excited about the prospects of their marriage, but there is also ambivalence and increasing uncertainty, as the bride contemplates leaving the comfort and familiarity of her own home, where as a "temporary guest" she has often been indulged, to live among strangers. Even in the best situation, she will now come under the close scrutiny of her husband's family. How she dresses, how she behaves, how she gets along with others, where she goes, how she spends her time, her domestic abilities—all of this and much more —will be observed and commented on by a whole new set of relations. Her interaction with her family of birth will be monitored and curtailed considerably. Not only will she leave their home, but with increasing geographic mobility, she may also live very far from them, perhaps even on another continent. Too much expression of her fondness for her own family, or her desire to visit them, may be interpreted as an inability to adjust to her new family, and may become a source of conflict. In an arranged marriage, the burden of adjustment is clearly heavier for a woman than for a man. And that is in the best of situations.

In less happy circumstances, the bride may be a target of resentment and hostility from her husband's family, particularly her mother-in-law or her husband's unmarried sisters, for whom she is now a source of competition for the affection, loyalty, and economic resources of their son or brother. If she is psychologically, or even physically abused, her options are limited, as returning to her parent's home, or divorce, are still very stigmatized. For most Indians, marriage and motherhood are still considered the only suitable roles for a woman, even for those who have careers, and few women can comfortably contemplate remaining unmarried. Most families still consider "marrying off" their daughters as a compelling religious duty and social necessity. This increases a bride's sense of obligation to make the marriage a success, at whatever cost to her own personal happiness.

The vulnerability of a new bride may also be intensified by the issue of dowry that, although illegal, has become a more pressing issue in the consumer conscious society of contemporary urban India. In many cases, where a groom's family is not satisfied with the amount of dowry a bride brings to her marriage, the young bride will be constantly harassed to get her parents to give more. In extreme cases, the bride may even be murdered, and the murder disguised as an accident or suicide. This also offers the husband's family an opportunity to arrange another match for him, thus bringing in another dowry. This phenomenon, called dowry death, calls attention not just to the "evils of dowry" but also to larger issues of the powerlessness of women as well.

Afterword by Serena Nanda, 2007

DISCUSSION QUESTIONS

1. What are the advantages and the disadvantages of arranged marriage? Do you feel that the disadvantages outweigh the advantages or vice versa?

2. What traits do parents in India look for when arranging a marriage for their sons and daughters?

3. When arranging a marriage for one's adult son, why would traditional Indian parents be reluctant to look for a bride from a family that has many daughters?

4. After reading this article, have your changed your mind about wanting an arranged marriage for yourself?

 **RESOURCES ON THE INTERNET**

 InfoTrac College Edition

infotrac-college.com

You can find further relevant readings by searching *InfoTrac College Edition*, an online library with access to thousands of scholarly and popular periodicals. Below are suggested search terms for this article:

- arranged marriage
- match-making
- arranging a marriage over the Internet

Anthropology Online: Wadsworth's Anthropology Resource Center

academic.cengage.com/anthropology

The Wadsworth Anthropology Resource Center contains a wealth of information and useful tools for students including information on careers in anthropology.

8

Death without Weeping

NANCY SCHEPER-HUGHES

Most anthropologists acknowledge a special emotional bond that exists between mother and child, owing to the physical nature of pregnancy and birth, in whatever culture they may be found. But can these strong psychological bonds undergo significant changes in the face of severe economic and social conditions? In this article about mothers in a Brazilian shanty-town, anthropologist Nancy Scheper-Hughes examines how extreme poverty, deprivation, hunger, and economic exploitation can cause mothers not to mourn the death of their children. She found that mothers living under these extreme conditions develop a strategy of delayed attachment to their children, withholding emotional involvement until they are reasonably sure the child will survive. Such a strategy—while appearing cruel and unfeeling to those of us in our comfortable, middle-class surroundings—is really an emotional coping strategy for mothers living with an extraordinarily high infant and child mortality rate. Rather than seeing "mother love" as an absolute cultural universal, Scheper-Hughes suggests that, under these extreme conditions, it is a luxury reserved for those children who survive. This article, and the book on which it is based written in 1992, provide a thoughtful and wrenching analysis of how poverty and injustice can lead to the demise of a mother's basic human right of weeping for her dead children.

Scheper-Hughes reminds us that cultures are not isolated, insulated entities that determine people's behavior. Instead we are compelled to look at the factors from the wider society—such as political, religious, and economic institutions—impinging on people's behavior.

> *I have seen death without weeping*
> *The destiny of the Northeast is death*
> *Cattle they kill*
> *To the people they do something worse*
>
> *—Anonymous Brazilian Singer (1965)*

"Why do the church bells ring so often?" I asked Nailza de Arruda soon after I moved into a corner of her tiny mud-walled hut near the top of the shantytown called the Alto do Cruzeiro (Crucifix Hill). I was then a Peace Corps volunteer and a community development/health worker. It was the dry and blazing hot summer of 1965, the months following the military coup in Brazil, and save for the rusty, clanging bells of N. S. das Dores Church, an eerie quiet had settled over the market

SOURCE: From *Natural History*, October, 1989, pp. 8, 10, 12, 14, 16. © 1989 by Nancy Scheper-Hughes. Reprinted by permission of the author.

town that I call Bom Jesus da Mata. Beneath the quiet, however, there was chaos and panic. "It's nothing," replied Nailza, "just another little angel gone to heaven."

Nailza had sent more than her share of little angels to heaven, and sometimes at night I could hear her engaged in a muffled but passionate discourse with one of them, two-year-old Joana. Joana's photograph, taken as she lay propped up in her tiny cardboard coffin, her eyes open, hung on a wall next to one of Nailza and Ze Antonio taken on the day they eloped.

Nailza could barely remember the other infants and babies who came and went in close succession. Most had died unnamed and were hastily baptized in their coffins. Few lived more than a month or two. Only Joana, properly baptized in church at the close of her first year and placed under the protection of a powerful saint, Joan of Arc, had been expected to live. And Nailza had dangerously allowed herself to love the little girl.

In addressing the dead child, Nailza's voice would range from tearful imploring to angry recrimination: "Why did you leave me? Was your patron saint so greedy that she could not allow me one child on this earth?" Ze Antonio advised me to ignore Nailza's odd behavior, which he understood as a kind of madness that, like the birth and death of children, came and went. Indeed, the premature birth of a stillborn son some months later "cured" Nailza of her "inappropriate" grief, and the day came when she removed Joana's photo and carefully packed it away.

More than fifteen years elapsed before I returned to the Alto do Cruzeiro, and it was anthropology that provided the vehicle of my return. Since 1982 I have returned several times in order to pursue a problem that first attracted my attention in the 1960s. My involvement with the people of the Alto do Cruzeiro now spans a quarter of a century and three generations of parenting in a community where mothers and daughters are often simultaneously pregnant.

The Alto do Cruzeiro is one of three shanty-towns surrounding the large market town of Bom Jesus in the sugar plantation zone of Pernambuco in Northeast Brazil, one of the many zones of neglect that have emerged in the shadow of the now tarnished economic miracle of Brazil. For the women and children of the Alto do Cruzeiro the only miracle is that some of them have managed to stay alive at all.

The Northeast is a region of vast proportions (approximately twice the size of Texas) and of equally vast social and developmental problems. The nine states that make up the region are the poorest in the country and are representative of the Third World within a dynamic and rapidly industrializing nation. Despite waves of migrations from the interior to the teeming shantytowns of coastal cities, the majority still live in rural areas on farms and ranches, sugar plantations and mills.

Life expectancy in the Northeast is only forty years, largely because of the appallingly high rate of infant and child mortality. Approximately one million children in Brazil under the age of five die each year. The children of the Northeast, especially those born in shantytowns on the periphery of urban life, are at a very high risk of death. In these areas, children are born without the traditional protection of breast-feeding, subsistence gardens, stable marriages, and multiple adult caretakers that exists in the interior. In the hillside shantytowns that spring up around cities or, in this case, interior market towns, marriages are brittle, single parenting is the norm, and women are frequently forced into the shadow economy of domestic work in the homes of the rich or into unprotected and often-times "scab" wage labor on the surrounding sugar plantations, where they clear land for planting and weed for a pittance, sometimes less than a dollar a day. The women of the Alto may not bring their babies with them into the homes of the wealthy, where the often sick infants are considered sources of contamination, and they cannot carry the little ones to the riverbanks where they wash clothes because the river is heavily infested with schistosomes and other deadly parasites. Nor can they carry their young children to the plantations, which are often several miles away. At wages of a dollar a day, the women of the Alto cannot hire baby sitters. Older children who are not in school will sometimes serve as somewhat indifferent caretakers. But any child not in school is also expected to find wage work. In most cases, babies are simply left at home alone, the door securely fastened. And so many also die alone and unattended.

Bom Jesus da Mata, centrally located in the plantation zone of Pernambuco, is within commuting distance of several sugar plantations and mills. Consequently, Bom Jesus has been a magnet for rural workers forced off their small subsistence plots by large landowners wanting to use every available piece of land for sugar cultivation. Initially, the rural migrants to Bom Jesus were squatters who were given tacit approval by the mayor to put up temporary straw huts on each of the three hills overlooking the town. The Alto do Cruzeiro is the oldest, the largest, and the poorest of the shantytowns. Over the past three decades many of the original migrants have become permanent residents, and the primitive and temporary straw huts have been replaced by small homes (usually of two rooms) made of wattle and daub, sometimes covered with plaster. The more affluent residents use bricks and tiles. In most Alto homes, dangerous kerosene lamps have been replaced by light bulbs. The once tattered rural garb, often fashioned from used sugar sacking, has likewise been replaced by store-bought clothes, often castoffs from a wealthy *patrão* (boss). The trappings are modern, but the hunger, sickness, and death that they conceal are traditional, deeply rooted in a history of feudalism, exploitation, and institutionalized dependency.

My research agenda never wavered. The questions I addressed first crystallized during a veritable "die-off" of Alto babies during a severe drought in 1965. The food and water shortages and the political and economic chaos occasioned by the military coup were reflected in the handwritten entries of births and deaths in the dusty, yellowed pages of the ledger books kept at the public registry office in Bom Jesus. More than 350 babies died in the Alto during 1965 alone—this from a shantytown population of little more than 5,000. But that wasn't what surprised me. There were reasons enough for the deaths in the miserable conditions of shantytown life. What puzzled me was the seeming indifference of Alto women to the death of their infants, and their willingness to attribute to their own tiny offspring an aversion to life that made their death seem wholly natural, indeed all but anticipated.

Although I found that it was possible, and hardly difficult, to rescue infants and toddlers from death by diarrhea and dehydration with a simple sugar, salt, and water solution (even bottled Coca-Cola worked fine), it was more difficult to enlist a mother herself in the rescue of a child she perceived as ill-fated for life or better off dead, or to convince her to take back into her threatened and besieged home a baby she had already come to think of as an angel rather than as a son or daughter.

I learned that the high expectancy of death, and the ability to face child death with stoicism and equanimity, produced patterns of nurturing that differentiated between those infants thought of as thrivers and survivors and those thought of as born already "wanting to die." The survivors were nurtured, while stigmatized, doomed infants were left to die, as mothers say, *a mingua,* "of neglect." Mothers stepped back and allowed nature to take its course. This pattern, which I call mortal selective neglect, is called passive infanticide by anthropologist Marvin Harris. The Alto situation, although culturally specific in the form that it takes, is not unique to Third World shantytown communities and may have its correlates in our own impoverished urban communities in some cases of "failure to thrive" infants.

I use as an example the story of Zezinho, the thirteen-month-old toddler of one of my neighbors, Lourdes. I became involved with Zezinho when I was called in to help Lourdes in the delivery of another child, this one a fair and robust little tyke with a lusty cry. I noted that while Lourdes showed great interest in the newborn, she totally ignored Zezinho who, wasted and severely malnourished, was curled up in a fetal position on a piece of urine- and feces-soaked cardboard placed under his mother's hammock. Eyes open and vacant, mouth slack, the little boy seemed doomed.

When I carried Zezinho up to the community day-care center at the top of the hill, the Alto women who took turns caring for one another's children (in order to free themselves for part-time work in the cane fields or washing clothes) laughed at my efforts to save Ze, agreeing with Lourdes that here was a baby without a ghost of a chance. Leave him alone, they cautioned. It makes no sense to fight with death. But I did do battle with Ze, and after several weeks of force-feeding (malnourished babies lose their interest in food), Ze began to succumb to my ministrations. He acquired some flesh across his taut chest bones, learned to sit up, and even tried to smile. When he seemed well enough, I returned him to Lourdes in her miserable scrap-material lean-to, but not without guilt about what I had done. I wondered whether returning Ze was at all fair to Lourdes and to his little brother. But I was busy and washed my hands of the matter. And Lourdes did seem more interested in Ze now that he was looking more human.

When I returned in 1982, there was Lourdes among the women who formed my sample of Alto mothers—still struggling to put together some semblance of life for a now grown Ze and her five other surviving children. Much was made of my reunion with Ze in 1982, and everyone enjoyed retelling the story of Ze's rescue and of how his mother had given him up for dead. Ze would laugh the loudest when told how I had had to force-feed him like a fiesta turkey. There was no hint of guilt on the part of Lourdes and no resentment on the part of Ze. In fact, when questioned in private as to who was the best friend he ever had in life, Ze took a long drag on his cigarette and answered without a trace of irony, "Why my mother, of course." "But of course," I replied.

Part of learning how to mother in the Alto do Cruzeiro is learning when to let go of a child who shows that it "wants" to die or that it has no "knack" or no "taste" for life. Another part is learning when it is safe to let oneself love a child. Frequent child death remains a powerful shaper of maternal thinking and practice. In the absence of firm expectation that a child will survive, mother love as we conceptualize it (whether in popular terms or in the psychobiological notion of maternal

bonding) is attenuated and delayed with consequences for infant survival. In an environment already precarious to young life, the emotional detachment of mothers toward some of their babies contributes even further to the spiral of high mortality—high fertility in a kind of macabre lock-step dance of death.

The average woman of the Alto experiences 9.5 pregnancies, 3.5 child deaths, and 1.5 stillbirths. Seventy percent of all child deaths in the Alto occur in the first six months of life, and 82 percent by the end of the first year. Of all deaths in the community each year, about 45 percent are of children under the age of five.

Women of the Alto distinguish between child deaths understood as natural (caused by diarrhea and communicable diseases) and those resulting from sorcery, the evil eye, or other magical or supernatural afflictions. They also recognize a large category of infant deaths seen as fated and inevitable. These hopeless cases are classified by mothers under the folk terminology "child sickness" or "child attack." Women say that there are at least fourteen different types of hopeless child sickness, but most can be subsumed under two categories—chronic and acute. The chronic cases refer to infants who are born small and wasted. They are deathly pale, mothers say, as well as weak and passive. They demonstrate no vital force, no liveliness. They do not suck vigorously; they hardly cry. Such babies can be this way at birth or they can be born sound but soon show no resistance, no "fight" against the common crises of infancy: diarrhea, respiratory infections, tropical fevers.

The acute cases are those doomed infants who die suddenly and violently. They are taken by stealth overnight, often following convulsions that bring on head banging, shaking, grimacing, and shrieking. Women say it is horrible to look at such a baby. If the infant begins to foam at the mouth or gnash its teeth or go rigid with its eyes turned back inside its head, there is absolutely no hope. The infant is "put aside"—left alone—often on the floor in a back room, and allowed to die. These symptoms (which accompany high fevers, dehydration, third-stage malnutrition, and encephalitis) are equated by Alto women with madness, epilepsy, and worst of all, rabies, which is greatly feared and highly stigmatized.

Most of the infants presented to me as suffering from chronic child sickness were tiny, wasted famine victims, while those labeled as victims of acute child attack seemed to be infants suffering from the deliriums of high fever or the convulsions that can accompany electrolyte imbalance in dehydrated babies.

Local midwives and traditional healers, praying women, as they are called, advise Alto women on when to allow a baby to die. One midwife explained: "If I can see that a baby was born unfortuitously, I tell the mother that she need not wash the infant or give it a cleansing tea. I tell her just to dust the infant with baby powder and wait for it to die." Allowing nature to take its course is not seen as sinful by these often very devout Catholic women. Rather, it is understood as cooperating with God's plan.

Often I have been asked how consciously women of the Alto behave in this regard. I would have to say that consciousness is always shifting between allowed and disallowed levels of awareness. For example, I was awakened early one morning in 1987 by two neighborhood children who had been sent to fetch me to a hastily organized wake for a two-month-old infant whose mother I had unsuccessfully urged to breast-feed. The infant was being sustained on sugar water, which the mother referred to as *soro* (serum), using a medical term for the infant's starvation regime in light of his chronic diarrhea. I had cautioned the mother that an infant could not live on *soro* forever.

The two girls urged me to console the young mother by telling her that it was "too bad" that her infant was so weak that Jesus had to take him. They were coaching me in proper Alto etiquette. I agreed, of course, but asked, "And what do *you* think?" Xoxa, the eleven-year-old, looked down at her dusty flip-flops and blurted out, "Oh, Dona Nanci, that baby never got enough to eat, but you must never say that!" And so the death of hungry babies remains one of the best kept secrets of life in Bom Jesus da Mata.

Most victims are waked quickly and with a minimum of ceremony. No tears are shed, and the neighborhood children form a tiny procession, carrying the baby to the town graveyard where it will join a multitude of others. Although a few fresh flowers may be scattered over the tiny grave, no stone or wooden cross will mark the place, and the same spot will be reused within a few months' time. The mother will never visit the grave, which soon becomes an anonymous one.

What, then, can be said of these women? What emotions, what sentiments motivate them? How are they able to do what, in fact, must be done? What does mother love mean in this inhospitable context? Are grief, mourning, and melancholia present, although deeply repressed? If so, where shall we look for them? And if not, how are we to understand the moral visions and moral sensibilities that guide their actions?

I have been criticized more than once for presenting an unflattering portrait of poor Brazilian women, women who are, after all, themselves the victims of severe social and institutional neglect. I have described these women as allowing some of their children to die, as if this were an unnatural and inhuman act rather than, as I would assert, the way any one of us might act, reasonably and rationally, under similarly desperate conditions. Perhaps I have not emphasized enough the real pathogens in this environment of high risk: poverty, deprivation, sexism, chronic hunger, and economic exploitation. If mother love is, as many psychologists and some feminists believe, a seemingly natural and universal maternal script, what does it mean to women for whom scarcity, loss, sickness, and deprivation have made that love frantic and robbed them of their grief, seeming to turn their hearts to stone?

Throughout much of human history—as in a great deal of the impoverished Third World today—women have had to give birth and to nurture children under ecological conditions and social arrangements hostile to child survival, as well as to their own well-being. Under circumstances of high childhood mortality, patterns of selective neglect and passive infanticide may be seen as active survival strategies.

They also seem to be fairly common practices historically and across cultures. In societies characterized by high childhood mortality and by a correspondingly high (replacement) fertility, cultural practices of infant and child care tend to be organized primarily around survival goals. But what this means is a pragmatic recognition that not all of one's children can be expected to live. The nervousness about child survival in areas of northeast Brazil, northern India, or Bangladesh, where a 30 percent or 40 percent mortality rate in the first years of life is common, can lead to forms of delayed attachment and a casual or benign neglect that serves to weed out the worst bets so as to enhance the life chances of healthier siblings, including those yet to be born. Practices similar to those that I am describing have been recorded for parts of Africa, India, and Central America.

Life in the Alto do Cruzeiro resembles nothing so much as a battlefield or an emergency room in an overcrowded inner-city public hospital. Consequently, morality is guided by a kind of "lifeboat ethics," the morality of triage. The seemingly studied indifference toward the suffering of some of their infants, conveyed in such sayings as "little critters have no feelings," is understandable in light of these women's obligation to carry on with their reproductive and nurturing lives.

In their slowness to anthropomorphize and personalize their infants, everything is mobilized so as to prevent maternal over-attachment and, therefore, grief at death. The bereaved mother is told not to cry, that her tears will dampen the wings of her little angel so that she cannot fly up to her heavenly home. Grief at the death of an angel is not only inappropriate, it is a symptom of madness and of a profound lack of faith.

Infant death becomes routine in an environment in which death is anticipated and bets are hedged. While the routinization of death in the context of shantytown life is not hard to understand, and quite possible to empathize with, its routinization in the formal institutions of public life in Bom Jesus is not as easy to accept uncritically. Here the social production of indifference takes on a different, even a malevolent, cast.

In a society where triplicates of every form are required for the most banal events (registering a car, for example), the registration of infant and child death is informal, incomplete, and rapid. It requires no documentation, takes less than five minutes, and demands no witnesses other than office clerks. No questions are asked concerning the circumstances of the death, and the cause of death is left blank, unquestioned and unexamined. A neighbor, grandmother, older sibling, or common-law husband may register the death. Since most infants die at home, there is no question of a medical record.

From the registry office, the parent proceeds to the town hall, where the mayor will give him or her a voucher for a free baby coffin. The fulltime municipal coffinmaker cannot tell you exactly how many baby coffins are dispatched each week. It varies, he says, with the seasons. There are more needed during the drought months and during the big festivals of Carnaval and Christmas and São Joao's Day because people are too busy, he supposes, to take their babies to the clinic. Record keeping is sloppy.

Similarly, there is a failure on the part of city-employed doctors working at two free clinics to recognize the malnutrition of babies who are weighed, measured, and immunized without comment and as if they were not, in fact, anemic, stunted, fussy, and irritated starvation babies. At best the mothers are told to pick up free vitamins or a health "tonic" at the municipal chambers. At worst, clinic personnel will give tranquilizers and sleeping pills to quiet the hungry cries of "sick-to-death" Alto babies.

The church, too, contributes to the routinization of, and indifference toward, child death. Traditionally, the local Catholic Church taught patience and resignation to domestic tragedies that were said to reveal the imponderable workings of God's will. If an infant died suddenly, it was because a particular saint had claimed the child. The infant would be an angel in the service of his or her heavenly patron. It would be wrong, a sign of a lack of faith, to weep for a child with such good fortune. The infant funeral was, in the past, an event celebrated with joy. Today, however, under the new

regime of "liberation theology," the bells of N.S. das Dores parish church no longer peal for the death of Alto babies, and no priest accompanies the procession of angels to the cemetery where their bodies are disposed of casually and without ceremony. Children bury children in Bom Jesus da Mata. In this most Catholic of communities, the coffin is handed to the disabled and irritable municipal gravedigger, who often chides the children for one reason or another. It may be that the coffin is larger than expected and the gravedigger can find no appropriate space. The children do not wait for the gravedigger to complete his task. No prayers are recited and no sign of the cross made as the tiny coffin goes into its shallow grave.

When I asked the local priest, Padre Marcos, about the lack of church ceremony surrounding infant and childhood death today in Bom Jesus, he replied: "In the old days, child death was richly celebrated. But those were the baroque customs of a conservative church that wallowed in death and misery. The new church is a church of hope and joy. We no longer celebrate the death of child angels. We try to tell mothers that Jesus doesn't want all the dead babies they send him." Similarly, the new church has changed its baptismal customs, now often refusing to baptize dying babies brought to the back door of a church or rectory. The mothers are scolded by the church attendants and told to go home and take care of their sick babies. Baptism, they are told, is for the living; it is not to be confused with the sacrament of extreme unction, which is the anointing of the dying. And so it appears to the women of the Alto that even the church has turned away from them, denying the traditional comfort of folk Catholicism.

The contemporary Catholic church is caught in the clutches of a double bind. The new theology of liberation imagines a kingdom of God on earth based on justice and equality, a world without hunger, sickness, or childhood mortality. At the same time, the church has not changed its official position on sexuality and reproduction, including its sanctions against birth control, abortion, and sterilization. The padre of Bom Jesus da Mata recognizes this contradiction intuitively, although he shies away from discussions on the topic, saying that he prefers to leave questions of family planning to the discretion and the "good consciences" of his impoverished parishioners. But this, of course, sidesteps the extent to which those good consciences have been shaped by traditional church teachings in Bom Jesus, especially by his recent predecessors. Hence, we can begin to see that the seeming indifference of Alto mothers toward the death of some of their infants is but a pale reflection of the official indifference of church and state to the plight of poor women and children.

Nonetheless, the women of Bom Jesus are survivors. One woman, Biu, told me her life history, returning again and again to the themes of child death, her first husband's suicide, abandonment by her father and later by her second husband, and all the other losses and disappointments she has suffered in her long forty-five years. She concluded with great force, reflecting on the days of Carnaval '88 that were fast approaching:

> No, Dona Nanci, I won't cry, and I won't waste my life thinking about it from morning to night…Can I argue with God for the state that I'm in? No! And so I'll dance and I'll jump and I'll play Carnaval! And yes, I'll laugh and people will wonder at a *pobre* like me who can have such a good time.

And no one did blame Biu for dancing in the streets during the four days of Carnaval—not even on Ash Wednesday, the day following Carnaval '88 when we all assembled hurriedly to assist in the burial of Mercea, Biu's beloved *casula,* her last-born daughter who had died at home of pneumonia during the festivities. The rest of the family barely had time to change out of their costumes. Severino, the child's uncle and godfather, sprinkled holy water over the little angel while he prayed: "Mercea, I don't know whether you were called, taken, or thrown out of this world. But look down at us from your heavenly home with tenderness, with pity, and with mercy." So be it.

DISCUSSION QUESTIONS

1. Why don't women in Bom Jesus, Brazil, grieve outwardly for their dead children?

2. Do you think that mother love is an innate human emotion? How do you think Scheper-Hughes would answer that question?

3. Are there any possible sociocultural changes in the overall social structure of Bom Jesus, Brazil, that might be made to change the way mothers deal with the death of their children?

 **RESOURCES ON THE INTERNET**

 InfoTrac College Edition

infotrac-college.com

You can find further relevant readings by searching *InfoTrac College Edition*, an online library with access to thousands of scholarly and popular periodicals. Below are suggested search terms for this article:

■   infant mortality rate

■   maternal love

Anthropology Online: Wadsworth's Anthropology Resource Center

academic.cengage.com/anthropology

The Wadsworth Anthropology Resource Center contains a wealth of information and useful tools for students including information on careers in anthropology.

9

Society and Sex Roles

ERNESTINE FRIEDL

Although it is possible to find societies in which gender inequalities are kept to a minimum, the overwhelming ethnographic and archaeological evidence suggests that females are subordinate to men in terms of exerting economic and political control. This gender asymmetry is so pervasive that some anthropologists over the years have concluded that this gender inequality is the result of biological differences between men and women. That is, men are dominant because of their greater size, physical strength, and innate aggressiveness. In this selection, Ernestine Friedl argues that the answer to this near universal male dominance lies more with economics than with biological predisposition.

A former president of the American Anthropological Association, Friedl argues that men tend to be dominant because they control the distribution of scarce resources in the society, both within and outside of the family. Quite apart from who produces the goods, "the person controlling the distribution of the limited and valued resources possesses the currency needed to create the obligations and alliances that are at the center of all political relations." Using ethnographic examples from foraging societies, Friedl shows how women have relative equality in those societies where they exercise some control over resources. Conversely, men are nearly totally dominant in those societies in which women have no control over scarce resources.

"Women must respond quickly to the demands of their husbands," says anthropologist Napoleon Chagnon describing the horticultural Yanomamo Indians of Venezuela. When a man returns from a hunting trip, "the woman, no matter what she is doing, hurries home and quietly but rapidly prepares a meal for her husband. Should the wife be slow in doing this, the husband is within his rights to beat her. Most reprimands...take the form of blows with the hand or with a piece of firewood....Some of them chop their wives with the sharp edge of a machete or axe, or shoot them with a barbed arrow in some nonvital area, such as the buttocks or leg."

Among the Semai agriculturalists of central Malaya, when one person refuses the request of another, the offended party suffers *punan,* a mixture of emotional pain and frustration. "Enduring *punan* is commonest when a girl has refused the victim her sexual favors," reports Robert Dentan. "The jilted man's 'heart becomes sad.' He loses his energy and his appetite. Much of the time he sleeps, dreaming of his lost love. In this state he is in fact very likely to injure himself 'accidentally.'" The Semai are afraid of violence; a man would never strike a woman.

The social relationship between men and women has emerged as one of the principal disputes

SOURCE: From "Society and Sex Roles" by Ernestine Friedl in *Human Nature,* April 1978, 1(4), pp. 68–75. Reprinted with permission of the author.

occupying the attention of scholars and the public in recent years. Although the discord is sharpest in the United States, the controversy has spread throughout the world. Numerous national and international conferences, including one in Mexico sponsored by the United Nations, have drawn together delegates from all walks of life to discuss such questions as the social and political rights of each sex, and even the basic nature of males and females.

Whatever their position, partisans often invoke examples from other cultures to support their ideas about the proper role of each sex. Because women are clearly subservient to men in many societies, like the Yanomamo, some experts conclude that the natural pattern is for men to dominate. But among the Semai no one has the right to command others, and in West Africa women are often chiefs. The place of women in these societies supports the argument of those who believe that sex roles are not fixed, that if there is a natural order, it allows for many different arrangements.

The argument will never be settled as long as the opposing sides toss examples from the world's cultures at each other like intellectual stones. But the effect of biological differences on male and female behavior can be clarified by looking at known examples of the earliest forms of human society and examining the relationship between technology, social organization, environment, and sex roles. The problem is to determine the conditions in which different degrees of male dominance are found, to try to discover the social and cultural arrangements that give rise to equality or inequality between the sexes, and to attempt to apply this knowledge to our understanding of the changes taking place in modern industrial society.

As Western history and the anthropological record have told us, equality between the sexes is rare; in most known societies females are subordinate. Male dominance is so widespread that it is virtually a human universal; societies in which women are consistently dominant do not exist and have never existed.

Evidence of a society in which women control all strategic resources like food and water, and in which women's activities are the most prestigious has never been found. The Iroquois of North America and the Lovedu of Africa came closest. Among the Iroquois, women raised food, controlled its distribution, and helped to choose male political leaders. Lovedu women ruled as queens, exchanged valuable cattle, led ceremonies, and controlled their own sex lives. But among both the Iroquois and the Lovedu, men owned the land and held other positions of power and prestige. Women were equal to men; they did not have ultimate authority over them. Neither culture was a true matriarchy.

Patriarchies are prevalent, and they appear to be strongest in societies in which men control significant goods that are exchanged with people outside the family. Regardless of who produces food, the person who gives it to others creates the obligations and alliances that are at the center of all political relations. The greater the male monopoly on the distribution of scarce items, the stronger their control of women seems to be. This is most obvious in relatively simple hunter-gatherer societies.

Hunter-gatherers, or foragers, subsist on wild plants, small land animals, and small river or sea creatures gathered by hand; large land animals and sea mammals hunted with spears, bows and arrows, and blow guns; and fish caught with hooks and nets. The 300,000 hunter-gatherers alive in the world today include the Eskimos, the Australian aborigines, and the Pygmies of Central Africa.

Foraging has endured for two million years and was replaced by farming and animal husbandry only 10,000 years ago; it covers more than 99 percent of human history. Our foraging ancestry is not far behind us and provides a clue to our understanding of the human condition.

Hunter-gatherers are people whose ways of life are technologically simple and socially and politically egalitarian. They live in small groups of 50 to 200 and have neither kings, nor priests, nor social classes. These conditions permit anthropologists to observe the essential bases for inequalities between the sexes without the distortions induced by the complexities of contemporary industrial society.

The source of male power among hunter-gatherers lies in their control of a scarce, hard to acquire, but necessary nutrient—animal protein. When men in a hunter-gatherer society return to camp with game, they divide the meat in some customary way. Among the !Kung San of Africa, certain parts of the animal are given to the owner of the arrow that killed the beast, to the first hunter to sight the game, to the one who threw the first spear, and to all men in the hunting party. After the meat has been divided, each hunter distributes his share to his blood relatives and his in-laws, who in turn share it with others. If an animal is large enough, every member of the band will receive some meat.

Vegetable foods, in contrast, are not distributed beyond the immediate household. Women give food to their children, to their husbands, to other members of the household, and rarely, to the occasional visitor. No one outside the family regularly eats any of the wild fruits and vegetables that are gathered by the women.

The meat distributed by the men is a public gift. Its source is widely known, and the donor expects a reciprocal gift when other men return from a successful hunt. He gains honor as a supplier of a scarce item and simultaneously obligates others to him.

These obligations constitute a form of power or control over others, both men and women. The opinions of hunters play an important part in decisions to move the village; good hunters attract the most desirable women; people in other groups join camps with good hunters; and hunters, because they already participate in an internal system of exchange, control exchange with other groups for flint, salt, and steel axes. The male monopoly on hunting unites men in a system of exchange and gives them power; gathering vegetable food does not give women equal power even among foragers who live in the tropics, where the food collected by women provides more than half the hunter-gatherer diet.

If dominance arises from a monopoly on big game hunting, why has the male monopoly remained unchallenged? Some women are strong enough to participate in the hunt and their endurance is certainly equal to that of men. Dobe San

women of the Kalahari Desert in Africa walk an average of 10 miles a day carrying from 15 to 33 pounds of food plus a baby.

Women do not hunt, I believe, because of four interrelated factors: variability in the supply of game; the different skills required for hunting and gathering; the incompatibility between carrying burdens and hunting; and the small size of semi-nomadic foraging populations.

Because the meat supply is unstable, foragers must make frequent expeditions to provide the band with gathered food. Environmental factors such as seasonal and annual variation in rainfall often affect the size of the wildlife population. Hunters cannot always find game, and when they do encounter animals, they are not always successful in killing their prey. In northern latitudes, where meat is the primary food, periods of starvation are known in every generation. The irregularity of the game supply leads hunter-gatherers in areas where plant foods are available to depend on these predictable foods a good part of the time. Someone must gather the fruits, nuts, and roots and carry them back to camp to feed unsuccessful hunters, children, the elderly, and anyone who might not have gone foraging that day.

Foraging falls to the women because hunting and gathering cannot be combined on the same expedition. Although gatherers sometimes notice signs of game as they work, the skills required to track game are not the same as those required to find edible roots or plants. Hunters scan the horizon and the land for traces of large game; gatherers keep their eyes to the ground, studying the distribution of plants and the texture of the soil for hidden roots and animal holes. Even if a woman who was collecting plants came across the track of an antelope, she could not follow it; it is impossible to carry a load and hunt at the same time. Running with a heavy load is difficult, and should the animal be sighted, the hunter would be off balance and could neither shoot an arrow nor throw a spear accurately.

Pregnancy and child care would also present difficulties for a hunter. An unborn child affects a woman's body balance, as does a child in her arms, on her back, or slung at her side. Until they are two years old, many hunter-gatherer children are carried at all times, and until they are four, they are carried some of the time.

An observer might wonder why young women do not hunt until they become pregnant, or why mature women and men do not hunt and gather on alternate days, with some women staying in camp to act as wet nurses for the young. Apart from the effects hunting might have on a mother's milk production, there are two reasons. First, young girls begin to bear children as soon as they are physically mature and strong enough to hunt, and second, hunter-gatherer bands are so small that there are unlikely to be enough lactating women to serve as wet nurses. No hunter-gatherer group could afford to maintain a specialized female hunting force.

Because game is not always available, because hunting and gathering are specialized skills, because women carrying heavy loads cannot hunt, and because women in hunter-gatherer societies are usually either pregnant or caring for young children, for most of the last two million years of human history men have hunted and women have gathered.

If male dominance depends on controlling the supply of meat, then the degree of male dominance in a society should vary with the amount of meat available and the amount supplied by the men. Some regions, like the East African grasslands and the North American woodlands, abounded with species of large mammals; other zones, like tropical forests and semideserts, are thinly populated with prey. Many elements affect the supply of game, but theoretically, the less meat provided exclusively by the men, the more egalitarian the society.

All known hunter-gatherer societies fit into four basic types: those in which men and women work together in communal hunts and as teams gathering edible plants, as did the Washo Indians of North America; those in which men and women each collect their own plant foods although the men supply some meat to the group, as do the Hadza of Tanzania; those in which male hunters and female gatherers work apart but return to camp each evening to share their acquisitions, as

do the Tiwi of North Australia; and those in which the men provide all the food by hunting large game, as do the Eskimo. In each case the extent of male dominance increases directly with the proportion of meat supplied by individual men and small hunting parties.

Among the most egalitarian of hunter-gatherer societies are the Washo Indians, who inhabited the valleys of the Sierra Nevada in what is now southern California and Nevada. In the spring they moved north to Lake Tahoe for the large fish runs of sucker and native trout. Everyone—men, women, and children—participated in the fishing. Women spent the summer gathering edible berries and seeds while the men continued to fish. In the fall some men hunted deer but the most important source of animal protein was the jack rabbit, which was captured in communal hunts. Men and women together drove the rabbits into nets tied end to end. To provide food for the winter, husbands and wives worked as teams in the late fall to collect pine nuts.

Since everyone participated in most food gathering activities, there were no individual distributors of food and relatively little difference in male and female rights. Men and women were not segregated from each other in daily activities; both were free to take lovers after marriage; both had the right to separate whenever they chose; menstruating women were not isolated from the rest of the group; and one of the two major Washo rituals celebrated hunting while the other celebrated gathering. Men were accorded more prestige if they had killed a deer, and men directed decisions about the seasonal movement of the group. But if no male leader stepped forward, women were permitted to lead. The distinctive feature of groups such as the Washo is the relative equality of the sexes.

The sexes are also relatively equal among the Hadza of Tanzania but this near-equality arises because men and women tend to work alone to feed themselves. They exchange little food. The Hadza lead a leisurely life in the seemingly barren environment of the East African Rift Gorge that is, in fact, rich in edible berries, roots, and small game. As a result of this abundance, from the time they are 10 years old, Hadza men and women gather much of their own food. Women take their young children with them into the bush, eating as they forage, and collect only enough food for a light family meal in the evening. The men eat berries and roots as they hunt for small game, and should they bring down a rabbit or a hyrax, they eat the meat on the spot. Meat is carried back to the camp and shared with the rest of the group only on those rare occasions when a poisoned arrow brings down a large animal—an impala, a zebra, an eland, or a giraffe.

Because Hadza men distribute little meat, their status is only slightly higher than that of the women. People flock to the camp of a good hunter and the camp might take on his name because of his popularity, but he is in no sense a leader of the group. A Hadza man and a woman have an equal right to divorce and each can repudiate a marriage simply by living apart for a few weeks. Couples tend to live in the same camp as the wife's mother but they sometimes make long visits to the camp of the husband's mother. Although a man may take more than one wife, most Hadza males cannot afford to indulge in this luxury. In order to maintain a marriage, a man must supply both his wife and his mother-in-law with some meat and trade goods, such as beads and cloth, and the Hadza economy gives few men the wealth to provide for more than one wife and mother-in-law. Washo equality is based on cooperation; Hadza equality is based on independence.

In contrast to both these groups, among the Tiwi of Melville and Bathurst Islands off the northern coast of Australia, male hunters dominate female gatherers. The Tiwi are representative of the most common form of foraging society, in which the men supply large quantities of meat, although less than half the food consumed by the group. Each morning Tiwi women, most with babies on their backs, scatter in different directions in search of vegetables, grubs, worms, and small game such as bandicoots, lizards, and opossums. To track the game, they use hunting dogs. On most days women return to camp with some meat and with baskets full of *korka,* the nut of a native palm, which is soaked and mashed to make a porridge-like dish.

The Tiwi men do not hunt small game and do not hunt every day, but when they do they often return with kangaroo, large lizards, fish, and game birds.

The porridge is cooked separately by each household and rarely shared outside the family, but the meat is prepared by a volunteer cook, who can be male or female. After the cook takes one of the parts of the animal traditionally reserved for him or her, the animal's "boss," the one who caught it, distributes the rest to all near kin and then to all others residing with the band. Although the small game supplied by the women is distributed in the same way as the big game supplied by the men, Tiwi men are dominant because the game they kill provides most of the meat.

The power of Tiwi men is clearest in their betrothal practices. Among the Tiwi, a woman must always be married. To ensure this, female infants are betrothed at birth and widows are remarried at the gravesides of their late husbands. Men form alliances by exchanging daughters, sisters, and mothers in marriage and some collect as many as 25 wives. Tiwi men value the quantity and quality of the food many wives can collect and the many children they can produce.

The dominance of the men is offset somewhat by the influence of adult women in selecting their next husbands. Many women are active strategists in the political careers of their male relatives, but to the exasperation of some sons attempting to promote their own futures, widowed mothers sometimes insist on selecting their own partners. Women also influence the marriages of their daughters and granddaughters, especially when the selected husband dies before the bestowed child moves to his camp.

Among the Eskimo, representative of the rarest type of forager society, inequality between the sexes is matched by inequality in supplying the group with food. Inland Eskimo men hunt caribou throughout the year to provision the entire society, and maritime Eskimo men depend on whaling, fishing, and some hunting to feed their extended families. The women process the carcasses, cut and sew skins to make clothing, cook, and care for the young; but they collect no food of their own and depend on the men to supply all the raw materials for their work. Since men provide all the meat, they also control the trade in hides, whale oil, seal oil, and other items that move between the maritime and inland Eskimos.

Eskimo women are treated almost exclusively as objects to be used, abused, and traded by men. After puberty all Eskimo girls are fair game for any interested male. A man shows his intentions by grabbing the belt of a woman and if she protests, he cuts off her trousers and forces himself upon her. These encounters are considered unimportant by the rest of the group. Men offer their wives' sexual services to establish alliances with trading partners and members of hunting and whaling parties.

Despite the consistent pattern of some degree of male dominance among foragers, most of these societies are egalitarian compared with agricultural and industrial societies. No forager has any significant opportunity for political leadership. Foragers, as a rule, do not like to give or take orders, and assume leadership only with reluctance. Shamans (those who are thought to be possessed by spirits) may be either male or female. Public rituals conducted by women in order to celebrate the first menstruation of girls are common, and the symbolism in these rituals is similar to that in the ceremonies that follow a boy's first kill.

In any society, status goes to those who control the distribution of valued goods and services outside the family. Equality arises when both sexes work side by side in food production, as do the Washo, and the products are simply distributed among the workers. In such circumstances, no person or sex has greater access to valued items than do others. But when women make no contribution to the food supply, as in the case of the Eskimo, they are completely subordinate.

When we attempt to apply these generalizations to contemporary industrial society, we can predict that as long as women spend their discretionary income from jobs on domestic needs, they will gain little social recognition and power. To be an effective source of power, money must be exchanged in ways that require returns and create obligations. In other words, it must be invested.

Jobs that do not give women control over valued resources will do little to advance their general status. Only as managers, executives, and professionals are women in a position to trade goods and services, to do others favors, and therefore to obligate others to them. Only as controllers of valued resources can women achieve prestige, power, and equality.

Within the household, women who bring in income from jobs are able to function on a more nearly equal basis with their husbands. Women who contribute services to their husbands and children without pay, as do some middle-class Western housewives, are especially vulnerable to dominance. Like Eskimo women, as long as their services are limited to domestic distribution they have little power relative to their husbands and none with respect to the outside world.

As for the limits imposed on women by their procreative functions in hunter-gatherer societies, childbearing and child care are organized around work as much as work is organized around reproduction. Some foraging groups space their children three to four years apart and have an average of only four to six children, far fewer than many women in other cultures. Hunter-gatherers nurse their infants for extended periods, sometimes for as long as four years. This custom suppresses ovulation and limits the size of their families. Sometimes, although rarely, they practice infanticide. By limiting reproduction, a woman who is gathering food has only one child to carry.

Different societies can and do adjust the frequency of birth and the care of children to accommodate whatever productive activities women customarily engage in. In horticultural societies, where women work long hours in gardens that may be far from home, infants get food to supplement their mothers' milk, older children take care of younger children, and pregnancies are widely spaced. Throughout the world, if a society requires a woman's labor, it finds ways to care for her children.

In the United States, as in some other industrial societies, the accelerated entry of women with preschool children into the labor force has resulted in the development of a variety of child-care arrangements.

Individual women have called on friends, relatives, and neighbors. Public and private child-care centers are growing. We should realize that the declining birth rate, the increasing acceptance of childless or single-child families, and a de-emphasis on mother-hood are adaptations to a sexual division of labor reminiscent of the system of production found in hunter-gatherer societies.

DISCUSSION QUESTIONS

1. How does Professor Friedl explain the perva-sive inequality between men and women found in the world today?

2. Which societies does Friedl cite as having rel-ative gender equality and which societies does she cite as having high levels of inequality?

3. Based on her cross-cultural findings, what suggestions does Friedl make for Western women to acquire greater power and status?

RESOURCES ON THE INTERNET

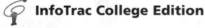

InfoTrac College Edition

infotrac-college.com
You can find further relevant readings by searching *InfoTrac College Edition*, an online library with access to thousands of scholarly and popular

In many countries where women no longer devote most of their productive years to childbear-ing, they are beginning to demand a change in the social relationship of the sexes. As women gain access to positions that control the exchange of resources, male dominance may become archaic, and industrial societies may one day become as egalitarian as the Washo.

periodicals. Below are suggested search terms for this article:

- gender inequality
- sex roles
- patriarchy

Anthropology Online: Wadsworth's Anthropology Resource Center

academic.cengage.com/anthropology
The Wadsworth Anthropology Resource Center contains a wealth of information and useful tools for students including information on careers in anthropology.

Women and Men in !Kung Society

MARJORIE SHOSTAK

This selection on gender roles among the !Kung of Botswana is taken from Shostak's Nisa: The Life and Words of a !Kung Woman, *an interesting collaboration between ethnographer and informant. Each of the fifteen chapters in the book begins with an ethnographic description of a particular aspect of !Kung culture written by Shostak. The second part of each chapter is a monologue on the subject by Shostak's main informant, Nisa, in her own words. A particularly rich source of cultural information, Nisa was a gifted storyteller willing to describe her own life in great detail and on a variety of topics. She was first married at age twelve, was separated, divorced, remarried, widowed, and gave birth to four children. The result of this collaboration between ethnographer and informant is a vivid account of !Kung life told from a very personal perspective.*

Residing in the Kalahari Desert, Nisa belongs to one of the last hunting and gathering societies in the world, although within the last several decades many have taken to horticulture and the keeping of small herds of goats. Known for hundreds of years as the !Kung or the !Kung Bushmen, they are today referred to as Ju/'hoansi. As a people they have very distinguishable physical features, including light skin, high cheek bones, and an average height of approximately five feet.

After Besa and I had lived together for a long time, he went to visit some people in the East. While there, he found work with a Tswana cattle herder. When he came back, he told me to pack; he wanted me to go and live with him there. So we left and took the long trip to Old Debe's village, a Zhun/twa village near a Tswana and European settlement. We lived there together for a long time.[1]

While we were there, my father died. My older brother, my younger brother, and my mother were with him when he died, but I wasn't; I was living where Besa had taken me. Others carried the news to me. They said that Dau had tried to cure my father, laying on hands and working hard to make him better. But God refused and Dau wasn't able to see what was causing the illness so he could heal him. Dau said, "God is refusing to give up my father."

I heard and said, "Eh, then today I'm going to see where he died." Besa and I and my children, along with a few others, left to take the long journey west. We walked the first day and slept that night. The next morning we started out and slept again that night; we slept another night on the road,

1. This chapter covers about five years, beginning when Nisa was in her early thirties (c. the mid 1950s).

SOURCE: Reprinted by permission of the publisher of "Women and Men" in *Nisa: The Life and Words of a !Kung Woman* by Marjorie Shostak, pp. 237–246, Cambridge, MA: Harvard University Press, Copyright © 1981 by Marjorie Shostak.

as well. As we walked, I cried and thought, "Why couldn't I have been with him when he died?" I cried as we walked, one day and the next and the next.

The sun was so hot, it was burning; it was killing us. One day we rested such a long time, I thought, "Is the sun going to stop me from seeing where my father died?" When it was cooler, we started walking again and slept on the road again that night.

We arrived at the village late in the afternoon. My younger brother, Kumsa, was the first to see us. When he saw me, he came and hugged me. We started to cry and cried together for a long time. Finally, our older brother stopped us, "That's enough for now. Your tears won't make our father alive again."

We stopped crying and we all sat down. My mother was also with us. Although my father never took her back again after the time she ran away with her lover, she returned and lived near him until he died. And even though she slept alone, she still loved him.

Later, my mother and I sat together and cried together.

We stayed there for a while, then Besa and I went back again to live in the East where he had been working for the Europeans. A very long time passed. Then, my brother sent word that my mother was dying. Once again we made the journey to my family and when we arrived I saw her: she was still alive.

We stayed there and lived there. One day, a group of people were going to the bush to live. I said, "Mother, come with us. I'll take care of you and can help me with my children." We traveled that day and slept that night; we traveled another day and slept another night. But the next night, the sickness that had been inside her grabbed her again and this time, held on. It was just as it had been with my father. The next day, she coughed up blood. I thought, "Oh, why is blood coming out like that? Is this what is going to kill her? Is this the

way she's going to die? What is this sickness going to do? She's coughing blood...she's already dead!" Then I thought, "If only Dau were here, he would be able to cure her. He would trance for her every day." But he and my younger brother had stayed behind. Besa was with us, but he didn't have the power to cure people. There were others with us as well, but they didn't help.

We slept again that night. The next morning, the others left, as is our custom, and then it was only me, my children, my husband, and my mother; we were the only ones who remained. But her life was really over by then, even though she was still alive.

I went to get her some water and when I came back, she said, "Nisa...Nisa...I am an old person and today, my heart...today you and I will stay together for a while longer; we will continue to sit beside each other. But later, when the sun stands over there in the afternoon sky and when the new slim moon first strikes, I will leave you. We will separate then and I will go away."

I asked, "Mother, what are you saying?" She said, "Yes, that's what I'm saying. I am an old person. Don't deceive yourself; I am dying. When the sun moves to that spot in the sky, that will be our final separation. We will no longer be together after that. So, take good care of your children."

I said, "Why are you talking like this? If you die as you say, because that's what you're telling me, who are you going to leave in your place?" She said, "Yes, I am leaving you. Your husband will take care of you now. Besa will be with you and your children."

We remained together the rest of the day as the sun crawled slowly across the sky. When it reached the spot she had spoken of, she said—just like a person in good health—"Mm, now...be well, all of you," and then she died.

That night I slept alone and cried and cried and cried. None of my family was with me[2] and I just cried the entire night. When morning came, Besa dug a grave and buried her. I said, "Let's pull our

---

2. In fact, her husband and children were with her.

things together and go back to the village. I want to tell Dau and Kumsa that our mother has died."

We walked that day and slept that night. We walked the next day and stopped again that night. The next morning, we met my brother Kumsa. Someone had told him that his mother was sick. When he heard, he took his bow and quiver and came looking for us. He left when the sun just rose and started walking toward us, even as we were walking toward him. We met when the sun was overhead. He stood and looked at me. Then he said, "Here you are, Nisa, with your son and your daughter and your husband. But Mother isn't with you...."

I sat down and started to cry. He said. "Mother must have died because you're crying like this," and he started to cry, too. Besa said, "Yes, your sister left your mother behind. Two days ago was when your mother and sister separated. That is where we are coming from now. Your sister is here and will tell you about it. You will be together to share your mourning for your mother. That will be good."

We stayed there and cried and cried. Later, Kumsa took my little son and carried him on his shoulders. I carried my daughter and we walked until we arrived back at the village. My older brother came with his wife, and when he saw us he, too, started to cry.

After that, we lived together for a while. I lived and cried, lived and cried. My mother had been so beautiful ... her face, so lovely. When she died, she caused me great pain. Only after a long time was I quiet again.

Before we returned to the East, I went with Besa to visit his family. While I was there, I became very sick. It came from having carried my mother. Because when she was sick, I carried her around on my back. After she died, my back started to hurt in the very place I had carried her. One of God's spiritual arrows must have struck me there and found its way into my chest.

I was sick for a long time and then blood started to come out of my mouth. My younger brother (he really loves me!) was visiting me at the time. When he saw how I was, he left to tell his older brother, "Nisa's dying the same way our mother died. I've come to tell you to come back with me and heal her." My older brother listened and the two of them traveled to where I was. They came when the sun was high in the afternoon sky. Dau started to trance for me. He laid on hands, healing me with his touch. He worked on me for a long time. Soon, I was able to sleep; then, the blood stopped coming from my chest and later, even if I coughed, there wasn't any more blood.

We stayed there for a few more days. Then, Dau said, "Now I'm going to take Nisa with me to my village." Besa agreed and we all left together. We stayed at my brother's village until I was completely better.

Besa and I eventually moved back East again. But after we had lived together for a long time, we no longer were getting along. One day I asked, "Besa, won't you take me back to my family's village so I can live there?" He said, "I'm no longer interested in you." I said, "What's wrong? Why do you feel that way?" But then I said, "Eh, if that's how it is, it doesn't matter."

I was working for a European woman at the time, and when I told her what Besa was saying to me, she told him, "Listen to me. You're going to chase your wife away. If you continue to speak to her like this, she'll be gone. Today, I'm pregnant. Why don't you just let her be and have her sit beside you. When I give birth, she will work for me and help me with the baby."

That's what we did. We continued to live together until she gave birth. After, I helped wash the baby's clothes and helped with other chores. I worked for her for a long time.

One day, Besa broke into a little box I had and stole the money she had paid me with. He took it and went to drink beer. I went to the European woman and told her Besa had taken five Rand[3] from me and had left with it. I asked her to help me get it back. We went to the Tswana but where

---

3. The rand is a South African currency that was then legal tender in Bechuanaland (pre-independence Botswana). It was worth between $1.20 and $1.50. Five rand was a very large sum of money to the !Kung at that time—perhaps as much as two months wages at a typical menial task.

everyone was drinking and went to the door. The European woman walked in, kicked over a bucket and the beer spilled out. She kicked over another and another and the beer was spilling everywhere. The Tswanas left. She turned to Besa and said, "Why are you treating this young Zhun/twa woman like this? Stop treating her this way." She told him to give her the money and when he gave it to her, she gave it to me. I went and put the money in the box, then took it and left it in her kitchen where it stayed.

Later Besa said, "Why did you tell on me? I'm going to beat you." I said, "Go ahead. Hit me. I don't care. I won't stop you."

Soon after that, I became pregnant with Besa's child. But when it was still very tiny, when I was still carrying it way inside, he left me. I don't know what it was that made him want to leave. Did he have a lover? I don't know. He said he was afraid of a sore I had on my face where a bug had bitten me. It had become swollen, and eventually the Europeans helped to heal it. Whatever it was, his heart had changed toward me and although my heart still liked him, he only liked me a very little then. That's why he left.

It happened the day he finished working for the Europeans. He came back when the sun was low in the sky and said, "Tomorrow, I'm going to visit my younger brother. I have finished my work and have been paid. I'm going, but you'll stay here. Later, Old Debe and his wife can take you back to your brothers' village." I said, "If you are leaving, won't I go with you?" He said, "No, you won't go with me." I said, "Why are you saying you'll go without me? If I go with you and give birth there, it will be good. Don't leave me here. Let me go with you and give birth in your brother's village." But he said, "No, Old Debe will bring you back to your family."

When I saw Old Debe, he asked me what was wrong. I said, "What is Besa doing to me? If he doesn't want me, why doesn't he just end it completely? I've seen for a long time that he doesn't want me." I thought, "Besa...he took me to this faraway village, got me pregnant, and now, is he just going to drop me in this foreign place where none of my people live?"

Later, I said to Besa, "Why did you take me from my people? My brothers are still alive, yet you won't take me to them. You say someone else will. But, why should someone else, a near stranger, take me to my family after you've given me this stomach. I say you should take me to them, take me there and say, 'Here is your sister. Today I am separating from her.' Instead, you're saying you'll just leave me here, with these strangers? I followed you here, to where you were working, because you wanted me to. Now you're just going to leave me? Why are you doing this? Can there be any good in it?"

I continued, "You're the one who came here to work. Yet, you have no money and have no blankets. But when you had no more work and no more money, I worked. I alone, a woman. I entered the work of the European and I alone bought us blankets and a trunk. I alone bought all those things and you covered yourself with my blankets. When you weren't working, you asked people to give you things. How can you leave me here in this foreign place after all that?" He answered, "What work could I have done when there wasn't any to be had?"

I said, "It doesn't matter, because I can see that you will only be here for a few more nights, then you will go. I know that now. But, if you leave me like this today, then tomorrow, after you have gone and have lived with your brother, if you ever decide to come to where I am living, I will refuse you and will no longer be your wife. Because you are leaving me when I am pregnant."

The next morning, early, he tied up his things and left. He packed everything from inside the hut, including all our blankets, and went to his brother's village to live. I thought, "Eh, it doesn't matter, after all. I'll just sit here and let him go." He left me with nothing; the people in the village had to give me blankets to sleep with.

Besa, that man is very bad. He left me hanging like that.

Once he left, I saw that I would be staying there for a while. I thought, "Today I'm no longer going to refuse other men, but will just be with them. Then, maybe I will miscarry. Because this is

Besa's child and didn't he leave it and go? I won't refuse other men and will just have them. I will drop this pregnancy; then I will go home."

That's when Numshe entered the hut with me. He spoke to me and I agreed. People said, "Yes, she will enter the hut with him. But when he tastes her,[4] the pregnancy will be ruined." Old Debe's wife said, "That won't be so bad. If her pregnancy is ruined, it won't be a bad thing. Because Besa dropped her. Therefore, I will sit here and take care of her. Later, I will bring her to her family."

I lived there for a long time. I lived alone and worked for the Europeans. Then one day, just as my heart had said, my body felt like fire and my stomach was in great pain. I told Old Debe's wife, "Eh-hey, today I'm sick." She asked, "Where does it hurt? Do you want some water? Where is the sickness hurting you?" I said, "My whole body hurts, it isn't just my stomach." I lay there and felt the pains, rising again and again and again. I thought, "That man certainly has made me feel bad; even today, I'm lying here in great pain."

She looked at my stomach and saw how it was standing out. She said, "Oh, my child. Are you going to drop your pregnancy? What is going to happen? Will you be able to give birth to this child or will it be a miscarriage? Here, there are just the two of us; I don't see anyone who will bring more help to you. If you miscarry, it will be only us two." I said, "Yes, that's fine. If I drop this pregnancy, it will be good. I want to drop it, then I can leave. Because my husband certainly doesn't want it."

We stayed together all day. When the sun was late in the sky, I told her it was time and we went together to the bush. I sat down and soon the baby was born. It was already big, with a head and arms and a little penis; but it was born dead. Perhaps my heart had ruined my pregnancy. I cried, "This man almost ruined me, did he not?" Debe's wife said, "Yes, he destroyed this baby, this baby which came from God. But if God hadn't been here helping you, you also would have died. Because when a child dies in a woman's stomach, it can kill the woman. But God…God gave you something beautiful in giving you this baby and although it had death in it, you yourself are alive." We left and walked back to the village. Then I lay down.

After that, I just continued to live there. One day I saw people visiting from Besa's village. I told them to tell him that our marriage had ended. I said, "Tell him that he shouldn't think, even with a part of his heart, that he still has a wife here or that when we meet another time in my village that he might still want me." That's what I said and that's what I thought.

Because he left me there to die.

Soon after, a man named Twi saw me and said, "Did your husband leave you?" I said, "Yes, he left me long ago." He asked, "Then won't you stay with me?" I refused the first time he asked as well as the second and the third. But when he asked the next time, I agreed and we started to live together. I continued to work for the European woman until my work was finished and she told me I could go home. She gave us food for our trip and then all of us—Old Debe, his wife, Twi, and me—traveled the long distance back to where my family was living.

Twi and I lived together in my brothers' village for a long time. Then, one day, Besa came from wherever he had been and said, "Nisa, I've come to take you back with me." I said, "What? What am I like today? Did I suddenly become beautiful? The way I used to be is the way I am now; the way I used to be is what you left behind when you dropped me. So what are you saying? First you drop me in the heart of where the white people live, then you come back and say I should once again be with you?" He said, "Yes, we will pick up our marriage again."

I was stunned! I said, "What are you talking about? This man, Twi, helped bring me back. He's the man who will marry me. You're the one who left me." We talked until he could say nothing more; he was humbled. Finally he said, "You're shit! That's what you are." I said, "I'm shit you

---

4. Tastes her: A euphemism for sexual intercourse.

say? That's what you thought about me long ago, and I knew it. That's why I told you while we were still living in the East that I wanted you to take me back to my family so we could end our marriage here. But today, I came here myself and you only came afterward. Now I refuse to have anything more to do with you."

That's when Besa brought us to the Tswana headman to ask for a tribal hearing. Once it started, the headman looked at everything. He asked me, "Among all the women who live here, among all those you see sitting around, do you see one who lives with two men?" I said, "No, the women who sit here...not one lives with two men; not one among them would I be able to find. I, alone, have two. But it was because this man, Besa, mistreated and hurt me. That's why I took this other man, Twi, who treats me well, who does things for me and gives me things to eat." Then I said, "He is also the man I want to marry; I want to drop the other one. Because Besa has no sense. He left me while I was pregnant and the pregnancy almost killed me. This other one is the one I want to marry."

We talked a long time. Finally, the headman told Besa, "I have questioned Nisa about what happened and she has tied you up with her talk; her talk has defeated you, without doubt. Because what she has said about her pregnancy is serious. Therefore, today she and Twi will continue to stay together. After more time passes, I will ask all of you to come back again." Later, Twi and I left and went back to my brothers' village to sleep.

The next day, my older brother saw a honey cache while walking in the bush. He came to tell us and take us back there with him; we planned to stay the night in the bush. We arrived and spent the rest of the day collecting honey. When we finished, we walked toward where we were planning to camp. That's when I saw Besa's tracks in the sand. I said, "Everyone! Come here! Besa's tracks are here! Has anyone seen them elsewhere?" One of the men said, "Nonsense! Would you know his tracks...." I interrupted, "My husband...the man who married me....I *know* his tracks." The man's wife came to look, "Yes, those are Besa's tracks; his wife really did see them."

The next morning, Besa walked into the camp. Besa and Twi started to fight. My older brother yelled, "Do you two want to kill Nisa? Today she is not taking another husband. Today she's just going to lie by herself." I agreed, "Eh, I don't want to marry again now."

Twi and I continued to live together after that. But later we separated. My older brother caused it, because he wanted Besa to be with me again. He liked him and didn't like Twi. That's why he forced Twi to leave. When Twi saw how much anger both Dau and Besa felt toward him, he became afraid, and finally he left.

I saw what my brother had done and was miserable; I had really liked Twi. I said, "So, this is what you wanted? Fine, but now that you have chased Twi away, I'll have nothing at all to do with Besa." That's when I began to refuse Besa completely. Besa went to the headman and said, "Nisa refuses to be with me." The headman said, "Nisa's been refusing you for a long time. What legal grounds could I possibly find for you now?"

After more time passed, a man who had been my lover years before, started with me again. Soon we were very much in love. He was so handsome! His nose...his eyes...everything was so beautiful! His skin was light and his nose was lovely. I really loved that man, even when I first saw him.

We lived together for a while, but then he died. I was miserable, "My lover has died. Where am I going to find another like him—another as beautiful, another as good, another with a European nose and with such lovely light skin? Now he's dead. Where will I ever find another like him?"

My heart was miserable and I mourned for him. I exhausted myself with mourning and only when it was finished did I feel better again.

After years of living and having everything that happened to me happen, that's when I started with Bo, the next important man in my life and the one I am married to today.

Besa and I lived separately, but he still wanted me and stayed near me. That man, he didn't hear; he didn't understand. He was without ears, because he still said, "This woman here, Nisa, I won't be finished with her."

People told Bo, "You're going to die. This man, Besa, he's going to kill you. Now, leave Nisa." But Bo refused, "Me...I won't go to another hut. I'll just stay with Nisa and even if Besa tries to kill me, I'll still be here and won't leave."

At first, Bo and I sneaked off together, but Besa suspected us; he was very jealous. He accused me all the time. Even when I just went to urinate, he'd say that I had been with Bo. Or when I went for water, he'd say, "Did you just meet your lover?" But I'd say, "What makes you think you can talk to me like that?" He'd say, "Nisa are you not still my wife? Why aren't we living together? What are you doing?" I'd say, "Don't you have other women or are they refusing you, too? You have others so why are you asking me about what I'm doing?"

One night, Bo and I were lying down inside my hut and as I looked out through the latched-branch door, I saw someone moving about. It was Besa; I was able to see his face. He wanted to catch us, hoping I would feel some remorse and perhaps return to him.

I said, "What? Besa's here! Bo...Bo...Besa's standing out there." Bo got up; Besa came and stood by the door. I got up and that's when Besa came in and grabbed me. He held onto me and threatened to throw me into the fire. I cursed him as he held me, "Besa-Big-Testicles! Long-Penis! First you left me and drank of women's genitals elsewhere. Now you come back, see me, and say I am your wife?" He pushed me toward the fire, but I twisted my body so I didn't land in it. Then he went after Bo. Bo is weaker and older than Besa, so Besa was able to grab him, pull him outside the hut, and throw him down. He bit him on the shoulder. Bo yelled out in pain.

My younger brother woke and ran to us, yelling, "Curses to your genitals!" He grabbed them and separated them. Bo cursed Besa. Besa cursed Bo, "Curses on your penis!" He yelled, "I'm going to kill you Bo, then Nisa will suffer! If I don't kill you, then maybe I'll kill her so that you will feel pain! Because what you have that is so full of pleasure, I also have. So why does her heart want you and refuse me?"

I yelled at him, "That's not it! It's you! It's who you are and the way you think! This one, Bo, his ways are good and his thoughts are good. But you, your ways are foul. Look, you just bit Bo; that, too, is part of your ways. You also left me to die. And death, that's something I'm afraid of. That's why you no longer have a hold over me. Today I have another who will take care of me well. I'm no longer married to you, Besa. I want my husband to be Bo."

Besa kept bothering me and hanging around me. He'd ask, "Why won't you come to me? Come to me, I'm a man. Why are you afraid of me?" I wouldn't answer. Once Bo answered. "I don't understand why, if you *are* a man, you keep pestering this woman? Is what you're doing going to do any good? Because I won't leave her. And even though you bit me and your marks are on me, you're the one who is going to move out of the way, not me. I intend to marry her."

Another time I told Bo, "Don't be afraid of Besa. You and I will marry; I'm not going to stay married to him. Don't let him frighten you. Because even if he comes here with arrows, he won't do anything with them." Bo said, "Even if he did, what good would that do? I am also a man and am a master of arrows. The two of us would just strike each other. That's why I keep telling him to let you go; I am the man you are with now."

The next time, Besa came with his quiver full of arrows, saying, "I'm going to get Nisa and bring her back with me." He left with another man and came to me at my village. When he arrived, the sun was high in the sky. I was resting. He said, "Nisa, come, let's go." I said, "What? Is your penis not well? Is it horny?"

People heard us fighting and soon everyone was there, my younger and older brothers as well. Besa and I kept arguing and fighting until, in a rage, I screamed, "All right! Today I'm no longer afraid!" and I pulled off all the skins that were covering me—first one, then another, and finally the leather apron that covered my genitals. I pulled them all off and laid them down on the ground. I cried, "There! There's my vagina! Look, Besa, look at me! This is what you want!"

The man he had come with said, "This woman, her heart is truly far from you. Besa, look. Nisa refuses you totally, with all her heart. She refuses to have sex with you. Your relationship with her is finished. See. She took off her clothes, put them down, and with her genitals is showing everyone how she feels about you. She doesn't want you, Besa. If I were you, I'd finish with her today." Besa finally said, "Eh, you're right. Now I am finished with her."

The two of them left. I took my leather apron, put it on, took the rest of my things and put them on.

Mother! That was just what I did.

Besa tried one last time. He went to the headman again, and when he came back he told me, "The headman wants to see you." I thought, "If he wants to see me, I won't refuse."

When I arrived, the headman said, "Besa says he still wants to continue your marriage." I said, "Continue our marriage? Why? Am I so stupid that I don't know my name? Would I stay in a marriage with a man who left me hanging in a foreign place? If Old Debe and his wife hadn't been there, I would have truly lost my way. Me, stay married to Besa? I can't make myself think of it."

I turned to Besa, "Isn't that what I told you when we were still in the East?" Besa said, "Mm, that's what you said." I said, "And, when you left, didn't I tell you that you were leaving me pregnant with your baby. Didn't I also tell you that?" He said, "Yes, that's what you said." I said, "And didn't I say that I wanted to go with you, that I wanted you to help make our pregnancy grow strong? Didn't I say that and didn't you refuse?" He said, "Yes, you said that." Then I said, "Mm. Therefore, that marriage you say today, in the lap of the headman, should be continued, that marriage no longer exists. Because I am Nisa and today, when I look at you, all I want to do is to throw up. Vomit is the only thing left in my heart for you now. As we sit together here and I see your face, that is all that rises within and grabs me."

The headman laughed, shook his head and said, "Nisa is impossible!" Then he said, "Besa,

you had better listen to her. Do you hear what she is saying? She says that you left her while she was pregnant, that she miscarried and was miserable. Today she will no longer take you for her husband." Besa said, "That's because she's with Bo now and doesn't want to leave him. But I still want her and want to continue our marriage."

I said, "What? Besa, can't you see me? Can't you see that I have really found another man? Did you think, perhaps, that I was too old and wouldn't find someone else?" The headman laughed again. "Yes, I am a woman. And that which you have, a penis, I also have something of equal worth. Like the penis of a chief... yes, something of a chief is what I have. And its worth is like money. Therefore, the person who drinks from it ... it's like he's getting money from me. But not you, because when you had it, you just left it to ruin."

The headman said, "Nisa is crazy; her talk is truly crazy now." Then he said, "The two of you sleep tonight and give your thoughts over to this. Nisa, think about all of it again. Tomorrow, I want both of you to come back."

Besa went and lay down. I went and lay down and thought about everything. In the morning, I went to the headman. I felt ashamed by my talk of the night before. I sat there quietly. The headman said, "Nisa, Besa says you should stay married to him." I answered, "Why should he stay married to me when yesterday I held his baby in my stomach and he dropped me. Even God doesn't want me to marry a man who leaves me, a man who takes my blankets when I have small children beside me, a man who forces other people to give me blankets to cover my children with. Tell him to find another woman to marry."

The headman turned to Besa, "Nisa has explained herself. There's nothing more I can see to say. Even you, you can hear that she has defeated you. So, leave Nisa and as I am headman, today your marriage to her is ended. She can now marry Bo."[5]

---

5. The procedure for divorce in traditional !Kung culture would have been less complicated and would have proceeded more quickly.

Besa went to the headman one more time. When he tried to discuss it again, saying, "Please, help me. Give Nisa back to me," the headman said, "Haven't you already talked to me about this? You talked and talked, and the words entered my ears. Are you saying that I have not already decided on this? That I am not an important person? That I am a worthless thing that you do not have to listen to? There is no reason to give Nisa back to you."

I was so thankful when I heard his words. My heart filled with happiness.

Bo and I married soon after that.[6] We lived together, sat together, and did things together. Our hearts loved each other very much and our marriage was very very strong.

Besa also married again not long after—this time to a woman much younger than me. One day he came to me and said, "Look how wrong you were to have refused me! Perhaps you thought you were the only woman. But you, Nisa, today you are old and you yourself can see that I have married a young woman, one who is beautiful!"

I said, "Good! I told you that if we separated, you'd find a young woman to marry and to sleep with. That is fine with me because there is nothing I want from you. But you know, of course, that just like me, another day she too will be old."

We lived on, but not long after, Besa came back. He said that his young wife was troubled and that he wanted me again. I refused and even told Bo about it. Bo asked me why I refused. I said, "Because I don't want him." But what he says about his wife is true. She has a terrible sickness, a type of madness. God gave it to her. She was such a beautiful woman, too. But no longer. I wonder why such a young woman has to have something like that....

Even today, whenever Besa sees me, he argues with me and says he still wants me. I say, "Look, we've separated. Now leave me alone." I even sometimes refuse him food. Bo tells me I shouldn't refuse, but I'm afraid he will bother me more if I give anything to him. Because his heart still cries for me.

Sometimes I do give him things to eat and he also gives things to me. Once I saw him in my village. He came over to me and said, "Nisa, give me some water to drink." I washed out a cup and poured him some water. He drank it and said, "Now, give me some tobacco." I took out some tobacco and gave it to him. Then he said, "Nisa, you really are adult; you know how to work. Today, I am married to a woman but my heart doesn't agree to her much. But you...you are one who makes me feel pain. Because you left me and married another man. I also married, but have made myself weary by having married something bad. You, you have hands that work and do things. With you, I could eat: You would get water for me to wash with. Today, I'm really in pain."

I said, "Why are you thinking about our dead marriage? Of course, we were married once, but we have gone our different ways. Now, I no longer want you. After all that happened when you took me East—living there, working there, my father dying, my mother dying, and all the misery you caused me—you say we should live together once again?"

He said that I wasn't telling it as it happened.

One day, he told me he wanted to take me from Bo. I said, "What? Tell me, Besa, what has been talking to you that you are saying this again?" He said, "All right, then have me as your lover. Won't you help my heart out?" I said, "Aren't there many men who could be my lover? Why should I agree to you?" He said, "Look here, Nisa...I'm a person who helped bring up your children, the children you and your husband gave birth to. You became pregnant again with my child and that was good. You held it inside you and lived with it until God came and killed it. That's why your heart is talking this way and refusing me."

I told him he was wrong. But he was right, too. Because, after Besa, I never had any more children.

---

6. Nisa and Bo married around 1957, when Nisa was about thirty-six years old.

He took that away from me. With Tashay, I had children, but Besa, he ruined me. Even the one time I did conceive, I miscarried. That's because of what he did to me; that's what everyone says.

DISCUSSION QUESTIONS

1. Based on this account, would you say that women are an exploited, low-status segment of !Kung society?

2. How does Shostak's account of !Kung social life differ from most other ethnographic accounts?

3. Given the obvious cultural differences between !Kung society and more industrialized, western societies, how different are the social relationships between men and women?

 **RESOURCES ON THE INTERNET**

 InfoTrac College Edition

infotrac-college.com
You can find further relevant readings by searching *InfoTrac College Edition*, an online library with access to thousands of scholarly and popular periodicals. Below are suggested search terms for this article:

- life story
- remarriage
- marital separation

Anthropology Online: Wadsworth's Anthropology Resource Center

academic.cengage.com/anthropology
The Wadsworth Anthropology Resource Center contains a wealth of information and useful tools for students including information on careers in anthropology.

11

The Kpelle Moot

JAMES L. GIBBS, JR.

A cultural universal found in all societies of the world is the notion of social control. More specifi-
cally, no society can function for very long without some well-understood mechanisms for settling
disputes. Some societies rely on formal mechanisms (such as courts of law), while others rely on more
informal mechanisms, many of which have different purposes, procedures, and functionaries.

In this selection, anthropologist James Gibbs describes how informal, ad hoc mechanisms of
conflict resolution (called "moots") operate among the Kpelle of Liberia. Found in many other
areas of Africa as well, these moots are local phenomena in which kinsmen, neighbors, and
friends come together to try to settle disputes and normalize relationships between the dispu-
tants. While moots coexist along with a more formal court system administered by political
chiefs, there are some significant differences between the two types of adjudicating structures.
Chiefly courts have as their major objective the administration of justice, whereby guilt is
determined and an appropriate penalty is levied. Moots, on the other hand, are not primarily
interested in making certain that the penalty fits the crime. Instead, moots are aimed at resolving
disagreements, extracting apologies, imposing token penalties, normalizing good relationships
between the disputants, and reintegrating them back into the community. Moots are particularly
effective mechanisms for resolving local conflicts between people who are part of the same small-
scale community. Thus, whereas the traditional courts tend to be more coercive and punitive, the
Kpelle moots are more conciliatory and therapeutic in nature.

Africa as a major culture area has been characterized
by many writers as being marked by a high development of law and legal procedures.[1] In the past few
years research on African law has produced a series of

1. The field work on which this paper is based was carried out in Liberia in 1957 and 1958 and was supported by a grant from the Ford Foundation, which is, of course, not responsible for any of the views presented here. The data were analyzed while the writer was the holder of a pre-doctoral National Science Foundation Fellowship. The writer wishes to acknowledge, with gratitude, the support of both foundations. This paper was read at the Annual Meeting of the American Anthropological Association in Philadelphia, Pennsylvania, in November 1961.

The dissertation, in which this material first appeared, was directed by Philip H. Gulliver, to whom I am in-debted for much stimulating and provocative discussion of many of the ideas here. Helpful comments and sugges-tions have also been made by Robert T. Holt and Robert S. Merrill.

Portions of the material included here were presented in a seminar on African Law conducted in the Department of Anthropology at the University of Minnesota by E. Adamson Hoebel and the writer. Members of the seminar were generous in their criticisms and comments.

SOURCE: From "The Kpelle Moot" by James L. Gibbs, Jr. in *Africa*, 33(1), January 1963. Reprinted by permis-sion from the author.

highly competent monographs such as those on law among the Tiv, the Barotse, and the Nuer.[2] These and related shorter studies have focused primarily on formal processes for the settlement of disputes, such as those which take place in a courtroom, or those which are, in some other way, set apart from simpler measures of social control. However, many African societies have informal, quasi-legal, dispute-settlement procedures, supplemental to formal ones, which have not been as well studied or—in most cases—adequately analysed.

In this paper I present a description and analysis of one such institution for the informal settlement of disputes, as it is found among the Kpelle of Liberia; it is the moot, the bɛrɛi mu meni saa or "house palaver." Hearings in the Kpelle moot contrast with those in a court in that they differ in tone and effectiveness. The genius of the moot lies in the fact that it is based on a covert application of the principles of psychoanalytic theory which underlie psychotherapy.

The Kpelle are a Mande-speaking, patrilineal group of some 175,000 rice cultivators who live in Central Liberia and the adjoining regions of Guinea. This paper is based on data gathered in a field study which I carried out in 1957 and 1958 among the Liberian Kpelle of Panta Chiefdom in north-east Central Province.

Strong corporate patrilineages are absent among the Kpelle. The most important kinship group is the virilocal polygynous family which sometimes becomes an extended family, almost always of the patrilineal variety. Several of these families form the core of a residential group, known as a village quarter, more technically, a clan-barrio.[3] This is headed by a quarter elder who is related to most of the household heads by real or putative patrilineal ties.

Kpelle political organization is centralized although there is no single king or paramount chief, but a series of chiefs of the same level of authority, each of whom is superordinate over district chiefs and town chiefs. Some political functions are also vested in the tribal fraternity, the Poro, which still functions vigorously. The form of political organization found in the area can thus best be termed the polycephalous associational state.

The structure of the Kpelle court system parallels that of the political organization. In Liberia the highest court of a tribal authority and the highest tribal court chartered by the Government is that of a paramount chief. A district chief's court is also an official court. Disputes may be settled in these official courts or in unofficial courts, such as those of town chiefs or quarter elders. In addition to this, grievances are settled informally in moots, and sometimes by associational groupings such as church councils or cooperative work groups.

In my field research I studied both the formal and informal methods of dispute settlement. The method used was to collect case material in as complete a form as possible. Accordingly, immediately after a hearing, my interpreter and I would prepare verbatim transcripts of each case that we heard. These transcripts were supplemented with accounts—obtained from respondents—of past cases or cases which I did not hear litigated. Transcripts from each type of hearing were analysed phrase by phrase in terms of a frame of reference derived from jurisprudence and ethno-law. The results of the analysis indicate two things: first, that courtroom hearings and moots are quite different in their procedures and tone, and secondly, why they show this contrast.

Kpelle courtroom hearings are basically coercive and arbitrary in tone. In another paper[4] I

---

2. Paul J. Bohannan, *Justice and Judgment among the Tiv*, Oxford University Press, London, 1957; Max Gluckman, *The Judicial Process among the Barotse of Northern Rhodesia*, Manchester University Press, 1954; P. P. Howell, *A Handbook of Nuer Law*, Oxford University Press, London, 1954.

3. Cf. George P. Murdock, *Social Structure*, Macmillan, New York, 1949, p. 74.

4. James L. Gibbs, Jr., "Poro Values and Courtroom Procedures in a Kpelle Chiefdom," *Southwestern Journal of Anthropology* (in press). A detailed analysis of Kpelle courtroom procedures and of procedures in the moot together with transcripts appears in: James L. Gibbs, Jr., *Some Judicial Implications of Marital Instability among the Kpelle* (unpublished Ph.D. Dissertation, Harvard University, Cambridge, Mass., 1960).

have shown that this is partly the result of the intrusion of the authoritarian values of the Poro into the courtroom. As a result, the court is limited in the manner in which it can handle some types of disputes. The court is particularly effective in settling cases such as assault, possession of illegal charms, or theft where the litigants are not linked in a relationship which must continue after the trial. However, most of the cases brought before a Kpelle court are cases involving disputed rights over women, including matrimonial matters which are usually cast in the form of suits for divorce. The court is particularly inept at settling these numerous matrimonial disputes because its harsh tone tends to drive spouses farther apart rather than to reconcile them. The moot, in contrast, is more effective in handling such cases. The following analysis indicates the reasons for this.[5]

The Kpelle *bɛrɛi mu meni saa,* or "house palaver," is an informal airing of a dispute which takes place before an assembled group which includes kinsmen of the litigants and neighbors from the quarter where the case is being heard. It is a completely ad hoc group, varying greatly in composition from case to case. The matter to be settled is usually a domestic problem: alleged mistreatment or neglect by a spouse, an attempt to collect money paid to a kinsman for a job which was not completed, or a quarrel among brothers over the inheritance of their father's wives.

In the procedural description which follows I shall use illustrative data from the Case of the Ousted Wife:

Wama Nya, the complainant, had one wife, Yua. His older brother died and he inherited the widow, Yokpo, who moved into his house. The two women were classificatory sisters. After Yokpo moved in, there was strife in the household. The husband accused her of staying out late at night, of harvesting rice without his knowledge, and of denying him food. He also accused Yokpo of having lovers and admitted having had a physical struggle with her, after which he took a basin of water and "washed his hands of her."

Yokpo countered by denying the allegations about having lovers, saying that she was accused falsely, although she had in the past confessed the name of one lover. She further complained that Wama Nya had assaulted her and, in the act, had committed the indignity of removing her headtie, and had expelled her from the house after the ritual handwashing. Finally, she alleged that she had been thus cast out of the house at the instigation of the other wife who, she asserted, had great influence over their husband.

KɔlɔWaa, the Town Chief and quarter elder, and the brother of Yokpo, was the mediator of the moot, which decided that the husband was mainly at fault, although Yua and Yokpo's children were also in the wrong. Those at fault had to apologize to Yokpo and bring gifts of apology as well as local rum[6] for the disputants and participants in the moot.

The moot is most often held on a Sunday—a day of rest for Christians and non-Christians alike— at the home of the complainant, the person who calls the moot. The mediator will have been selected by the complainant. He is a kinsman who also holds an office such as town chief or quarter

---

5. What follows is based on a detailed case study of moots in Panta Chiefdom and their contrast with courtroom hearings before the paramount chief of that chiefdom. Moots, being private, are less susceptible to the surveillance of the anthropologist than courtroom hearings, thus I have fewer transcripts of moots than of court cases. The analysis presented here is valid for Panta Chiefdom and also valid, I feel, for most of the Liberian Kpelle area, particularly the north-east where people are, by and large, traditional.

6. This simple distilled rum, bottled in Monrovia and retailing for twenty-five cents a bottle in 1958, is known in the Liberian Hinterland as "cane juice" and should not be confused with imported varieties.

elder, and therefore has some skill in dispute settlement. It is said that he is chosen to preside by virtue of his kin tie, rather than because of his office.

The proceedings begin with the pronouncing of blessings by one of the oldest men of the group. In the Case of the Ousted Wife, Gbenai Zua, the elder who pronounced the blessings, took a rice-stirrer in his hand and, striding back and forth, said:

> This man has called us to fix the matter between him and his wife. May αala [the supreme, creator deity] change his heart and let his household be in good condition. May αala bless the family and make them fruitful. May He bless them so they can have food this year. May He bless the children and the rest of the family so they may always be healthy. May He bless them to have good luck. When Wama Nya takes a gun and goes in the bush, may he kill big animals. May αala bless us to enjoy the meat. May He bless us to enjoy life and always have luck. May αala bless all those who come to discuss this matter.

The man who pronounces the blessings always carries a stick or a whisk *(kpung),* which he waves for effect as he paces up and down chanting his injunctions. Participation of spectators is demanded, for the blessings are chanted by the elder (*kpung namu* or "*kpung* owner") as a series of imperatives, some of which he repeats. Each phrase is responded to by the spectators who answer in unison with a formal response, either *e ka ti* (so be it), or a low, drawn-out *eeee.* The *kpung namu* delivers his blessings faster and faster, building up a rhythmic interaction pattern with the other participants. The effect is to unite those attending in common action before the hearing begins. The blessing focuses attention on the concern with maintaining harmony and the well-being of the group as a whole.

Everyone attending the moot wears their next-to-best clothes or, if it is not Sunday, everyday clothes. Elders, litigants, and spectators sit in mixed fashion, pressed closely upon each other, often overflowing onto a veranda. This is in contrast to the vertical spatial separation between litigants and adjudicators in the courtroom. The mediator, even though he is a chief, does not wear his robes. He and the oldest men will be given chairs as they would on any other occasion.

The complainant speaks first and may be interrupted by the mediator or anyone else present. After he has been thoroughly quizzed, the accused will answer and will also be questioned by those present. The two parties will question each other directly and question others in the room also. Both the testimony and the questioning are lively and uninhibited. Where there are witnesses to some of the actions described by the parties, they may also speak and be questioned. Although the proceedings are spirited, they remain orderly. The mediator may fine anyone who speaks out of turn by requiring them to bring some rum for the group to drink.

The mediator and others present will point out the various faults committed by both the parties. After everyone has been heard, the mediator expresses the consensus of the group. For example, in the Case of the Ousted Wife, he said to Yua: "The words you used towards your sister were not good, so come and beg her pardon."

The person held to be mainly at fault will then formally apologize to the other person. This apology takes the form of the giving of token gifts to the wronged person by the guilty party. These may be an item of clothing, a few coins, clean hulled rice, or a combination of all three. It is also customary for the winning party in accepting the gifts of apology to give, in return, a smaller token such as a twenty-five cent piece[7] to show his "white heart" or good will. The losing party is also lightly "fined"; he must present rum or beer to the mediator and the others who heard the case. This is consumed by all in attendance. The old man then pronounces blessings again and offers thanks for the restoration of harmony within the group, and asks that all continue to act with good grace and unity.

---

7. American currency is the official currency of Liberia and is used throughout the country.

An initial analysis of the procedural steps of the moot isolates the descriptive attributes of the moot and shows that they contrast with those of the courtroom hearing. While the airing of grievances is incomplete in courtroom hearings, it is more complete in the moot. This fuller airing of the issues results, in many marital cases, in a more harmonious solution. Several specific features of the house palaver facilitate this wider airing of grievances. First, the hearing takes place soon after a breach has occurred, before the grievances have hardened. There is no delay until the complainant has time to go to the paramount chief's or district chief's headquarters to institute suit. Secondly, the hearing takes place in the familiar surroundings of a home. The robes, writs, messengers, and other symbols of power which subtly intimidate and inhibit the parties in the courtroom, by reminding them of the physical force which underlies the procedures, are absent. Thirdly, in the courtroom the conduct of the hearing is firmly in the hands of the judge but in the moot the investigatory initiative rests much more with the parties themselves. Jurisprudence suggests that, in such a case, more of the grievances lodged between the parties are likely to be aired and adjusted. Finally, the range of relevance applied to matters which are brought out is extremely broad. Hardly anything mentioned is held to be irrelevant. This too leads to a more thorough ventilation of the issues.

There is a second surface difference between court and moot. In a courtroom hearing, the solution is, by and large, one which is imposed by the adjudicator. In the moot the solution, is more consensual. It is, therefore, more likely to be accepted by both parties and hence more durable. Several features of the moot contribute to the consensual solution: first, there is no unilateral ascription of blame, but an attribution of fault to both parties. Secondly, the mediator, unlike the chief in the courtroom, is not backed by political authority and the physical force which underlies it. He

cannot jail parties, nor can he levy a heavy fine. Thirdly, the sanctions which are imposed are not so burdensome as to cause hardship to the losing party or to give him or her grounds for a new grudge against the other party. The gifts for the winning party and the potables for the spectators are not as expensive as the fines and the court costs in a paramount chief's court. Lastly, the ritualized apology of the moot symbolizes very concretely the consensual nature of the solution.[8] The public offering and acceptance of the tokens of apology indicate that each party has no further grievances and that the settlement is satisfactory and mutually acceptable. The parties and spectators drink together to symbolize the restarted solidarity of the group and the rehabilitation of the offending party.

This type of analysis describes the courtroom hearing and the moot, using a frame of reference derived from jurisprudence and ethno-law which is explicitly comparative and evaluative. Only by using this type of comparative approach can the researcher select features of the hearings which are not only unique to each of them, but theoretically significant in that their contribution to the social-control functions of the proceedings can be hypothesized. At the same time, it enables the researcher to pin-point in procedures the cause for what he feels intuitively: that the two hearings contrast in tone, even though they are similar in some ways.

However, one can approach the transcripts of the trouble cases with a second analytical framework and emerge with a deeper understanding of the implications of the contrasting descriptive attributes of the court and the house palaver. Remember that the coercive tone of the courtroom hearing limits the court's effectiveness in dealing with matrimonial disputes, especially in effecting reconciliations. The moot, on the other hand, is particularly effective in bringing about reconciliations between spouses. This is because the moot is not only conciliatory, but *therapeutic*. Moot procedures

---

8. Cf. J. F. Holleman, "An Anthropological Approach to Bantu Law (with special reference to Shona law)" in the *Journal of the Rhodes-Livingstone Institute*, vol. x, 1950, pp. 27–41. Holleman feels that the use of tokens for effecting apologies—or marriages—shows the proclivity for reducing events of importance to something tangible.

are therapeutic in that, like psychotherapy, they re-educate the parties through a type of social learning brought about in a specially structured interpersonal setting.

Talcott Parsons[9] has written that therapy involves four elements: support, permissiveness, denial of reciprocity, and manipulation of rewards. Writers such as Frank,[10] Klapman,[11] and Opler[12] have pointed out that the same elements character-ize not only individual psychotherapy, but group psychotherapy as well. All four elements are writ large in the Kpelle moot.

The patient in therapy will not continue treat-ment very long if he does not feel support from the therapist or from the group. In the moot the parties are encouraged in the expression of their com-plaints and feelings because they sense group support. The very presence of one's kinsmen and neighbors demonstrates their concern. It indicates to the parties that they have a real problem and that the others are willing to help them to help themselves in solving it. In a parallel vein, Frank, speaking of group psychotherapy, notes that: "Even anger may be supportive if it implies to a patient that others take him seriously enough to get angry at him, especially if the object of the anger feels it to be directed toward his neurotic behavior rather than himself as a person."[13] In the moot the feeling of support also grows out of the pronouncement of the blessings which stress the unity of the group and its harmonious goal, and it is also undoubtedly increased by the absence of the publicity and expressive symbols of political power which are found in the courtroom.

Permissiveness is the second element in therapy. It indicates to the patient that everyday restrictions on making anti-social statements or acting out anti-social impulses are lessened. Thus, in the Case of the Ousted Wife, Yua felt free enough to turn to her ousted co-wife (who had been married leviratically) and say:

> You don't respect me. You don't rely on me any more. When your husband was living, and I was with my husband, we slept on the farm. Did I ever refuse to send you what you asked me for when you sent a message? Didn't I always send you some of the meat my husband killed? Did I refuse to send you anything you wanted? When your husband died and we became co-wives, did I disrespect you? Why do you always make me ashamed? The things you have done to me make me sad.

Permissiveness in the therapeutic setting (and in the moot) results in catharsis, in a high degree of stimulation of feelings in the participants and an equally high tendency to verbalize these feelings.[14] Frank notes that: "Neurotic responses must be ex-pressed in the therapeutic situation if they are to be changed by it."[15] In the same way, if the solution to a dispute reached in a house palaver is to be stable, it is important that there should be nothing left to embitter and undermine the decision. In a familiar setting, with familiar people, the parties to the moot feel at ease and free to say *all* that is on their minds. Yokpo, judged to be the wronged party in the Case

9. Talcott Parsons, *The Social System*, The Free Press, Glencoe, Ill., 1951, pp. 314–19.

10. Jerome D. Frank, "Group Methods in Psychotherapy" in *Mental Health and Mental Disorder: A Sociological Approach*, edited by Arnold Rose, W. W. Norton Co., New York, pp. 524–35.

11. J. W. Klapman, *Group Psychotherapy: Theory and Practice*, Grune & Stratton, New York, 1959.

12. Marvin K. Opler, "Values in Group Psychotherapy," *International Journal of Social Psychiatry*, vol. iv, 1959, pp. 296–98.

13. Frank, op. cit., p. 531.

14. Ibid.

15. Ibid.

of the Ousted Wife, in accepting an apology, gave expression to this when she said:

> I agree to everything that my people said, and I accept the things they have given me—I don't have *anything else* about them on my mind. (*My italics*.)

As we shall note below, this thorough airing of complaints also facilitates the gaining of insight into and the unlearning of idiosyncratic behaviour which is socially disruptive. Permissiveness is rooted in the lack of publicity and the lack of symbols of power. But it stems, too, from the immediacy of the hearing, the locus of investigatory initiative with the parties, and the wide range of relevance.

Permissiveness in therapy is impossible without the denial of reciprocity. This refers to the fact that the therapist will not respond in kind when the patient acts in a hostile manner or with inappropriate affection. It is a type of privileged indulgence which comes with being a patient. In the moot, the parties are treated in the same way and are allowed to hurl recriminations that, in the courtroom, might bring a few hours in jail as punishment for the equivalent of contempt of court. Even though inappropriate views are not responded to in kind, neither are they simply ignored. There is denial of *congruent* response, not denial of *any* response whatsoever. In the *bɛrɛi mu meni saa,* as in group psychotherapy, "private ideation and conceptualization are brought out into the open and all their facets or many of their facets exposed. The individual gets a "reading" from different bearings on the compass, so to speak,[16] and perceptual patterns... are joggled out of their fixed positions...."[17]

Thus, Yua's outburst against Yokpo quoted above was not responded to with matching hostility, but its inappropriateness was clearly pointed out to her by the group. Some of them called her aside in a huddle and said to her:

You are not right. If you don't like the woman, or she doesn't like you, don't be the first to say anything. Let her start and then say what you have to say. By speaking, if she heeds some of your words, the wives will scatter, and the blame will be on you. Then your husband will cry for your name that you have scattered his property.

In effect, Yua was being told that, in view of the previous testimony, her jealousy of her co-wife was not justified. In reality testing, she discovered that her view of the situation was not shared by the others and, hence, was inappropriate. Noting how the others responded, she could see why her treatment of her co-wife had caused so much dissension. Her interpretation of her new co-wife's actions and resulting premises were not shared by the co-wife, nor by the others hearing a description of what had happened. Like psychotherapy, the moot is gently corrective of behavior rooted in such misunderstandings.

Similarly, Wama Nya, the husband, learned that others did not view as reasonable his accusing his wife of having a lover and urging her to go off and drink with the suspected paramour when he passed their house and wished them all a good evening. Reality testing for him taught him that the group did not view this type of mildly paranoid sarcasm as conducive to stable marital relationships.

The reaction of the moot to Yua's outburst indicates that permissiveness in this case was certainly not complete, but only relative, being much greater than in the courtroom. But without this moderated immunity the airing of grievances would be limited, and the chance for social relearning lessened. Permissiveness in the moot is incomplete because, even there, prudence is not thrown to the winds. Note that Yua was not told not to express her feelings at all, but to express them only after the co-wife had spoken so that, if the moot failed, she would not be in an untenable position. In court there would be objection to her blunt speaking out. In the moot

---

16. Klapman, op. cit., p. 39.

17. Ibid., p. 15.

the objection was, in effect, to her speaking *out of turn*. In other cases the moot sometimes fails, foundering on this very point, because the parties are *too* prudent, all waiting for the others to make the first move in admitting fault.

The manipulation of rewards is the last dimension of therapy treated by Parsons. In this final phase of therapy[18] the patient is coaxed to conformity by the granting of rewards. In the moot one of the most important rewards is the group approval which goes to the wronged person who accepts an apology and to the person who is magnanimous enough to make one.

In the Case of the Ousted Wife, KɔlɔWaa, the mediator, and the others attending decided that the husband and the co-wife, Yua, had wronged Yokpo. Waa said to the husband:

> From now on, we don't want to hear of your fighting. You should live in peace with these women. If your wife accepts the things which the people have brought you should pay four chickens and ten bottles of rum as your contribution.

The husband's brother and sister also brought gifts of apology, although the moot did not explicitly hold them at fault.

By giving these prestations, the wrong-doer is restored to good grace and is once again acting like an "upright Kpelle" (although, if he wishes, he may refuse to accept the decision of the moot). He is eased into this position by being grouped with others to whom blame is also allocated, for, typically, he is not singled out and isolated in being labelled deviant. Thus, in the Case of the Ousted Wife, the children of Yokpo were held to be at fault in "being mean" to their stepfather, so that blame was not only shared by one "side," but ascribed to the other also.

Moreover, the prestations which the losing party is asked to hand over are not expensive. They are significant enough to touch the pocketbook a little; for the Kpelle say that if an apology does not cost something other than words, the wrong-doer is more likely to repeat the offending action. At the same time, as we noted above, the tokens are not so costly as to give the loser additional reason for anger directed at the other party which can undermine the decision.

All in all, the rewards for conformity to group expectations and for following out a new behaviour pattern are kept within the deviant's sight. These rewards are positive, in contrast to the negative sanctions of the courtroom. Besides the institutionalized apology, praise and acts of concern and affection replace fines and jail sentences. The mediator, speaking to Yokpo as the wronged party, said:

> You have found the best of the dispute. Your husband has wronged you. All the people have wronged you. You are the only one who can take care of them because you are the oldest. Accept the things they have given to you.

The moot in its procedural features and procedural sequences is, then, strongly analogous to psychotherapy. It is analogous to therapy in the structuring of the role of the mediator also. Parsons has indicated that, to do his job well, the therapist must be a member of two social systems: one containing himself and his patient; and the other, society at large.[19] He must not be seduced into thinking that he belongs only to the therapeutic dyad, but must gradually pull the deviant back into a relationship with the wider group. It is significant, then, that the mediator of a moot is a kinsman who is also a chief of some sort. He thus represents both the group involved in the dispute and the wider community. His task is to utilize his position as kinsman as a lever to manipulate the parties into living up to the normative requirements of the wider society, which, as chief, he

---

18. For expository purposes the four elements of therapy are described as if they always occur serially. They may, and do, occur simultaneously also. Thus, all four of the factors may be implicit in a single short behavioural sequence. Parsons (op. cit.) holds that these four elements are common not only to psychotherapy but to all measures of social control.

19. Parsons, op. cit., p. 314. Cf. loc. cit., chap. 10.

upholds. His major orientation must be to the wider collectivity, not to the particular goals of his kinsmen.

When successful, the moot stops the process of alienation which drives two spouses so far apart that they are immune to ordinary social control measures such as a smile, a frown, or a pointed aside.[20] A moot is not always successful, however. Both parties must have a genuine willingness to cooperate and a real concern about their discord. Each party must be willing to list his grievances, to admit his guilt, and make an open apology. The moot, like psychotherapy, is impotent without well-motivated clients.

The therapeutic elements found in the Kpelle moot are undoubtedly found in informal procedures for settling disputes in other African societies also; some of these are reported in literature and others are not. One such procedure which seems strikingly parallel to the Kpelle *bɛrɛi mu meni saa* has been described by J. H. M. Beattie.[21] This is the court of neighbors or *rukurato rw'enzarwa* found in the Banyoro kingdom of Uganda. The group also meets as an ad hoc assembly of neighbors to hear disputes involving kinsmen or neighbors.[22]

The intention of the Nyoro moot is to "reintegrate the delinquent into the community and, if possible, to achieve reconciliation without causing bitterness and resentment; in the words of an informant, the institution exists 'to finish off people's quarrels and to abolish bad feeling.'"[23] This therapeutic goal is manifested in the manner in which the dispute is resolved. After a decision is reached the penalty imposed is always the same. The party held to be in the wrong is asked to bring beer (four pots, modified downwards according to the circumstances) and meat, which is shared with the other party and all those attending the *rukurato*. The losing party is also expected to "humble himself, not only to the man he has injured but to the whole assembly."[24]

Beattie correctly points out that, because the council of neighbors has no power to enforce its decision, the shared feast is *not* to be viewed primarily as a penalty, for the wrong-doer acts as a host and also shares in the food and drink. "And it is a praiseworthy thing; from a dishonourable status he is promoted to an honourable one..."[25] and reintegrated into the community.[26]

Although Beattie does not use a psychoanalytic frame of reference in approaching his material, it is clear that the communal feast involves the manipulation of rewards as the last step in a social-control measure which breaks the progressive alienation of the deviance cycle. The description of procedures in the *rukurato* indicates that it is highly informal in nature, convening in a room in a house with everyone "sitting around." However, Beattie does not provide enough detail to enable one to determine whether or not the beginning and intermediate steps in the Nyoro moot show the permissiveness, support, and denial of reciprocity which characterize the Kpelle moot. Given the structure and outcome of most

---

20. Cf. Parsons, op. cit., chap. 7. Parsons notes that in any social-control action the aim is to avoid the process of alienation, that "vicious-cycle" phenomenon whereby each step taken to curb the non-conforming activity of the deviant has the effect of driving him further into his pattern of deviance. Rather, the need is to "reach" the deviant and bring him back to the point where he is susceptible to the usual everyday informal sanctions.

21. J. H. M. Beattie, "Informal Judicial Activity in Bunyoro," *Journal of African Administration*, vol. ix, 1957, pp. 188–95.

22. Disputes include matters such as a son seducing his father's wives, a grown son disobeying his father, or a husband or wife failing in his or her duties to a spouse. Disputes between unrelated persons involve matters like quarrelling, abuse, assault, false accusations, petty theft, adultery, and failure to settle debts. (Ibid., p. 190.)

23. Ibid., p. 194.

24. Beattie, op. cit., p. 194.

25. Ibid., p. 193.

26. Ibid., p. 195. Moreover, Beattie also recognizes the functional significance of the Nyoro moots, for he notes that: "It would be a serious error to represent them simply as clumsy, 'amateur' expedients for punishing wrong-doers or settling civil disputes at an informal, sub official level." (Ibid.)

Nyoro councils, one would surmise that a close examination of their proceedings[27] would reveal the implicit operation of therapeutic principles.

The fact that the Kpelle court is basically coercive and the moot therapeutic does not imply that one is dysfunctional while the other is eufunctional. Like Beattie, I conclude that the court and informal dispute-settlement procedures have separate but complementary functions. In marital disputes the moot is oriented to a couple as a dyadic social system and serves to reconcile them wherever possible. This is eufunctional from the point of view of the couple, to whom divorce would be dysfunctional. Kpelle courts customarily treat matrimonial matters by granting a divorce. While this may be dysfunctional from the point of view of the couple, because it ends their marriage, it may be eufunctional from the point of view of society. Some marriages, if forced to continue, would result in adultery or physical violence at best, and improper socialization of children at worst. It is clear that the Kpelle moot is to the Kpelle court as the domestic and family relations courts (or commercial and labour arbitration boards) are to ordinary courts in our own society. The essential point is that both formal and informal dispute-settlement procedures serve significant functions in Kpelle society and neither can be fully understood if studied alone.[28]

DISCUSSION QUESTIONS

1. What types of cases are usually heard by moots? What types are heard by traditional courts?

2. How do the procedures of Kpelle moots differ from the procedures of traditional courts?

3. Gibbs says that the Kpelle moot tends to be more consensual than formal courts. In what specific ways are moots more consensual?

 **RESOURCES ON THE INTERNET**

 InfoTrac College Edition

infotrac-college.com

You can find further relevant readings by searching *InfoTrac College Edition*, an online library with access to thousands of scholarly and popular periodicals. Below are suggested search terms for this article:

- moot
- conflict resolution
- social control

Anthropology Online: Wadsworth's Anthropology Resource Center

academic.cengage.com/anthropology

The Wadsworth Anthropology Resource Center contains a wealth of information and useful tools for students including information on careers in anthropology.

---

27. The type of examination of case materials that is required demands that field workers should not simply record cases that meet the "trouble case" criterion (cf. K. N. Llewellyn and E. A. Hoebel, *The Cheyenne Way*, Norman, Okla., University of Oklahoma Press, 1941; and E. A. Hoebel, *The Law of Primitive Man*, Cambridge, Mass., Harvard University Press, 1954), but that cases should be recorded in some transcript-like form.

28. The present study has attempted to add to our understanding of informal dispute-settlement procedures in one African society by using an eclectic but organized collection of concepts from jurisprudence, ethno-law, and psychology. It is based on the detailed and systematic analysis of a few selected cases, rather than a mass of quantitative data. In further research a greater variety of cases handled by Kpelle moots should be subjected to the same analysis to test its merit more fully.

12

Anthropology and Counterinsurgency

MONTGOMERY McFATE

While cultural anthropology in recent decades has been applied successfully to a number of different areas in the United States (e.g., medicine, education, and business), it has been conspicuously absent in our military establishment. This has become painfully apparent in the current Iraq War and counterinsurgency, which has revealed just how uninformed our national security leadership has been regarding the social and cultural realities of the adversaries. This has held true for both U.S. political leaders who chose to wage a preemptive war in Iraq as well as the military leadership that was expected to win the war and secure the peace.

According to Montgomery McFate, this lack of cultural understanding was the result of two concurrent tendencies during the past forty years. First, the U.S. military/national security establishment has almost completely ignored the field of cultural anthropology—the discipline that focuses on understanding other cultures. And second, anthropologists have avoided working with the national security establishment out of fear of jeopardizing their ethical responsibility to protect the lives of the people they study. In this selection McFate raises an important practical question that both anthropologists and the national security establishment have avoided since the Vietnam conflict:

> *Regardless of whether anthropologists decide to enter the national security arena, cultural information will inevitably be used as the basis of military operations and public policy. And, if anthropologists refuse to contribute, how reliable will that information be?*

Something mysterious is going on inside the U.S. Department of Defense (DOD). Over the past two years, senior leaders have been calling for something unusual and unexpected—cultural knowledge of the adversary. In July 2004, retired Major General Robert H. Scales, Jr., wrote an article for the Naval War College's *Proceedings* magazine that opposed the commonly held view within the U.S. military that success in war is best achieved by overwhelming technological advantage. Scales argues that the type of conflict we are now witnessing in Iraq requires "an exceptional ability to understand people, their culture, and their motivation." In October 2004, Arthur Cebrowski, Director of the Office of Force Transformation, concluded that "knowledge of one's enemy and his culture and society may be more important than knowledge of his order of battle." In November 2004, the Office of Naval Research and the Defense Advanced Research Projects Agency (DARPA) sponsored the Adversary Cultural Knowledge and National Security Conference, the first major DOD conference on the social sciences since 1962.

SOURCE: From *Military Review,* March/April, 2005, pp. 24–38.

Why has cultural knowledge suddenly become such an imperative? Primarily because traditional methods of war-fighting have proven inadequate in Iraq and Afghanistan. U.S. technology, training, and doctrine designed to counter the Soviet threat are not designed for low-intensity counterinsurgency operations where civilians mingle freely with combatants in complex urban terrain.

The major combat operations that toppled Saddam Hussein's regime were relatively simple because they required the U.S. military to do what it does best—conduct maneuver warfare in flat terrain using overwhelming firepower with air support. However, since the end of the "hot" phase of the war, coalition forces have been fighting a complex war against an enemy they do not understand. The insurgents' organizational structure is not military, but tribal. Their tactics are not conventional, but asymmetrical. Their weapons are not tanks and fighter planes, but improvised explosive devices (IEDs). They do not abide by the Geneva Conventions, nor do they appear to have any informal rules of engagement.

Countering the insurgency in Iraq requires cultural and social knowledge of the adversary. Yet, none of the elements of U.S. national power—diplomatic, military, intelligence, or economic—explicitly take adversary culture into account in the formation or execution of policy. This cultural knowledge gap has a simple cause—the almost total absence of anthropology within the national-security establishment.

Once called "the handmaiden of colonialism," anthropology has had a long, fruitful relationship with various elements of national power, which ended suddenly following the Vietnam War. The strange story of anthropology's birth as a war-fighting discipline, and its sudden plunge into the abyss of postmodernism, is intertwined with the U.S. failure in Vietnam. The curious and conspicuous lack of anthropology in the national-security arena since the Vietnam War has had grave consequences for countering the insurgency in Iraq, particularly because political policy and military operations based on partial and incomplete cultural knowledge are often worse than none at all.

A LACK OF CULTURAL AWARENESS

In a conflict between symmetric adversaries, where both are evenly matched and using similar technology, understanding the adversary's culture is largely irrelevant. The Cold War, for all its complexity, pitted two powers of European heritage against each other. In a counterinsurgency operation against a non-Western adversary, however, culture matters. U.S. Department of the Army Field Manual (FM) (interim) 3-07.22, Counterinsurgency Operations, defines *insurgency* as an "organized movement aimed at the overthrow of a constituted government through use of subversion and armed conflict. It is a protracted politico-military struggle designed to weaken government control and legitimacy while increasing insurgent control. Political power is *the* central issue in an insurgency [emphasis added]." Political considerations must therefore circumscribe military action as a fundamental matter of strategy. As British Field Marshall Gerald Templar explained in 1953, "The answer lies not in pouring more troops into the jungle, but rests in the hearts and minds of the … people." Winning hearts and minds requires understanding the local culture.

Aside from Special Forces, most U.S. soldiers are not trained to understand or operate in foreign cultures and societies. One U.S. Army captain in Iraq said, "I was never given classes on how to sit down with a sheik. … He is giving me the traditional dishdasha and the entire outfit of a sheik because he claims that I am a new sheik in town so I must be dressed as one. I don't know if he is trying to gain favor with me because he wants something [or if it is] something good or something bad." In fact, as soon as coalition forces toppled Saddam Hussein, they became de facto players in the Iraqi social system. The young captain had indeed become the new sheik in town and was being properly honored by his Iraqi host.

As this example indicates, U.S. forces frequently do not know who their friends are, and just as often they do not know who their enemies are. A returning commander from the 3d Infantry

Division observed: "I had perfect situational awareness. What I lacked was cultural awareness. I knew where every enemy tank was dug in on the outskirts of Tallil. Only problem was, my soldiers had to fight fanatics charging on foot or in pickups and firing AK-47s and RPGs [rocket-propelled grenades]. Great technical intelligence. Wrong enemy."

While the consequences of a lack of cultural knowledge might be most apparent (or perhaps most deadly) in a counterinsurgency, a failure to understand foreign cultures has been a major contributing factor in multiple national-security and intelligence failures. In her 1962 study, "Pearl Harbor: Warning and Decision," Roberta Wohlstetter demonstrated that although the U.S. Government picked up Japanese signals (including conversations, decoded cables, and ship movements), it failed to distinguish signals from noise—to understand which signals were meaningful—because it was unimaginable that the Japanese might do something as "irrational" as attacking the headquarters of the U.S. Pacific fleet.

Such ethnocentrism (the inability to put aside one's own cultural attitudes and imagine the world from the perspective of a different group) is especially dangerous in a national-security context because it can distort strategic thinking and result in assumptions that the adversary will behave exactly as one might behave. India's nuclear tests on 11 and 13 May 1998 came as a complete surprise because of this type of "mirror-imaging" among CIA analysts. According to the internal investigation conducted by former Vice Chairman of the Joint Chiefs of Staff David Jeremiah, the real problem was an assumption by intelligence analysts and policymakers that the Indians would not test their nuclear weapons because Americans would not test nuclear weapons in similar circumstances. According to Jeremiah, "The intelligence and the policy communities had an underlying mind-set going into these tests that the B.J.P. [Bharatiya Janata Party] would behave as we [would] behave."

The United States suffers from a lack of cultural knowledge in its national-security establishment for two primary, interrelated reasons. First, anthropology is largely and conspicuously absent as a discipline within our national-security enterprise, especially within the intelligence community and DOD. Anthropology is a social science discipline whose primary object of study has traditionally been non-Western, tribal societies. The methodologies of anthropology include participant observation, fieldwork, and historical research. One of the central epistemological tenets of anthropology is cultural relativism—understanding other societies from within their own framework.

The primary task of anthropology has historically been translating knowledge gained in the "field" back to the West. While it might seem self-evident that such a perspective would be beneficial to the national security establishment, only one of the national defense universities (which provide master's degree level education to military personnel) currently has an anthropologist on its faculty. At West Point, which traditionally places a heavy emphasis on engineering, anthropology is disparagingly referred to by cadets as "nuts and huts." And, although political science is well represented as a discipline in senior policymaking circles, there has never been an anthropologist on the National Security Council.

The second and related reason for the current lack of cultural knowledge is the failure of the U.S. military to achieve anything resembling victory in Vietnam. Following the Vietnam War, the Joint Chiefs of Staff collectively put their heads in the sand and determined they would never fight an unconventional war again. From a purely military perspective, it was easier for them to focus on the threat of Soviet tanks rolling through the Fulda Gap, prompting a major European land war—a war they could easily fight using existing doctrine and technology and that would have a clear, unequivocal winner.

The preference for the use of overwhelming force and clear campaign objectives was formalized in what has become known as the Weinberger doctrine. In a 1984 speech, Secretary of Defense Caspar Weinberger articulated six principles designed to ensure the nation would never become involved in another Vietnam. By the mid-1980s, there was cause for concern: deployment of troops to El Salvador seemed likely and the involvement in Lebanon had proved disastrous following the bombing of the U.S. Marine barracks in Beirut. Responding to these events, Weinberger believed troops should be committed only if U.S. national interests were at stake; only in support of clearly defined political and military objectives; and only "with the clear intention of winning."

In 1994, Chairman of the Joint Chiefs of Staff Colin Powell (formerly a military assistant to Weinberger) rearticulated the Weinberger doctrine's fundamental elements, placing a strong emphasis on the idea that force, when used, should be overwhelming and disproportionate to the force used by the enemy. The Powell-Weinberger doctrine institutionalized a preference for "major combat operations"—big wars—as a matter of national preference. Although the Powell-Weinberger doctrine was eroded during the Clinton years; during operations other than war in Haiti, Somali, and Bosnia; and during the second Bush Administration's preemptive strikes in Afghanistan and Iraq, no alternative doctrine has emerged to take its place.

We have no doctrine for "nation-building," which the military eschews as a responsibility because it is not covered by Title 10 of the U.S. Code, which outlines the responsibilities of the military as an element of national power. Field Manual 3-07, Stability Operations and Support Operations, was not finalized until February 2003, despite the fact the U.S. military was already deeply engaged in such operations in Iraq. Field Manual 3-07.22—meant to be a temporary document—is still primarily geared toward fighting an enemy engaged in Maoist revolutionary warfare, a type of insurgency that has little application to the situation in Iraq where multiple organizations are competing for multiple, confusing objectives.

Since 1923, the core tenet of U.S. war-fighting strategy has been that overwhelming force deployed against an equally powerful state will result in military victory. Yet in a counterinsurgency situation such as the one the United States currently

faces in Iraq, "winning" through overwhelming force is often inapplicable as a concept, if not problematic as a goal. While negotiating in Hanoi a few days before Saigon fell, U.S. Army Colonel Harry Summers, Jr., said to a North Vietnamese colonel, "You know, you never defeated us on the battlefield." The Vietnamese colonel replied, "That may be so, but it is also irrelevant." The same could be said of the conflict in Iraq.

Winning on the battlefield is irrelevant against an insurgent adversary because the struggle for power and legitimacy among competing factions has no purely military solution. Often, the application of overwhelming force has the negative, unintended effect of strengthening the insurgency by creating martyrs, increasing recruitment, and demonstrating the "brutality" of state forces.

The alternative approach to fighting insurgency, such as the British eventually adopted through trial and error in Northern Ireland, involves the following: A comprehensive plan to alleviate the political conditions behind the insurgency; civil-military cooperation; the application of minimum force; deep intelligence; and an acceptance of the protracted nature of the conflict. Deep cultural knowledge of the adversary is inherent to the British approach.

Although cultural knowledge of the adversary matters in counterinsurgency, it has little importance in major combat operations. Because the Powell-Weinberger doctrine meant conventional, large-scale war was the only acceptable type of conflict, no discernable present or future need existed to develop doctrine and expertise in unconventional war, including counterinsurgency. Thus, there was no need to incorporate cultural knowledge into doctrine, training, or war-fighting. Until now, that is.

On 21 October 2003, the House Armed Services Committee held a hearing to examine lessons learned from Operation Iraqi Freedom. Scales' testimony at the hearing prompted U.S. Representative "Ike" Skelton to write a letter to Secretary of Defense Donald Rumsfeld in which he said: "In simple terms, if we had better understood the Iraqi culture and mindset, our war plans would have been even better than they were, the plan for the postwar period and all of its challenges would have been far better, and we [would have been] better prepared for the 'long slog' ... to win the peace in Iraq."

Even such DOD luminaries as Andrew Marshall, the mysterious director of the Pentagon's Office of Net Assessment, are now calling for "anthropology level knowledge of a wide range of cultures" because such knowledge will prove essential to conducting future operations. Although senior U.S. Government officials such as Skelton are calling for "personnel in our civilian ranks who have cultural knowledge and understanding to inform the policy process," there are few anthropologists either available or willing to play in the same sandbox with the military.

THE CURRENT STATE OF THE DISCIPLINE

Although anthropology is the only academic discipline that explicitly seeks to understand foreign cultures and societies, it is a marginal contributor to U.S. national-security policy at best and a punch line at worst. Over the past 30 years, as a result of anthropologists' individual career choices and the tendency toward reflexive self-criticism contained within the discipline itself, the discipline has become hermetically sealed within its Ivory Tower.

Unlike political science or economics, anthropology is primarily an academic discipline. The majority of newly minted anthropologists brutally compete for a limited number of underpaid university faculty appointments, and although there is an increasing demand from industry for applied anthropologists to advise on product design, marketing, and organizational culture, anthropologists still prefer to study the "exotic and useless," in the words of A.L. Kroeber.

The retreat to the Ivory Tower is also a product of the deep isolationist tendencies within the discipline. Following the Vietnam War, it was fashionable among anthropologists to reject the disci-

pline's historic ties to colonialism. Anthropologists began to reinvent their discipline, as demonstrated by Kathleen Cough's 1968 article, "Anthropology: Child of Imperialism," followed by Dell Hymes' 1972 anthology, *Reinventing Anthropology,* and culminating in editor Talal Asad's *Anthropology and the Colonial Encounter.*

Rejecting anthropology's status as the handmaiden of colonialism, anthropologists refused to "collaborate" with the powerful, instead vying to represent the interests of indigenous peoples engaged in neocolonial struggles. In the words of Gayatri Chakravorti Spivak, anthropologists would now speak for the "subaltern." Thus began a systematic interrogation of the contemporary state of the discipline as well as of the colonial circumstances from which it emerged. Armed with critical hermeneutics, frequently backed up by self-reflexive neo-Marxism, anthropology began a brutal process of self-flagellation, to a degree almost unimaginable to anyone outside the discipline.

The turn toward postmodernism within anthropology exacerbated the tendency toward self-flagellation, with the central goal being "the deconstruction of the centralized, logocentric master narratives of European culture." This movement away from descriptive ethnography has produced some of the worst writing imaginable. For example, *Cultural Anthropology,* one of the most respected anthropology journals in the United States, commonly publishes such incomprehensible articles as "Recovering True Selves in the Electro-Spiritual Field of Universal Love" and "Material Consumers, Fabricating Subjects: Perplexity, Global Connectivity Discourses, and Transnational Feminist Research."

Anthropologist Stephen Tyler recently took fourth place in the Bad Writing Contest with this selection from *Writing Culture,* a remarkable passage describing postmodern ethnography:

> It thus relativizes discourse not just to form—that familiar perversion of the modernist; nor to authorial intention— that conceit of the romantics; nor to a foundational world beyond discourse— that desperate grasping for a separate reality

of the mystic and scientist alike; nor even to history and ideology—those refuges of the hermeneuticist; nor even less to language—that hypostasized abstraction of the linguist; nor, ultimately, even to discourse—that Nietzschean playground of world-lost signifiers of the structuralist and grammatologist, but to all or none of these, for it is anarchic, though not for the sake of anarchy, but because it refuses to become a fetishized object among objects—to be dismantled, compared, classified, and neutered in that parody of scientific scrutiny known as criticism.

THE COLONIAL ERA

From the foregoing discussion, it might be tempting to conclude that anthropology is absent from the policy arena because it really is "exotic and useless." However, this was not always the case. Anthropology actually evolved as an intellectual tool to consolidate imperial power at the margins of empire.

In Britain the development and growth of anthropology was deeply connected to colonial administration. As early as 1908, anthropologists began training administrators of the Sudanese civil service. This relationship was quickly institutionalized: in 1921, the International Institute of African Languages and Cultures was established with financing from various colonial governments, and Lord Lugard, the former governor of Nigeria, became head of its executive council. The organization's mission was based on Bronislaw Malinowski's article, "Practical Anthropology," which argued that anthropological knowledge should be applied to solve the problems faced by colonial administrators, including those posed by "savage law, economics, customs, and institutions." Anthropological knowledge was frequently useful, especially in understanding the power dynamics in traditional societies. In 1937, for example, the Royal Anthropological Institute's Standing Committee on Applied Anthropology noted that anthropological research would "indicate

the persons who hold key positions in the community and whose influence it would be important to enlist on the side of projected reforms." In the words of Lord Hailey, anthropologists were indeed "of great assistance in providing Government with knowledge which must be the basis of administrative policy."

Anthropology as a tool of empire was, however, not without its detractors. In 1951, Sir Philip E. Mitchell wrote: "Anthropologists busied themselves [with] all the minutiae of obscure trial and personal practices, especially if they were agreeably associated with sex or flavoured with obscenity. There resulted a large number of painstaking and often accurate records of interesting habits and practices, of such length that no one had time to read them and [which were] often, in any case, irrelevant...."

THE WORLD WAR I ERA

After the classic age of empire came to a close, anthropologists and archeologists became key players in the new game in town—espionage. Their habits of wandering in remote areas and skill at observation proved to be quite useful to the government. Although a number of anthropologists worked as spies during World War I (including Arthur Carpenter, Thomas Gann, John Held, Samuel Lothrop, and Herbert Spinden), the most famous was Harvard-trained archaeologist Sylvanus Morley, who had discovered the ancient city of Naachtun and had directed the reconstruction of Chichen Itza while serving as head of the Carnegie Archaeological Program from 1914 to 1929. Morley, who was one of the most respected archeologists of the early 20th century, was also the "best secret agent the United States produced during World War I."

In 1916, when German agents were allegedly attempting to establish a Central American base for submarine warfare, the Office of Naval Intelligence recruited Morley, who used archeological fieldwork as cover to traverse 2,000 miles of remote Central American coastline, enduring "ticks, mosquitoes, fleas, sand flies, saddle-sores, seasickness, barrunning, indifferent grub, and sometimes no grub at all, rock-hard beds, infamous hostelries, and even earthquakes." While Morley and company found no German submarine bases, he did produce nearly 10,000 pages of intelligence reports documenting everything from navigable shoreline features to the economic impact of sisal production.

Morley's activities were not well regarded by many anthropologists. On 20 December 1919, Franz Boas, the most well-known anthropologist in America, published a letter in the *Nation,* to the effect that Morley and others (although they were not named directly) "have prostituted science by using it as a cover for their activities as spies. A soldier whose business is murder as a fine art … accept[s] the code of morality to which modern society still conforms. Not so the scientist. The very essence of his life is the service of truth."

A German Jew by birth, Boas was an adamant pacifist and an outspoken critic of the war, writing multiple editorials and newspaper articles expressing his opinion that World War I was a war of imperialist aggression. (Ironically, many of Boas' students, including Margaret Mead and Ruth Benedict, went on to work for the military in roles Boas would have, no doubt, questioned.)

For his public allegations against the unnamed anthropologists, the American Anthropological Association censured Boas in 1919. The criticism of Morley by his peers for his espionage activities and the resulting scuffle within the American Anthropological Association (AAA) foreshadowed the reemergence of the issue of covert anthropological support to the U.S. Government during the 1960s.

THE WORLD WAR II ERA

During World War II, the role of anthropologists within the national-security arena was greatly expanded. Many anthropologists served in the Office of Strategic Services (OSS), the institutional predecessor to both the CIA and Special Forces. Anthropologists served in a research capacity and as operatives. Carleton Coon, a professor of anthropology at Harvard, trained Moroccan resistance groups in sabotage, fought in the battle of Kasserine Pass, and

smuggled arms to French resistance groups in German-occupied Morocco. His book about life in the OSS, *A North Africa Story: The Anthropologist as OSS Agent,* contains a highly amusing account of developing an IED in the shape of a donkey dropping.

Other anthropologists also saw direct action: British ethnologist Tom Harrison parachuted into Borneo to train indigenous guerrillas to fight the Japanese. Cora Du Bois, who served as Chief of the Indonesia section in the OSS Research and Analysis Branch, became the head of the Southeast Asia Command in Ceylon, where she ran resistance movements in Southeast Asian countries under Japanese occupation. Du Bois received the Exceptional Civilian Service Award in 1945 for her work with the Free Thai underground movement.

Perhaps the most famous anthropologist who served in the OSS was Gregory Bateson. Bateson, a British citizen, spent many years conducting ethnographic research in New Guinea, the results of which were published in 1936 as *Naven.* At the beginning of World War II, having failed to find a position with the British War Office, Bateson returned to the United States and was recruited by the OSS, where he served as a civilian member of a forward intelligence unit in the Arakan Mountains of Burma.

In addition to intelligence analysis, Bateson designed and produced "black propaganda" radio broadcasts intended to undermine Japanese propaganda in the Pacific Theater. He found the work distasteful, however, because he believed that truth, especially the unpleasant truth, was healthy. Despite his misgivings about deceitful propaganda, Bateson was a willing and competent operative. In 1945, he volunteered to penetrate deep into enemy territory to attempt the rescue of three OSS agents who had escaped from their Japanese captors. For this service, Bateson was awarded the Pacific Campaign Service Ribbon.

Bateson had remarkable strategic foresight concerning the effect of new technology on warfare. While in the Pacific Theater, he wrote to the legendary director of the OSS, "Wild Bill" Donovan, that the existence of the nuclear bomb would change the nature of conflict, forcing nations to engage in indirect methods of warfare. Bateson recommended to Donovan that the United States not rely on conventional forces for defense but to establish a third agency to employ clandestine operations, economic controls, and psychological pressures in the new warfare. This organization is, of course, now known as the Central Intelligence Agency.

Later in his career, Bateson was allegedly involved with a number of experimental psychological warfare initiatives, including the CIA's Operation MK-Ultra, which conducted mind-control research. It is generally accepted that Bateson "turned on" the Beat poet Allen Ginsberg to LSD at the Mental Research Institute, where Bateson was working on the causes of schizophrenia.

Among anthropologists, Bateson is generally remembered not for his activities in the OSS, but as Mead's husband. In 1932, he met Mead in the remote Sepik River area of New Guinea. After conducting fieldwork together in New Guinea, Bateson and Mead co-produced ethnographic films and photo documentation of Balinese kinesics.

Like her husband, Mead was also involved in the war effort. In addition to producing pamphlets for the Office of War Information, she produced a study for the National Research Council on the cultural food habits of people from different national backgrounds in the United States. She also investigated food distribution as a method of maintaining morale during wartime in the United States. Along with Bateson and Geoffrey Gorer, Mead helped the OSS establish a psychological warfare training unit for the Far East.

Like Bateson, Mead had reservations about the use of deceitful propaganda, believing that such methods have "terrible possibilities of backfiring." Mead's larger concern, however, was the "tremendous amount of resentment" against using anthropological insights during the war. In particular, she noted that using anthropologists to advise advisers is ineffective; to be useful, anthropologists must work directly with policymakers.

In 1942, Mead published *And Keep Your Powder Dry,* a book on U.S. military culture. According to Mead, Americans see aggression as a response rather than a primary behavior; believe in the use of violence for altruistic, never for selfish purposes; and view organized conflict as a finite task to be completed. Once finished, Americans walk away and move on to the next task. William O. Beeman points out that Mead's observations of U.S. national strategic character seem to be borne out by the current administration's characterization of the conflict in Iraq as a defensive war, prompted by the imminent threat of weapons of mass destruction ready for imminent use and undertaken for altruistic reasons, such as "bringing democracy to Iraq," that would be short and limited in scope.

In 1943, Benedict, Mead's long-time friend and collaborator, became the head (and initially the sole member) of the Basic Analysis Section of the Bureau of Overseas Intelligence of the Office of War Information (OWI), a position Benedict sought to use "to get policy makers to take into account different habits and customs of other parts of the world." While at OWI, Benedict coauthored "The Races of Mankind," a government pamphlet which refuted the Nazi pseudo-theories of Aryan racial superiority. Conservative congressmen attacked the pamphlet as communist propaganda, and the publicity surrounding it led to the sale of 750,000 copies, its translation into seven languages, and the production of a musical version in New York City.

Benedict also undertook research on Japanese personality and culture, the effect of which cannot be overstated. Near the end of the war, senior military leaders and U.S. President Franklin Delano Roosevelt were convinced the Japanese were "culturally incapable of surrender" and would fight to the last man. Benedict and other OWI anthropologists were asked to study the view of the emperor in Japanese society. The ensuing OWI position papers convinced Roosevelt to leave the emperor out of the conditions of surrender (rather than demanding unconditional surrender as he did of dictators Adolph Hitler and Benito Mussolini). Much of Benedict's research for OWI was published in 1946 as *The Chrysanthemum and the Sword,* considered by many as a classic ethnography of Japanese military culture, despite Benedict never having visited the country.

Since fieldwork in the traditional sense was impossible during wartime, culture had to be studied remotely. The theoretical contribution of World War II anthropologists to the discipline is commonly known as "culture at a distance." Following the war, from 1947 to 1952, Mead, Benedict, and others established a research program at Columbia University. Working under contract to the U.S. Office of Naval Research, anthropologists developed techniques for evaluating cultural artifacts, such as immigrant and refugee testimonies, art, and travelers' accounts, to build up a picture of a particular culture.

Most of the culture-at-a-distance studies were rooted in the premises of developmental psychology, such as that the so-called national character of any group of people could be traced to commonalities in psychological-development processes. While some of their conclusions now seem ridiculous (for example, Gorer's "swaddling hypothesis" to explain the bipolar swings in Russian culture from emotional repression to aggressive drinking), other research results were not only accurate but useful in a military context.

SMALL WARS

In January 1961, U.S. President John F. Kennedy met with national security adviser Walt Whitman Rostow to discuss various national-security threats. Kennedy and Rostow turned their attention to the subject of Vietnam, and Kennedy said: "This is the worst one we've got. You know, Eisenhower never mentioned it. He talked at length about Laos, but never uttered the word Vietnam."

Kennedy and Rostow's discussion (and Kennedy's approval of the "Counterinsurgency Plan" for Vietnam 10 days after taking office) was inspired by Major General Edward G. Lansdale's report on the situation in Vietnam. Lansdale, who was widely believed to have been the model for Alden Pyle in Graham Greene's *The Quiet American,* was a former advertising executive who almost single-handedly prevented a communist takeover of the Philippines. Lansdale helped install

Ngo Dinh Diem as president of the American-backed government of South Vietnam and, later, ran Operation Mongoose, the covert plot to overthrow by any means necessary Fidel Castro's government in Cuba.

Much of Lansdale's counterinsurgency operations in the Philippines can best be described as applied military anthropology. For example, in the 1950s, as part of his counterinsurgency campaign against the Huk rebels of the Philippines, he conducted research into local superstitions, which he exploited in "psywar": "One psywar operation played upon the popular dread of an asuang, or vampire....When a Huk patrol came along the trail, the ambushers silently snatched the last man of the patrol....They punctured his neck with two holes, vampire-fashion, held the body up by the heels, drained it of blood, and put the corpse back on the trail. When the Huks returned to look for the missing man and found their bloodless comrade, every member of the patrol believed that the asuang had got him and that one of them would be next...." Lansdale noted that such tactics were remarkably effective.

During the Huk Rebellion, the real guerrilla-warfare expert was Captain Charles Bohannan, who later coauthored one of the best studies of practical counterinsurgency, *Counter-Guerrilla Operations: The Philippine Experience.* Bohannan, who fought as an anti-Japanese guerrilla in New Guinea and the Philippines during World War II, remained in the Philippines as an Army counterintelligence officer. He was a natural pick for the team when Lansdale returned to the Philippines in 1950. Bohannan continued to work with Lansdale in Vietnam (and apparently Laos) throughout the 1950s and 1960s, serving as deputy commander of the covert "Saigon Military Mission" that Lansdale headed. Quite likely, Bohannan was also the military planner for the Bay of Pigs.

Bohannan had completed advanced graduate work in anthropology and was a strong advocate of local cultural knowledge and "total immersion" during training and operations. He was particularly interested in "operations intended to influence the thinking of people." In 1959, for example, he was a member of the secret U.S. "survey team" sent to Colombia to evaluate the insurgency and provide a plan for U.S.-Colombian action. Much like anthropologists conducting fieldwork, the team traveled more than 23,000 kilometers and interviewed more than 2,000 officials, civilians, and guerrilla leaders. Their three-volume report reviewed the history of the violence, the underlying socioeconomic conditions, and issued recommendations for social, civil, and military reform to the Colombian and U.S. governments.

Bohannan was a believer in the use of minimum force in counterinsurgency. In an unpublished 1964 paper from a Vietnam posting, he objects to totalitarian methods of counterinsurgency as being potentially counterproductive: "Mass arrests, wholesale searches, and other seemingly easy methods of 'population control' can only strengthen opposition to the government." And, according to Lansdale, overwhelming force was simply not effective for fighting an insurgency: "Only unabashedly totalitarian governments, Communist or colonialist, with relatively unlimited resources, can seriously think of, or attempt, killing or capturing most of the insurgents and their supports."

Bohannan's mentor, Rufus Phillips (a former CIA operative who later headed the Rural Affairs Section of the U.S. Agency for the International Development Mission in Vietnam) observed in a 1964 memorandum that the U.S. military was bound by "conventional military thinking." The American command was guided by neither a British-style dedication to a political objective—however abusive the measures used to achieve it—nor any particular interest in the nonmilitary side of U.S. counterinsurgency: "Everybody talks about civic action and psychological warfare, but little command emphasis is placed on it and it is not understood. The major emphasis remains on 'killing Viet Cong.'"

THE VIETNAM WAR

Despite the authority of men like Lansdale and Bohannan within high-level military and policy circles during the Vietnam War, the military pref-

erence for overwhelming force frequently trumped the hearts-and-minds aspect of counterinsurgency. Anthropologists such as Gerald Hickey, who went to Vietnam as a University of Chicago graduate student and remained throughout the war as a researcher for the RAND Corporation, found that their deep knowledge of Vietnam (valuable for counterinsurgency) was frequently ignored by U.S. military leaders who increasingly adopted a conventional-war approach as the conflict progressed. Mickey's career raises a number of issues that even now plague anthropological research in a military context, such as the politics of research inside the beltway, the inability to change counterproductive policies, and backbiting by other anthropologists hostile to the military enterprise.

Hickey, who wrote *Village in Vietnam,* a classic ethnography of a southern Vietnamese lowland village, was recruited by RAND in 1961 to produce a study funded by DARPA. The study followed the newly established Strategic Hamlet Program that sought to consolidate governmental authority in pacified areas through a defense system and administrative reorganization at the village level. Central to the study was the question of how highland tribes could be encouraged to support the South Vietnamese Government.

Hickey's research indicated that the strategic hamlets might be successful if farmers saw evidence their communal labor and contribution of time, land, and building materials actually resulted in physical and economic security. Although Hickey's observations were probably correct, his views were often dismissed as too pacifistic. When Hickey debriefed Marine General Victor Krulak, the general pounded his fist on his desk and said, "We are going to make the peasants do what's necessary for strategic hamlets to succeed!" As Hickey noted, peasants have many methods of passive and active resistance, and force is often counterproductive as a motivator. Disliking the results of the study, the Pentagon pressured RAND to change the findings and, in the interest of impartial research, RAND refused. In the end, none of Hickey's findings were implemented, and the Strategic Hamlet Program was a failure.

In 1964, a major uprising of Montagnard high-land tribal groups occurred under the banner of FULRO (The United Front for the Struggle of Oppressed Races). Although the Montagnards sided with the United States against the communist north and were supplied by (and fought alongside) U.S. troops, they violently opposed the South Vietnamese Government's efforts to control their region and assimilate the population.

Dealing with the revolt was a major imperative for the military and the South Vietnamese Government because the central highlands were of strategic importance and included the Ho Chi Minh Trail, which was the main North Vietnamese infil-tration and supply route. Hickey, who had worked closely with the Montagnards for years, advised the senior commander of U.S. forces in Vietnam, General William Westmoreland, on the reasons for the rise of ethno-nationalism among the tribes and how to cope with the revolt. Hickey also successfully acted as an intermediary between highland leaders and the U.S. and South Vietnamese governments.

As the war dragged on, Hickey became increas-ingly frustrated with the military-strategy viewpoint held by officers such as U.S. Army General William E. Depuy, who believed a war of attrition would defeat the communists. Hickey's view was that the war in Vietnam was a political struggle that could only be resolved in political terms, not through pure military force. As an anthropologist, he recog-nized that elements of Vietnam's own culture could be used to promote peace between the existing nationalist political parties, religious groups, and minorities—none of whom welcomed com-munist rule.

In a remarkable paper titled "Accommodation in South Vietnam: The Key to Sociopolitical Solidarity," Hickey explored the indigenous Viet-namese cultural concept of accommodation. While Taoist roots of the Vietnamese value system stressed individualism, in the Vietnamese worldview, ac-commodation was also necessary to restore har-mony with the universe. In Washington, D.C., Hickey's views on accommodation were treated as heresy. In 1967, at the conclusion of Hickey's brief to a Pentagon audience, Richard Holbrooke said,

"What you're saying, Gerry, is that we're not going to win a military victory in Vietnam." Because it did not conform to the prevailing view of the con-flict, Hickey's message was promptly dismissed. Regardless of the improbability of a military vic-tory, to U.S. leaders, "accommodation" meant "giving in," and that was not an acceptable alterna-tive. In the end, the American solution to the conflict was the use of overwhelming force in the form of strategic bombing and the Accelerated Pacification Campaign, neither of which resulted in victory.

For his "ethnographic studies," "contributions to the enhancement of U.S. Advisor/Vietnamese Counterpart relationship," and "presence and coun-sel during periods of attack by Viet Cong Forces and Montagnard uprisings," Hickey was awarded the medal for Distinguished Public Service by Secretary of Defense Robert McNamara. Despite his medal (or perhaps because of it), Hickey was not able to get an academic job when he returned to the United States. He was refused a position at the University of Chicago by fellow anthropologists who objected to his association with RAND. Ironically, Hickey was also forced out of RAND because it was no longer interested in counterinsur-gency. Following the lead of the Joint Chiefs of Staff, RAND was no longer going to undertake research on unconventional warfare, but turn its attention to "longer-range problems of tactical, limited war and deterrence under the Nixon Doctrine."

PROJECT CAMELOT

Testifying before the U.S. Congress in 1965, R.L. Sproul, director of DARPA said: "It is [our] pri-mary thesis that remote area warfare is controlled in a major way by the environment in which the warfare occurs, by the sociological and anthropo-logical characteristics of the people involved in the war, and by the nature of the conflict itself."

The recognition within DOD that research and development efforts to support counterinsurgency operations must be oriented toward the local human terrain led to the establishment of the Special Operations Research Office (SORO) at American University in Washington, D.C. With anthropologists and other social scientists on staff, SORO functioned as a research center into the human dimension of counterinsurgency. Many SORO reports took a unique approach. In 1964, the Army commissioned an unusual paper titled "Witchcraft, Sorcery, Magic, and Other Psychological Phenomena, and Their Implications on Military and Paramilitary Operations in the Congo." Authored by James R. Price and Paul Jureidini, the report is a treatise on paranormal combat, discussing "counter-magic" tactics to suppress rebels who are backed by witch doctors, charms, and magic potions.

In 1964, SORO also designed the infamous Project Camelot. According to a letter from the Office of the Director of the Special Operations Research Office, Project Camelot was "a study whose objective [was] to determine the feasibility of developing a general social systems model which would make it possible to predict and influence politically significant aspects of social change in the developing nations of the world." The project's objectives were "to devise procedures for assessing the potential for internal war within national societies; to identify with increased degrees of confidence those actions which a government might take to relieve conditions which are assessed as giving rise to a potential for internal war; [and] to assess the feasibility of prescribing the characteristics of a system for obtaining and using the essential information needed for doing the above two things."

Project Camelot, which was initiated during a time when the military took counterinsurgency seriously as an area of competency, recognized the need for social science insights. According to the director's letter: "Within the Army there is especially ready acceptance of the need to improve the general understanding of the processes of social change if the Army is to discharge its responsibilities in the overall counterinsurgency program of the U.S. Government."

Chile was to be the first case study for Project Camelot. Norwegian sociologist Johan Galtung was invited to design a seminar for Project Camelot. Although he refused, he shared information about the project with colleagues. Meanwhile, Hugo Nuttini, who taught anthropology at the University of Pittsburgh, accepted an assignment for Project Camelot in Chile. While there, he concealed Camelot's military origin, but word leaked out. Protests arose from Chile's newspapers and legislature and the Chilean Government lodged a diplomatic protest with the U.S. Ambassador. In Washington, D.C., following congressional hearings on the subject, McNamara canceled Project Camelot in 1965.

THE THAI SCANDAL

Shortly after the Project Camelot scandal, the issue of clandestine research surfaced again in Thailand. In March 1970, documents that appeared to implicate social scientists in U.S. counterinsurgency programs in Thailand were stolen from a university professor's file cabinet. The documents were given to the Student Mobilization Committee to End the War in Vietnam and were subsequently published in *The Student Mobilizer*. A number of anthropologists and other social scientists were allegedly gathering data for DOD and the Royal Thai Government to support a counterinsurgency program that would use development aid to encourage tribal villages to remain loyal to the Thai Government rather than joining the insurgents. Although anthropologists claimed to have been using their expertise to prevent Thai villages from being harmed, heated debates took place within the AAA's Committee on Ethics.

As a result of Project Camelot and the Thai scandal, government funding and use of social science research became suspect. Anthropologists feared that, were such research to continue, the indigenous people they studied would assume they were all spies, closing off future field opportunities abroad. Many anthropologists also believed the information would be used to control, enslave, and even annihilate many of the communities studied. The result of these debates is the determination that for anthropologists to give secret briefings is ethically unacceptable. The AAA's current

"Statement of Professional Responsibility" says: "Anthropologists should undertake no secret research or any research whose results cannot be freely derived and publicly reported.... No secret research, no secret reports or debriefings of any kind should be agreed to or given." These guidelines reflect a widespread view among anthropologists that any research undertaken for the military is de facto evil and ethically unacceptable.

THE PERILS OF INCOMPLETE KNOWLEDGE

DOD yearns for cultural knowledge, but anthropologists en masse, bound by their own ethical code and sunk in a mire of postmodernism, are unlikely to contribute much of value to reshaping national security policy or practice. Yet, if anthropologists remain disengaged, who will provide the relevant subject matter expertise? As Anna Simons, an anthropologist who teaches at the Naval Postgraduate School, points out: "If anthropologists want to put their heads in the sand and not assist, then who will the military, the CIA, and other agencies turn to for information? They'll turn to people who will give them the kind of information that should make anthropologists want to rip their hair out because the information won't be nearly as directly connected to what's going on on the local landscape."

Regardless of whether anthropologists decide to enter the national-security arena, cultural information will inevitably be used as the basis of military operations and public policy. And, if anthropologists refuse to contribute, how reliable will that information be? The result of using incomplete "bad" anthropology is, invariably, failed operations and failed policy. In a May 2004 *New Yorker* article, "The Gray Zone: How a Secret Pentagon Program Came to Abu Ghraib," Seymour Hersh notes that Raphael Patai's 1973 study of Arab culture and psychology, *The Arab Mind,* was the basis of the military's understanding of the psychological vulnerabilities of Arabs, particularly to sexual shame and humiliation.

Patai says: "The segregation of the sexes, the veiling of the women…, and all the other minute rules that govern and restrict contact between men and women, have the effect of making sex a prime mental preoccupation in the Arab world." Apparently, the goal of photographing the sexual humiliation was to blackmail Iraqi victims into becoming informants against the insurgency. To prevent the dissemination of photos to family and friends, it was believed Iraqi men would do almost anything.

As Bernard Brodie said of the French Army in 1914, "This was neither the first nor the last time that bad anthropology contributed to bad strategy." Using sexual humiliation to blackmail Iraqi men into becoming informants could never have worked as a strategy since it only destroys honor, and for Iraqis, lost honor requires its restoration through the appeasement of blood. This concept is well developed in Iraqi culture, and there is even a specific Arabic word for it: al-sharaf, upholding one's manly honor. The alleged use of Patai's book as the basis of the psychological torment at Abu Ghraib, devoid of any understanding of the broader context of Iraqi culture, demonstrates the folly of using decontextualized culture as the basis of policy.

Successful counterinsurgency depends on attaining a holistic, total understanding of local culture. This cultural understanding must be thorough and deep if it is to have any practical benefit at all. This fact is not lost on the Army. In the language of interim FM 3-07.22: "The center of gravity in counterinsurgency operations is the population. Therefore, understanding the local society and gaining its support is critical to success. For U.S. forces to operate effectively among a local population and gain and maintain their support, it is important to develop a thorough understanding of the society and its culture, including its history, tribal/family/social structure, values, religions, customs, and needs."

To defeat the insurgency in Iraq, U.S. and coalition forces must recognize and exploit the underlying tribal structure of the country; the power wielded by traditional authority figures; the use of Islam as a political ideology; the competing interests of the Shia, the Sunni, and the Kurds; the psychological effects of totalitarianism; and the divide between urban and rural, among other things.

Interim FM 3-07.22 continues: "Understanding and working within the social fabric of a local area is initially the most influential factor in the conduct of counterinsurgency operations. Unfortunately, this is often the factor most neglected by U.S. forces."

And, unfortunately, anthropologists, whose assistance is urgently needed in time of war, entirely neglect U.S. forces. Despite the fact that military applications of cultural knowledge might be distasteful to ethically inclined anthropologists, their assistance is necessary.

DISCUSSION QUESTIONS

1. What was the Powell–Weinberger Doctrine?
2. Why has anthropology as a discipline avoided studying the conduct of war and counterinsurgency?
3. What was Project Camelot and how did it contribute to anthropologists' reluctance to conduct research for the national security establishment?
4. Explain how the abuses of detainees at Abu Ghraib were based on erroneous cultural information.

 **RESOURCES ON THE INTERNET**

 InfoTrac College Edition

infotrac-college.com

You can find further relevant readings by searching *InfoTrac College Edition*, an online library with access to thousands of scholarly and popular periodicals. Below are suggested search terms for this article:

- counterinsurgency
- Powell–Weinberger Doctrine
- Project Camelot
- Abu Ghraib

Anthropology Online: Wadsworth's Anthropology Resource Center

academic.cengage.com/anthropology

The Wadsworth Anthropology Resource Center contains a wealth of information and useful tools for students including information on careers in anthropology.

13

The Notion of Witchcraft Explains
Unfortunate Events

E. E. EVANS-PRITCHARD

Although the book from which this selection was drawn was published in 1937 (and based on fieldwork conducted in the 1920s), Evans-Pritchard's work on the meaning of witchcraft among the Azande of the Sudan is still relevant to modern anthropology. When most westerners hear the term witchcraft, they associate it with a host of scary phenomena, including Halloween, the witch trials of colonial America, and high levels of psychological derangement on the part of both witches and the people who believe in their existence. For the Azande, however, there is nothing particularly frightening about witches, because witchcraft provides a perfectly rational system for explaining why events occur.

To understand the Azande system of witchcraft as a system of explanation, we need only to acknowledge some mysterious powers of humans, not the supernatural powers of deities. In a very real sense, the use of witchcraft to explain unfortunate events is not appreciably different from any system of explanation that lacks absolute proof, such as a conspiracy theory of history or the belief in the power of prayer. Such a belief system, which westerners often dismiss as superstitious, childlike, and irrational, in no way contradicts what westerners would call natural, scientific, or empirical explanations for events. To illustrate, the Azande parents of a child who recently died of malaria would not deny that the immediate cause of death was the bite of an infected female anopheles mosquito. But these same parents would ask an additional question: "Why did the mosquito bite my child, when my neighbor's child was not bitten?" For the Azande parent, the answer to the question would seem obvious: our child was bewitched. And, as Evans-Pritchard shows in this piece, such an explanation would be no less reasonable than ascribing the child's death to "the will of God."

I

Witches, as the Azande conceive them, clearly cannot exist. None the less, the concept of witchcraft provides them with a natural philosophy by which the relations between men and unfortunate events are explained and a ready and stereotyped means of reacting to such events. Witchcraft beliefs also embrace a system of values which regulate human conduct.

Witchcraft is ubiquitous. It plays its part in every activity of Zande life; in agricultural, fishing, and hunting pursuits; in domestic life of homesteads as well as in communal life of district and court; it is an important theme of mental life in which it forms the background of a vast panorama of oracles and

SOURCE: From *Witchcraft, Oracles and Magic Among the Azandes* by E. E. Evans-Pritchard, pp. 18–32, 1937.
Reprinted by permission of Oxford University Press.

magic; its influence is plainly stamped on law and morals, etiquette and religion; it is prominent in technology and language; there is no niche or corner of Zande culture into which it does not twist itself. If blight seizes the ground-nut crop it is witchcraft; if the bush is vainly scoured for game it is witchcraft; if women laboriously bale water out of a pool and are rewarded by but a few small fish it is witchcraft; if termites do not rise when their swarming is due and a cold useless night is spent in waiting for their flight it is witchcraft; if a wife is sulky and unresponsive to her husband it is witchcraft; if a prince is cold and distant with his subject it is witchcraft; if a magical rite fails to achieve its purpose it is witchcraft; if, in fact, any failure or misfortune falls upon anyone at any time and in relation to any of the manifold activities of his life it may be due to witchcraft. The Zande attributes all these misfortunes to witchcraft unless there is strong evidence, and subsequent oracular confirmation, that sorcery or some other evil agent has been at work, or unless they are clearly to be attributed to incompetence, breach of a taboo, or failure to observe a moral rule.

To say that witchcraft has blighted the ground-nut crop, that witchcraft has scared away game, and that witchcraft has made so-and-so ill is equivalent to saying in terms of our own culture that the ground-nut crop has failed owing to blight, that game is scarce this season, and that so-and-so has caught influenza. Witchcraft participates in all misfortunes and is the idiom in which Azande speak about them and in which they explain them. To us witchcraft is something which haunted and disgusted our credulous forefathers. But the Zande expects to come across witchcraft at any time of the day or night. He would be just as surprised if he were not brought into daily contact with it as we would be if confronted by its appearance. To him there is nothing miraculous about it. It is expected that a man's hunting will be injured by witches, and he has at his disposal means of dealing with them. When misfortunes occur he does not become awestruck at the play of supernatural forces. He is not terrified at the presence of an occult enemy. He is, on the other hand, extremely annoyed. Someone,

out of spite, has ruined his ground-nuts or spoilt his hunting or given his wife a chill, and surely this is cause for anger! He has done no one harm, so what right has anyone to interfere in his affairs? It is an impertinence, an insult, a dirty, offensive trick! It is the aggressiveness and not the eeriness of these actions which Azande emphasize when speaking of them, and it is anger and not awe which we observe in their response to them.

Witchcraft is not less anticipated than adultery. It is so intertwined with everyday happenings that it is part of a Zande's ordinary world. There is nothing remarkable about a witch—you may be one yourself, and certainly many of your closest neighbours are witches. Nor is there anything awe-inspiring about witchcraft. We do not become psychologically transformed when we hear that someone is ill—we expect people to be ill—and it is the same with Zande. They expect people to be ill, i.e., to be bewitched, and it is not a matter for surprise or wonderment.

I found it strange at first to live among Azande and listen to naïve explanations of misfortunes which, to our minds, have apparent causes, but after a while I learnt the idiom of their thought and applied notions of witchcraft as spontaneously as themselves in situations where the concept was relevant. A boy knocked his foot against a small stump of wood in the centre of a bush path, a frequent happening in Africa, and suffered pain and inconvenience in consequence. Owing to its position on his toe it was impossible to keep the cut free from dirt and it began to fester. He declared the witchcraft had made him knock his foot against the stump. I always argued with Azande and criticized their statements, and I did so on this occasion. I told the boy that he had knocked his foot against the stump of wood because he had been careless, and that witchcraft had not placed it in the path, for it had grown there naturally. He agreed that witchcraft had nothing to do with the stump of wood being in his path but added that he had kept his eyes open for stumps, as indeed every Zande does most carefully, and that if he had not been bewitched he would have seen the stump. As a conclusive argument for his view he remarked that all cuts do not take days to heal but, on the contrary, close quickly, for that is the nature of cuts. Why, then, had his sore festered and remained open if there were no witchcraft behind it? This, as I discovered before long, was to be regarded as the Zande explanation of sickness.

Shortly after my arrival in Zandeland we were passing through a government settlement and noticed that a hut had been burnt to the ground on the previous night. Its owner was overcome with grief as it had contained the beer he was preparing for a mortuary feast. He told us that he had gone the previous night to examine his beer. He had lit a handful of straw and raised it above his head so that light would be cast on the pots, and in so doing he had ignited the thatch. He, and my companions also, were convinced that the disaster was caused by witchcraft.

One of my chief informants, Kisanga, was a skilled wood-carver, one of the finest carvers in the whole kingdom of Gbudwe. Occasionally the bowls and stools which he carved split during the work, as one may well imagine in such a climate. Though the hardest woods be selected they sometimes split in process of carving or on completion of the utensil even if the craftsman is careful and well acquainted with the technical rules of his craft. When this happened to the bowls and stools of this particular craftsman he attributed the misfortune to witchcraft and used to harangue me about the spite and jealousy of his neighbours. When I used to reply that I thought he was mistaken and that people were well disposed towards him he used to hold the split bowl or stool towards me as concrete evidence of his assertions. If people were not bewitching his work, how would I account for that? Likewise a potter will attribute the cracking of his pots during firing to witchcraft. An experienced potter need have no fear that his pots will crack as a result of error. He selects the proper clay, kneads it thoroughly till he has extracted all grit and pebbles, and builds it up slowly and carefully. On the night before digging out his clay he abstains from sexual intercourse. So he would have nothing to fear. Yet pots sometimes break, even when they are the handiwork of expert potters, and this can only be accounted for by witchcraft. "It is broken—there is witchcraft," says the potter simply....

II

In speaking to Azande about witchcraft and in observing their reactions to situations of misfortune it was obvious that they did not attempt to account for the existence of phenomena, or even the action of phenomena, by mystical causation alone. What they explained by witchcraft were the particular conditions in a chain of causation which related an individual to natural happenings in such a way that he sustained injury. The boy who knocked his foot against a stump of wood did not account for the stump by reference to witchcraft, nor did he suggest that whenever anybody knocks his foot against a stump it is necessarily due to witchcraft, nor yet again did he account for the cut by saying that it was caused by witchcraft, for he knew quite well that it was caused by the stump of wood. What he attributed to witchcraft was that on this particular occasion, when exercising his usual care, he struck his foot against a stump of wood, whereas on a hundred other occasions he did not do so, and that on this particular occasion the cut, which he expected to result from the knock, festered whereas he had had dozens of cuts which had not festered. Surely these peculiar conditions demand an explanation. Again, every year hundreds of Azande go and inspect their beer by night and they always take with them a handful of straw in order to illuminate the hut in which it is fermenting. Why then should this particular man on this single occasion have ignited the thatch of his hut? Again, my friend the wood-carver had made scores of bowls and stools without mishap and he knew all there was to know about the selection of wood, use of tools, and conditions of carving. His bowls and stools did not split like the products of craftsmen who were unskilled in their work, so why on rare occasions should his bowls and stools split when they did not split usually and when he had exercised all his usual knowledge and care? He knew the answer well enough and so, in his opinion, did his envious, back-biting neighbours. In the same way, a potter wants to know why his pots should break on an occasion when he uses the same material and technique as on other occasions;

or rather he already knows, for the reason is known in advance, as it were. If the pots break it is due to witchcraft.

We shall give a false account of Zande philosophy if we say that they believe witchcraft to be the sole cause of phenomena. This proposition is not contained in Zande patterns of thought, which only assert that witchcraft brings a man into relation with events in such a way that he sustains injury.

In Zandeland sometimes an old granary collapses. There is nothing remarkable in this. Every Zande knows that termites eat the supports in course of time and that even the hardest woods decay after years of service. Now a granary is the summerhouse of a Zande homestead and people sit beneath it in the heat of the day and chat or play the African hole-game or work at some craft. Consequently it may happen that there are people sitting beneath the granary when it collapses and they are injured, for it is a heavy structure made of beams and clay and may be stored with eleusine as well. Now why should these particular people have been sitting under this particular granary at the particular moment when it collapsed? That it should collapse is easily intelligible, but why should it have collapsed at the particular moment when these particular people were sitting beneath it? Through years it might have collapsed, so why should it fall just when certain people sought its kindly shelter? We say that the granary collapsed because its supports were eaten away by termites; that is the cause that explains the collapse of the granary. We also say that people were sitting under it at the time because it was in the heat of the day and they thought that it would be a comfortable place to talk and work. This is the cause of people being under the granary at the time it collapsed. To our minds the only relationship between these two independently caused facts is their coincidence in time and space. We have no explanation of why the two chains of causation intersected at a certain time and in a certain place, for there is no interdependence between them.

Zande philosophy can supply the missing link. The Zande knows that the supports were undermined by termites and that people were sitting beneath the granary in order to escape the heat and glare of the sun. But he knows besides why these two events occurred at a precisely similar moment in time and space. It was due to the action of witchcraft. If there had been no witchcraft people would have been sitting under the granary and it would not have fallen on them, or it would have collapsed but the people would not have been sheltering under it at the time. Witchcraft explains the coincidence of these two happenings.

III

I hope I am not expected to point out that the Zande cannot analyse his doctrines as I have done for him. It is no use saying to a Zande "Now tell me what you Azande think about witchcraft" because the subject is too general and indeterminate, both too vague and too immense, to be described concisely. But it is possible to extract the principles of their thought from dozens of situations in which witchcraft is called upon to explain happenings and from dozens of other situations in which failure is attributed to some other cause. Their philosophy is explicit, but is not formally stated as a doctrine. A Zande would not say "I believe in natural causation but I do not think that that fully explains coincidences, and it seems to me that the theory of witchcraft offers a satisfactory explanation of them," but he expresses his thought in terms of actual and particular situations. He says "a buffalo charges," "a tree falls," "termites are not making their seasonal flight when they are expected to do so," and so on. Herein he is stating empirically ascertained facts. But he also says "a buffalo charged and wounded so-and-so," "a tree fell on so-and-so and killed him," "my termites refuse to make their flight in numbers worth collecting but other people are collecting theirs all right," and so on. He tells you that these things are due to witchcraft, saying in each instance, "So-and-so has been bewitched." The facts do not explain themselves or only partly explain themselves. They can only be explained fully if one takes witchcraft into consideration.

One can only obtain the full range of a Zande's ideas about causation by allowing him to fill in the gaps himself, otherwise one will be led astray by linguistic conventions. He tells you "So-and-so was bewitched and killed himself" or even simply that "So-and-so was killed by witchcraft." But he is telling you the ultimate cause of his death and not the secondary causes. You can ask him "How did he kill himself?" and he will tell you that he committed suicide by hanging himself from the branch of a tree. You can also ask "Why did he kill himself?" and he will tell you that it was because he was angry with his brothers. The cause of his death was hanging from a tree, and the cause of his hanging from a tree was his anger with his brothers. If you then ask a Zande why he should say that the man was bewitched if he committed suicide on account of his anger with his brothers, he will tell you that only crazy people commit suicide, and that if everyone who was angry with his brothers committed suicide there would soon be no people left in the world, and that if this man had not been bewitched he would not have done what he did do. If you persevere and ask why witchcraft caused the man to kill himself the Zande will reply that he supposes someone hated him, and if you ask him why someone hated him your informant will tell you that such is the nature of men.

For if Azande cannot enunciate a theory of causation in terms acceptable to us they describe happenings in an idiom that is explanatory. They are aware that it is particular circumstances of events in their relation to man, their harmfulness to a particular person, that constitutes evidence of witchcraft. Witchcraft explains *why* events are harmful to man and not *how* they happen. A Zande perceives how they happen just as we do. He does not see a witch charge a man, but an elephant. He does not see a witch push over a granary, but termites gnawing away its supports. He does not see a psychical flame igniting thatch, but an ordinary lighted bundle of straw. His perception of how events occur is as clear as our own.

IV

Zande belief in witchcraft in no way contradicts empirical knowledge of cause and effect. The world known to the senses is just as real to them as it is to us.

We must not be deceived by their way of expressing causation and imagine that because they say a man was killed by witchcraft they entirely neglect the secondary causes that, as we judge them, were the true causes of his death. They are foreshortening the chain of events, and in a particular social situation are selecting the cause that is socially relevant and neglecting the rest. If a man is killed by a spear in war, or by a wild beast in hunting, or by the bite of a snake, or from sickness, witchcraft is the socially relevant cause, since it is the only one which allows intervention and determines social behaviour.

Belief in death from natural causes and belief in death from witchcraft are not mutually exclusive. On the contrary, they supplement one another, the one accounting for what the other does not account for. Besides, death is not only a natural fact but also a social fact. It is not simply that the heart ceases to beat and the lungs to pump air in an organism, but it is also the destruction of a member of a family and kin, of a community and tribe. Death leads to consultation of oracles, magic rites, and revenge. Among the causes of death witchcraft is the only one that has any significance for social behaviour. The attribution of misfortune to witchcraft does not exclude what we call its real causes but is superimposed on them and gives to social events their moral value.

Zande thought expresses the notion of natural and mystical causation quite clearly by using a hunting metaphor to define their relations. Azande always say of witchcraft that it is the *umbaga* or second spear. When Azande kill game there is a division of meat between the man who first speared the animal and the man who plunged a second spear into it. These two are considered to have killed the beast and the owner of the second spear is called the *umbaga*. Hence if a man is killed by an elephant Azande say that the elephant is the first spear and that witchcraft is the second spear and that together they killed the man. If a man spears another in war the slayer is the first spear and witchcraft is the second spear and together they killed him.

Since Azande recognize plurality of causes, and it is the social situation that indicates the relevant one, we can understand why the doctrine of witchcraft is not used to explain every failure and misfortune.

It sometimes happens that the social situation demands a common-sense, and not a mystical, judgment of cause. Thus, if you tell a lie, or commit adultery, or steal, or deceive your prince, and are found out, you cannot elude punishment by saying that you were bewitched. Zande doctrine declares emphatically "Witchcraft does not make a person tell lies"; "Witchcraft does not make a person commit adultery"; "Witchcraft does not put adultery into a man. 'Witchcraft' is in yourself (you alone are responsible), that is, your penis becomes erect. It sees the hair of a man's wife and it rises and becomes erect because the only 'witchcraft' is, itself" ("witchcraft" is here used metaphorically); "Witchcraft does not make a person steal"; "Witchcraft does not make a person disloyal." Only on one occasion have I heard a Zande plead that he was bewitched when he had committed an offence and this was when he lied to me, and even on this occasion everybody present laughed at him and told him that witchcraft does not make people tell lies.

If a man murders another tribesman with knife or spear he is put to death. It is not necessary in such a case to seek a witch, for an objective towards which vengeance may be directed is already present. If, on the other hand, it is a member of another tribe who has speared a man his relatives, or his prince, will take steps to discover the witch responsible for the event.

It would be treason to say that a man put to death on the orders of his king for an offence against authority was killed by witchcraft. If a man were to consult the oracles to discover the witch responsible for the death of a relative who had been put to death at the orders of his king he would run the risk of being put to death himself. For here the social situation excludes the notion of witchcraft as on other occasions it pays no attention to natural agents and emphasizes only witchcraft. Also, if a man were killed in vengeance because the oracles said that he was a witch and had murdered another man with his witchcraft then his relatives could not say that he had been killed by witchcraft. Zande doctrine lays it down that he died at the hand of avengers because he was a homicide. If a man were to have expressed the view that his

kinsman had been killed by witchcraft and to have acted upon his opinion by consulting the poison oracle, he might have been punished for ridiculing the king's poison oracle, for it was the poison oracle of the king that had given official confirmation of the man's guilt, and it was the king himself who had permitted vengeance to take its course.

In these situations witchcraft is irrelevant and, if not totally excluded, is not indicated as the principal factor in causation. As in our own society a scientific theory of causation, if not excluded, is deemed irrelevant in questions of moral and legal responsibility, so in Zande society the doctrine of witchcraft, if not excluded, is deemed irrelevant in the same situations. We accept scientific explanations of the causes of disease, and even of the causes of insanity, but we deny them in crime and sin because here they militate against law and morals which are axiomatic. The Zande accepts a mystical explanation of the causes of misfortune, sickness, and death, but he does not allow this explanation if it conflicts with social exigencies expressed in law and morals.

For witchcraft is not indicated as a cause for failure when a taboo has been broken. If a child becomes sick, and it is known that its father and mother have had sexual relations before it was weaned, the cause of death is already indicated by breach of a ritual prohibition and the question of witchcraft does not arise. If a man develops leprosy and there is a history of incest in his case then incest is the cause of leprosy and not witchcraft. In these cases, however, a curious situation arises because when the child or the leper dies it is necessary to avenge their deaths and the Zande sees no difficulty in explaining what appears to us to be most illogical behaviour. He does so on the same principles as when a man has been killed by a wild beast, and he invokes the same metaphor of "second spear." In the cases mentioned above there are really three causes of a person's death. There is the illness from which he dies, leprosy in the case of the man, perhaps some fever in the case of the child. These sicknesses are not in themselves products of witchcraft, for they exist in their own right just as a buffalo or a granary exist in their own right. Then there is the breach of a taboo, in the one case of weaning, in the other case of incest. The child, and the man, developed fever, and leprosy, because a taboo was broken. The breach of a taboo was the cause of their sickness, but the sickness would not have killed them if witchcraft had not also been operative. If witchcraft had not been present as "second spear" they would have developed fever and leprosy just the same, but they would not have died from them. In these instances there are two socially significant causes, breach of taboo and witchcraft, both of which are relative to different social processes, and each is emphasized by different people.

But where there has been a breach of taboo and death is not involved witchcraft will not be evoked as a cause of failure. If a man eats a forbidden food after he has made powerful punitive magic he may die, and in this case the cause of his death is known beforehand, since it is contained in the conditions of the situation in which he died even if witchcraft was also operative. But it does not follow that he will die. What does inevitably follow is that the medicine he has made will cease to operate against the person for whom it is intended and will have to be destroyed lest it turn against the magician who sent it forth. The failure of the medicine to achieve its purpose is due to breach of a taboo and not to witchcraft. If a man has had sexual relations with his wife and on the next day approaches the poison oracle it will not reveal the truth and its oracular efficacy will be permanently undermined. If he had not broken a taboo it would have been said that witchcraft had caused the oracle to lie, but the condition of the person who had attended the seance provides a reason for its failure to speak the truth without having to bring in the notion of witchcraft as an agent. No one will admit that he has broken a taboo before consulting the poison oracle, but when an oracle lies everyone is prepared to admit that a taboo may have been broken by someone.

Similarly, when a potter's creations break in firing witchcraft is not the only possible cause of the calamity. Inexperience and bad workmanship may also be reasons for failure, or the potter may himself have had sexual relations on the preceding night. The potter himself will attribute his failure

to witchcraft, but others may not be of the same opinion.

Not even all deaths are invariably and unanimously attributed to witchcraft or to the breach of some taboo. The deaths of babies from certain diseases are attributed vaguely to the Supreme Being. Also, if a man falls suddenly and violently sick and dies, his relatives may be sure that a sorcerer has made magic against him and that it is not a witch who has killed him. A breach of the obligations of blood-brotherhood may sweep away whole groups of kin, and when one after another of brothers and cousins die it is the blood and not witchcraft to which their deaths are attributed by outsiders, though the relatives of the dead will seek to avenge them on witches. When a very old man dies unrelated people say that he has died of old age, but they do not say this in the presence of kinsmen, who declare that witchcraft is responsible for his death.

It is also thought that adultery may cause misfortune, though it is only one participating factor, and witchcraft is also believed to be present. Thus is it said that a man may be killed in warfare or in a hunting accident as a result of his wife's infidelities. Therefore, before going to war or on a large-scale hunting expedition a man might ask his wife to divulge the names of her lovers.

Even where breaches of law and morals do not occur witchcraft is not the only reason given for failure. Incompetence, laziness, and ignorance may be selected as causes. When a girl smashes her water-pot or a boy forgets to close the door of the hen-house at night they will be admonished severely by their parents for stupidity. The mistakes of children are due to carelessness or ignorance and they are taught to avoid them while they are still young. People do not say that they are effects of witchcraft, or if they are prepared to concede the possibility of witchcraft they consider stupidity the main cause. Moreover, the Zande is not so naïve that he holds witchcraft responsible for the cracking of a pot during firing if subsequent examination shows that a pebble was left in the clay, or for an animal escaping his net if someone frightened it away by a move or a sound. People do not blame witchcraft if a woman burns her porridge nor if she presents it undercooked to her husband. And when an inexperienced craftsman makes a stool which lacks polish or which splits, this is put down to his inexperience.

In all these cases the man who suffers the misfortune is likely to say that it is due to witchcraft, but others will not say so. We must bear in mind nevertheless that a serious misfortune, especially if it results in death, is normally attributed by everyone to the action of witchcraft, especially by the sufferer and his kin, however much it may have been due to a man's incompetence or absence of self-control. If a man falls into a fire and is seriously burnt, or falls into a game-pit and breaks his neck or his leg, it would undoubtedly be attributed to witchcraft. Thus when six or seven of the sons of Prince Rikita were entrapped in a ring of fire and burnt to death when hunting cane-rats their death was undoubtedly due to witchcraft.

Hence we see that witchcraft has its own logic, its own rules of thought, and that these do not exclude natural causation. Belief in witchcraft is quite consistent with human responsibility and a rational appreciation of nature. First of all a man must carry out an activity according to traditional rules of technique, which consist of knowledge checked by trial and error in each generation. It is only if he fails in spite of adherence to these rules that people will impute his lack of success to witchcraft.

V

It is often asked whether primitive peoples distinguish between the natural and the supernatural, and the query may be here answered in a preliminary manner in respect to the Azande. The question as it stands may mean, do primitive peoples distinguish between the natural and the supernatural in the abstract? We have a notion of an ordered world conforming to what we call natural laws, but some people in our society believe that mysterious things can happen which cannot be accounted for by reference to natural laws and which therefore are held to transcend them, and we call these happenings supernatural. To us supernatural means very

much the same as abnormal or extraordinary. Azande certainly have no such notions of reality. They have no conceptions of "natural" as we understand it, and therefore neither of the "supernatural" as we understand it. Witchcraft is to Azande an ordinary and not an extraordinary, even though it may in some circumstances be an infrequent, event. It is a normal, and not an abnormal happening. But if they do not give to the natural and supernatural the meanings which educated Europeans give to them they nevertheless distinguish between them. For our question may be formulated, and should be formulated, in a different manner. We ought rather to ask whether primitive peoples perceive any difference between the happenings which we, the observers of their culture, class as natural and the happenings which we class as mystical. Azande undoubtedly perceive a difference between what we consider the workings of nature on the one hand and the workings of magic and ghosts and witchcraft on the other hand, though in the absence of a formulated doctrine of natural law they do not, and cannot, express the difference as we express it.

The Zande notion of witchcraft is incompatible with our ways of thought. But even to the Azande there is something peculiar about the action of witchcraft. Normally it can be perceived only in dreams. It is not an evident notion but transcends sensory experience. They do not profess to understand witchcraft entirely. They know that it exists and works evil, but they have to guess at the manner in which it works. Indeed, I have frequently been struck when discussing witchcraft with Azande by the doubt they express about the subject, not only in what they say, but even more in their manner of saying it, both of which contrast with their ready knowledge, fluently imparted, about social events and economic techniques. They feel out of their depth in trying to describe the way in which witchcraft accomplishes its ends. That it kills people is obvious, but how it kills them cannot be known precisely. They tell you that perhaps if you were to ask an older man or a witch-doctor he might give you more information. But the older men and the witch-doctors can tell you little more than youth and laymen. They only know what the others know: that the soul of witchcraft goes by night and devours the soul of its victim. Only witches themselves understand these matters fully. In truth Azande experience feelings about witchcraft rather than ideas, for their intellectual concepts of it are weak and they know better what to do when attacked by it than how to explain it. Their response is action and not analysis.

There is no elaborate and consistent representation of witchcraft that will account in detail for its workings, nor of nature which expounds its conformity to sequences and functional interrelations. The Zande actualizes these beliefs rather than intellectualizes them, and their tenets are expressed in socially controlled behaviour rather than in doctrines. Hence the difficulty of discussing the subject of witchcraft with Azande, for their ideas are imprisoned in action and cannot be cited to explain and justify action.

DISCUSSION QUESTIONS

1. What is the rationale for witchcraft in Azande society?

2. How does witchcraft function in Azande society? Can you think of any positive roles that witchcraft plays which contribute to the overall well-being of Azande society?

3. According to the Azande system of explanation, in what situations would witchcraft not be used to explain events?

RESOURCES ON THE INTERNET

InfoTrac College Edition

infotrac-college.com

You can find further relevant readings by searching *InfoTrac College Edition*, an online library with access to thousands of scholarly and popular periodicals. Below are suggested search terms for this article:

- witchcraft
- supernatural

Anthropology Online: Wadsworth's Anthropology Resource Center

academic.cengage.com/anthropology

The Wadsworth Anthropology Resource Center contains a wealth of information and useful tools for students including information on careers in anthropology.

14

Baseball Magic

GEORGE GMELCH

Americans like to think of themselves as being grounded in scientific rationality rather than in superstition, magic, and ritual. Yet, when we turn the anthropological lens upon our own culture, we can see that magic and appeals to supernatural forces are employed in the United States for the very same reasons they are in the Trobriand Islands or among the Azande in the Southern Sudan—that is, to ensure success in human activities. Middle-class North Americans—and others—are likely to call on supernatural forces in those situations that are unpredictable and over which they have relatively little control.

In this article, George Gmelch, an anthropologist as well as a former professional baseball player, reminds us that U.S. baseball players are more likely to use magic (ritual, taboos, and fetishes) on those aspects of the game that are unpredictable (hitting and pitching) than on fielding, over which players have greater control. Even if this baseball magic doesn't always produce the desired outcome, it continues to be used because it functions to reduce anxiety and provide players with at least the illusion of control.

> *We find magic wherever the elements of chance and accident, and the emotional play between hope and fear have a wide and extensive range. We do not find magic wherever the pursuit is certain, reliable, and well under the control of rational methods.*
>
> —*Bronislaw Malinowski*

Professional baseball is a nearly perfect arena in which to test Malinowski's hypothesis about magic. The great anthropologist was not, of course, talking about sleight of hand but of rituals, taboos and fetishes that men resort to when they want to ensure that things go their own way. Baseball is rife with this sort of magic, but, as we shall see, the players use it in some aspects of the game far more than in others.

Everyone knows that there are three essentials of baseball—hitting, pitching and fielding. The point is, however, that the first two, hitting and pitching, involve a high degree of chance. The pitcher is the player least able to control the outcome of his own efforts. His best pitch may be hit for a bloop single while his worst pitch may be hit directly to one of his fielders for an out. He may limit the opposition to a single hit and lose, or he may give up a dozen hits and win. It is not uncommon for pitchers to perform well and lose, and vice versa; one has only to look at the frequency with which pitchers end a season with poor won-lost percentages but low earned run averages (number of runs given up per game). The opposite is equally

SOURCE: Reprinted by permission of Springer-SBM, B.V. "Superstition and Ritual in American Baseball" by George Gmelch in *Society* 8(8): 39–41. Copyright © 1971 by Transaction Publishers.

true: some pitchers play poorly, giving up many runs, yet win many games. In brief, the pitcher, regardless of how well he performs, is dependent upon the proficiency of his teammates, the inefficiency of the opposition and the supernatural (luck).

But luck, as we all know, comes in two forms, and many fans assume that the pitcher's tough losses (close games in which he gave up very few runs) are eventually balanced out by his "lucky" wins. This is untrue, as a comparison of pitchers' lifetime earned run averages to their overall won-lost records shows. If the player could apply a law of averages to individual performance, there would be much less concern about chance and uncertainty in baseball. Unfortunately, he cannot and does not.

Hitting, too, is a chancy affair. Obviously, skill is required in hitting the ball hard and on a line. Once the ball is hit, however, chance plays a large role in determining where it will go, into a waiting glove or whistling past a falling stab.

With respect to fielding, the player has almost complete control over the outcome. The average fielding percentage or success rate of .975 compared to a .245 success rate for hitters (the average batting average), reflects the degree of certainty in fielding. Next to the pitcher or hitter, the fielder has little to worry about when he knows that better than 9.7 times in ten he will execute his task flawlessly.

If Malinowski's hypothesis is correct, we should find magic associated with hitting and pitching, but none with fielding. Let us take the evidence by category—ritual, taboo and fetish.

RITUAL

After each pitch, ex-major leaguer Lou Skeins used to reach into his back pocket to touch a crucifix, straighten his cap and clutch his genitals. Detroit Tiger infielder Tim Maring wore the same clothes and put them on exactly in the same order each day during a batting streak. Baseball rituals are almost infinitely various. After all, the ballplayer can ritualize any activity he considers necessary for a success-ful performance, from the type of cereal he eats in the morning to the streets he drives home on.

Usually, rituals grow out of exceptionally good performances. When the player does well he cannot really attribute his success to skill alone. He plays with the same amount of skill one night when he gets four hits as the next night when he goes hitless. Through magic, such as ritual, the player seeks greater control over his performance, actually control over the elements of chance. The player, knowing that his ability is fairly constant, attributes the inconsistencies in his performance to some form of behavior or a particular food that he ate. When a player gets four hits in a game, especially "cheap" hits, he often believes that there must have been something he did, in addition to his ability, that shifted luck to his side. If he can attribute his good fortune to the glass of iced tea he drank before the game or the new shirt he wore to the ballpark, then by repeating the same behavior the following day he can hope to achieve similar results. (One expression of this belief is the myth that eating certain foods will give the ball "eyes," that is, a ball that seeks the gaps between fielders.) In hopes of maintaining a batting streak, I once ate fried chicken every day at 4:00 P.M., kept my eyes closed during the national anthem and changed sweat shirts at the end of the fourth inning each night for seven consecutive nights until the streak ended.

Fred Caviglia, Kansas City minor league pitcher, explained why he eats certain foods before each game: "Everything you do is important to winning. I never forget what I eat the day of a game or what I wear. If I pitch well and win I'll do it all exactly the same the next day I pitch. You'd be crazy not to. You just can't ever tell what's going to make the difference between winning and losing."

Rituals associated with hitting vary considerably in complexity from one player to the next, but they have several components in common. One of the most popular is tagging a particular base when leaving and returning to the dugout each inning. Tagging second base on the way to the outfield is habitual with some players. One informant reported that during a successful month of the season he stepped on third base on his way to the dugout after the third, sixth and ninth innings of each game. Asked if he ever purposely failed to step on the bag he replied, "Never! I wouldn't dare, it would destroy my confidence to hit." It is not uncommon for a hitter who is playing poorly to try different combinations of tagging and not tagging particular bases in an attempt to find a successful combination. Other components of a hitter's ritual may include tapping the plate with his bat a precise number of times or taking a precise number of warm-up swings with the leaded bat.

One informant described a variation of this in which he gambled for a certain hit by tapping the plate a fixed number of times. He touched the plate once with his bat for each base desired: one tap for a single, two for a double and so on. He even built in odds that prevented him from asking for a home run each time. The odds of hitting a single with one tap were one in three, while the chances of hitting a home run with four taps were one in 12.

Clothing is often considered crucial to both hitters and pitchers. They may have several athletic supporters and a number of sweat shirts with ritual significance. Nearly all players wear the same uniform and undergarments each day when playing well, and some even wear the same street clothes. In 1954, the New York Giants, during a 16-game winning streak, wore the same clothes in each game and refused to let them be cleaned for fear that their good fortune might be washed away with the dirt. The route taken to and from the stadium can also have significance; some players drive the same streets to the ballpark during a hitting streak and try different routes during slumps.

Because pitchers only play once every four days, the rituals they practice are often more complex than the hitters', and most of it, such as tugging the cap between pitches, touching the rosin bag after each bad pitch or smoothing the dirt on the mound before each new batter, takes place on the field. Many baseball fans have observed this behavior never realizing that it may be as important to the pitcher as throwing the ball.

Dennis Grossini, former Detroit farmhand, practiced the following ritual on each pitching day for the first three months of a winning season. First, he arose from bed at exactly 10:00 A.M. and not a minute earlier or later. At 1:00 P.M. he went to the nearest restaurant for two glasses of iced tea and a tuna fish sandwich. Although the afternoon was free, he observed a number of taboos such as no movies, no reading and no candy. In the clubhouse he changed into the sweat shirt and jock he wore during his last winning game, and one hour before the game he chewed a wad of Beechnut chewing tobacco. During the game he touched his letters (the team name on his uniform) after each pitch and straightened his cap after each ball. Before the start of each inning he replaced the pitcher's rosin bag next to the spot where it was the inning before. And after every inning in which he gave up a run he went to the clubhouse to wash his hands. I asked him which part of the ritual was most important. He responded: "You can't really tell what's most important so it all becomes important. I'd be afraid to change anything. As long as I'm winning I do everything the same. Even when I can't wash my hands [this would occur when he must bat] it scares me going back to the mound.... I don't feel quite right."

One ritual, unlike those already mentioned, is practiced to improve the power of the baseball bat. It involves sanding the bat until all the varnish is removed, a process requiring several hours of labor, then rubbing rosin into the grain of the bat before finally heating it over a flame. This ritual treatment supposedly increases the distance the ball travels after being struck. Although some North Americans prepare their bats in this fashion it is more popular among Latin Americans. One informant admitted that he was not certain of the effectiveness of the treatment. But, he added, "There may not be a God, but I go to church just the same."

Despite the wide assortment of rituals associated with pitching and hitting, I never observed any ritual related to fielding. In all my 20 interviews only one player, a shortstop with acute fielding problems, reported any ritual even remotely connected to fielding.

TABOO

Mentioning that a no-hitter is in progress and crossing baseball bats are the two most widely observed taboos. It is believed that if the pitcher hears the words "no-hitter" his spell will be broken and the no-hitter lost. As for the crossing of bats, that is sure to bring bad luck; batters are therefore extremely careful not to drop their bats on top of another. Some players elaborate this taboo even further. On one occasion a teammate became quite upset when another player tossed a bat from the batting cage and it came to rest on top of his. Later he explained that the top bat would steal hits from the lower one. For him, then, bats contain a finite number of hits, a kind of baseball "image of limited good." Honus Wagner, a member of baseball's Hall of Fame, believed that each bat was good for only 100 hits and no more. Regardless of the quality of the bat he would discard it after its 100th hit.

Besides observing the traditional taboos just mentioned, players also observe certain personal prohibitions. Personal taboos grow out of exceptionally poor performances, which a player often attributes to some particular behavior or food. During my first season of professional baseball I once ate pancakes before a game in which I struck out four times. Several weeks later I had a repeat performance, again after eating pancakes. The result was a pancake taboo in which from that day on I never ate pancakes during the season. Another personal taboo, born out of similar circumstances, was against holding a baseball during the national anthem.

Taboos are also of many kinds. One athlete was careful never to step on the chalk foul lines or the chalk lines of the batter's box. Another would never put on his cap until the game started and would not wear it at all on the days he did not pitch. Another had a movie taboo in which he refused to watch a movie the day of a game. Often certain uniform numbers become taboo. If a player has a poor spring training or a bad year, he may refuse to wear the same uniform number again. I would not wear double numbers, especially 44 and 22. On several occasions, teammates who were playing poorly requested a change of uniform during the middle of the season. Some players consider it so important that they will wear the wrong size uniform just to avoid a certain number or to obtain a good number.

Again, with respect to fielding, I never saw or heard of any taboos being observed, though of course there were some taboos, like the uniform numbers, that were concerned with overall performance and so included fielding.

FETISHES

These are standard equipment for many baseball players. They include a wide assortment of objects: horsehide covers of old baseballs, coins, bobby pins, protective cups, crucifixes and old bats. Ordinary objects are given this power in a fashion similar to the formation of taboos and rituals. The player during an exceptionally hot batting or pitching streak, especially one in which he has "gotten all the breaks," credits some unusual object, often a new possession, for his good fortune. For example, a player in a slump might find a coin or an odd stone just before he begins a hitting streak. Attributing the improvement in his performance to the new object, it becomes a fetish, embodied with supernatural power. While playing for Spokane, Dodger pitcher Alan Foster forgot his baseball shoes on a road trip and borrowed a pair from a teammate to pitch. That night he pitched a no-hitter and later, needless to say, bought the shoes from his teammate. They became his most prized possession.

Fetishes are taken so seriously by some players that their teammates will not touch them out of fear of offending the owner. I once saw a fight caused by the desecration of a fetish. Before the game, one player stole the fetish, a horsehide baseball cover, out of a teammate's back pocket. The prankster did not return the fetish until after the game, in which the owner of the fetish went hitless, breaking a batting streak. The owner, blaming his inability to hit on the loss of the fetish, lashed out at the thief when the latter tried to return it.

Rube Waddel, an old-time Philadelphia Athletic pitching great, had a hairpin fetish. However, the hairpin he possessed was only powerful as long as he won. Once he lost a game he would look for another hairpin, which had to be found on the street, and he would not pitch until he found another.

The use of fetishes follows the same pattern as ritual and taboo in that they are connected only with hitting or pitching. In nearly all cases the player expressed a specific purpose for carrying a fetish, but never did a player perceive his fetish as having any effect on his fielding.

I have said enough, I think, to show that many of the beliefs and practices of professional baseball players are magical. Any empirical connection between the ritual, taboo and fetishes and the desired event is quite absent. Indeed, in several instances the relationship between the cause and effect,

such as eating tuna fish sandwiches to win a ball game, is even more remote than is characteristic of primitive magic. Note, however, that unlike many forms of primitive magic, baseball magic is usually performed to achieve one's own end and not to block someone else's. Hitters do not tap their bats on the plate to hex the pitcher but to improve their own performance.

Finally, it should be plain that nearly all the magical practices that I participated in, observed or elicited, support Malinowski's hypothesis that magic appears in situations of chance and uncertainty. The large amount of uncertainty in pitching and hitting best explains the elaborate magical practices used for these activities. Conversely, the high success rate in fielding, .975, involving much less uncertainty offers the best explanation for the absence of magic in this realm.

DISCUSSION QUESTIONS

1. How would you distinguish among a ritual, a taboo, and a fetish?

2. Of the three aspects of the game of baseball (fielding, hitting, and pitching), which are the most susceptible to baseball magic?

3. Can you think of how magic is used in other American sports?

RESOURCES ON THE INTERNET

InfoTrac College Edition

infotrac-college.com

You can find further relevant readings by searching *InfoTrac College Edition*, an online library with

access to thousands of scholarly and popular periodicals. Below are suggested search terms for this article:

- magic
- taboo
- fetish

Anthropology Online: Wadsworth's Anthropology Resource Center

academic.cengage.com/anthropology

The Wadsworth Anthropology Resource Center contains a wealth of information and useful tools for students including information on careers in anthropology.

15

Steel Axes for Stone-Age Australians

LAURISTON SHARP

For decades, anthropologists have recognized that cultures are more than the sum of their parts (things, ideas, and behavior patterns). Rather, cultures are integrated wholes, the parts of which are integrated. This means, of course, that a change in one part of a culture is likely to bring about changes in other parts of the culture. In this classic selection on the aboriginal Yir Yoront of Australia, Lauriston Sharp shows how the introduction of steel axes to Yir Yoront culture in the 1930s by well-meaning but shortsighted missionaries changed the relationship among family members and trading partners and eventually contributed to the demise of the culture.

This general principle of integrated cultures—so dramatically illustrated by Sharp—has important implications for anyone today working with people from other cultures, such as Peace Corps volunteers, foreign aid personnel, or international businesspeople. To illustrate, the introduction of a seemingly harmless commercial product or agricultural development program could have profoundly disruptive effects on the very fabric of the local culture. By knowing how the various parts of a culture are interconnected ahead of time, the humane and responsible foreign aid worker or global businessperson will be able to predict possible harmful effects of introducing changes into other cultures.

I

Like other Australian aboriginals, the Yir Yoront group which lives at the mouth of the Coleman River on the west coast of Cape York Peninsula originally had no knowledge of metals. Technologically their culture was of the old stone age or paleolithic type. They supported themselves by hunting and fishing, and obtained vegetables and other materials from the bush by simple gathering techniques. Their only domesticated animal was the dog; they had no cultivated plants of any kind. Unlike some other aboriginal groups, however, the Yir Yoront did have polished stone axes hafted in short handles which were most important in their economy.

Towards the end of the 19th century metal tools and other European artifacts began to filter into the Yir Yoront territory. The flow increased with the gradual expansion of the white frontier outward from southern and eastern Queensland. Of all the items of western technology thus made available, the hatchet, or short handled steel axe, was the most acceptable to and the most highly valued by all aboriginals.

In the mid 1930s an American anthropologist lived alone in the bush among the Yir Yoront for 13 months without seeing another white man. The Yir Yoront were thus still relatively isolated and continued to live an essentially independent economic existence, supporting themselves entirely

SOURCE: From "Steel Axes for Stone-Age Australians" in *Human Organization*, Summer 1952, pp. 17–22. Reprinted with permission from the Society for Applied Anthropology.

by means of their old stone age techniques. Yet their polished stone axes were disappearing fast and being replaced by steel axes which came to them in considerable numbers, directly or indirectly, from various European sources to the south.

What changes in the life of the Yir Yoront still living under aboriginal conditions in the Australian bush could be expected as a result of their increasing possession and use of the steel axe?

II: THE COURSE OF EVENTS

Events leading up to the introduction of the steel axe among the Yir Yoront begin with the advent of the second known group of Europeans to reach the shores of the Australian continent. In 1623 a Dutch expedition landed on the coast where the Yir Yoront now live.[1] In 1935 the Yir Yoront were still using the few cultural items recorded in the Dutch log for the aboriginals they encountered. To this cultural inventory the Dutch added beads and pieces of iron which they offered in an effort to attract the frightened "Indians." Among these natives metal and beads have disappeared, together with any memory of this first encounter with whites.

The next recorded contact in this area was in 1864. Here there is more positive assurance that the natives concerned were the immediate ancestors of the Yir Yoront community. These aboriginals had the temerity to attack a party of cattle men who were driving a small herd from southern Queensland through the length of the then unknown Cape York Peninsula to a newly established government station at the northern tip.[2] Known as the "Battle of the Mitchell River," this was one of the rare instances in which Australian aboriginals stood up to European gunfire for any length of time. A diary kept by the cattle men records that: "…10 carbines poured volley after volley into them

from all directions, killing and wounding with every shot with very little return, nearly all their spears having already been expended.... About 30 being killed, the leader thought it prudent to hold his hand, and let the rest escape. Many more must have been wounded and probably drowned, for 59 rounds were counted as discharged." The European party was in the Yir Yoront area for three days; they then disappeared over the horizon to the north and never returned. In the almost three-year long anthropological investigation conducted some 70 years later—in all the material of hundreds of free association interviews, in texts of hundreds of dreams and myths, in genealogies, and eventually in hundreds of answers to direct and indirect questioning on just this particular matter—there was nothing that could be interpreted as a reference to this shocking contact with Europeans.

The aboriginal accounts of their first remembered contact with whites begin in about 1900 with references to persons known to have had sporadic but lethal encounters with them. From that time on whites continued to remain on the southern periphery of Yir Yoront territory. With the establishment of cattle stations (ranches) to the south, cattle men made occasional excursions among the "wild black-fellows" in order to inspect the country and abduct natives to be trained as cattle boys and "house girls." At least one such expedition reached the Coleman River where a number of Yir Yoront men and women were shot for no apparent reason.

About this time the government was persuaded to sponsor the establishment of three mission stations along the 700-mile western coast of the Peninsula in an attempt to help regulate the treatment of natives. To further this purpose a strip of coastal territory was set aside as an aboriginal reserve and closed to further white settlement.

In 1915, an Anglican mission station was established near the mouth of the Mitchell River, about

---

1. An account of this expedition from Amboina is given in R. Logan Jack, *Northmost Australia* (2 vols.), London, 1921, Vol. 1, pp. 18–57.

2. R. Logan Jack, *op. cit.,* pp. 298–335.

a three-day march from the heart of the Yir Yoront country. Some Yir Yoront refused to have anything to do with the mission, others visited it occasionally, while only a few eventually settled more or less permanently in one of the three "villages" established at the mission.

Thus the majority of the Yir Yoront continued to live their old self-supporting life in the bush, protected until 1942 by the government reserve and the intervening mission from the cruder realities of the encroaching new order from the south. To the east was poor, uninhabited country. To the north were other bush tribes extending on along the coast to the distant Archer River Presbyterian mission with which the Yir Yoront had no contact. Westward was the shallow Gulf of Carpentaria on which the natives saw only a mission lugger making its infrequent dry season trips to the Mitchell River. In this protected environment for over a generation the Yir Yoront were able to recuperate from shocks received at the hands of civilized society. During the 1930s their raiding and fighting, their trading and stealing of women, their evisceration and two- or three-year care of their dead, and their totemic ceremonies continued, apparently uninhibited by western influence. In 1931 they killed a European who wandered into their territory from the east, but the investigating police never approached the group whose members were responsible for the act.

As a direct result of the work of the Mitchell River mission, all Yir Yoront received a great many more western artifacts of all kinds than ever before. As part of their plan for raising native living standards, the missionaries made it possible for aboriginals living at the mission to earn some western goods, many of which were then given or traded to natives still living under bush conditions; they also handed out certain useful articles gratis to both mission and bush aboriginals. They prevented guns, liquor, and damaging narcotics, as well as decimating diseases, from reaching the tribes of this area, while encouraging the introduction of goods they considered "improving." As has been noted, no item of western technology available, with the possible exception of trade tobacco, was in greater demand among all groups of aboriginals than the short handled steel axe. The mission always kept a good supply of these axes in stock; at Christmas parties or other mission festivals they were given away to mission or visiting aboriginals indiscriminately and in considerable numbers. In addition, some steel axes as well as other European goods were still traded in to the Yir Yoront by natives in contact with cattle stations in the south. Indeed, steel axes had probably come to the Yir Yoront through established lines of aboriginal trade long before any regular contact with whites had occurred.

III: RELEVANT FACTORS

If we concentrate our attention on Yir Yoront behavior centering about the original stone axe (rather than on the axe—the object—itself) as a cultural trait or item of cultural equipment, we should get some conception of the role this implement played in aboriginal culture. This, in turn, should enable us to foresee with considerable accuracy some of the results stemming from the displacement of the stone axe by the steel axe.

The production of a stone axe required a number of simple technological skills. With the various details of the axe well in mind, adult men could set about producing it (a task not considered appropriate for women or children). First of all a man had to know the location and properties of several natural resources found in his immediate environment: pliable wood for a handle, which could be doubled or bent over the axe head and bound tightly; bark, which could be rolled into cord for the binding; and gum, to fix the stone head in the haft. These materials had to be correctly gathered, stored, prepared, cut to size and applied or manipulated. They were in plentiful supply, and could be taken from anyone's property without special permission. Postponing consideration of the stone head, the axe could be made by any normal man who had a simple knowledge of nature and of the technological skills involved, together with fire (for heating the gum), and a few simple cutting tools—perhaps the sharp shells of plentiful bivalves.

The use of the stone axe as a piece of capital equipment used in producing other goods indicates its very great importance to the subsistence economy of the aboriginal. Anyone—man, woman, or child—could use the axe; indeed, it was used primarily by women, for theirs was the task of obtaining sufficient wood to keep the family campfire burning all day, for cooking or other purposes, and all night against mosquitoes and cold (for in July, winter temperature might drop below 40 degrees). In a normal lifetime a woman would use the axe to cut or knock down literally tons of firewood. The axe was also used to make other tools or weapons, and a variety of material equipment required by the aboriginal in his daily life. The stone axe was essential in the construction of the wet season domed huts which keep out some rain and some insects; of platforms which provide dry storage; of shelters which give shade in the dry summer when days are bright and hot. In hunting and fishing and in gathering vegetable or animal food the axe was also a necessary tool, and in this tropical culture, where preservatives or other means of storage are lacking, the natives spend more time obtaining food than in any other occupation—except sleeping. In only two instances was the use of the stone axe strictly limited to adult men: for gathering wild honey, the most prized food known to the Yir Yoront; and for making the secret paraphernalia for ceremonies. From this brief listing of some of the activities involving the use of the axe, it is easy to understand why there was at least one stone axe in every camp, in every hunting or fighting party, and in every group out on a "walkabout" in the bush.

The stone axe was also prominent in interpersonal relations. Yir Yoront men were dependent upon interpersonal relations for their stone axe heads, since the flat, geologically-recent, alluvial country over which they range provides no suitable stone for this purpose. The stone they used came from quarries 400 miles to the south, reaching the Yir Yoront through long lines of male trading partners. Some of these chains terminated with the Yir

Yoront men, others extended on farther north to other groups, using Yir Yoront men as links. Almost every older adult man had one or more regular trading partners, some to the north and some to the south. He provided his partner or partners in the south with surplus spears, particularly fighting spears tipped with the barbed spines of sting ray which snap into vicious fragments when they penetrate human flesh. For a dozen such spears, some of which he may have obtained from a partner to the north, he would receive one stone axe head. Studies have shown that the sting ray barb spears increased in value as they move south and farther from the sea. One hundred and fifty miles south of Yir Yoront one such spear may be exchanged for one stone axe head. Although actual investigations could not be made, it was presumed that farther south, nearer the quarries, one sting ray barb spear would bring several stone axe heads. Apparently people who acted as links in the middle of the chain and who made neither spears nor axe heads would receive a certain number of each as a middleman's profit.

Thus trading relations, which may extend the individual's personal relationships beyond that of his own group, were associated with spears and axes, two of the most important items in a man's equipment. Finally, most of the exchanges took place during the dry season, at the time of the great aboriginal celebrations centering about initiation rites or other totemic ceremonials which attracted hundreds and were the occasion for much exciting activity in addition to trading.

Returning to the Yir Yoront, we find that adult men kept their axes in camp with their other equipment, or carried them when travelling. Thus a woman or child who wanted to use an axe—as might frequently happen during the day—had to get one from a man, use it promptly, and return it in good condition. While a man might speak of "my axe," a woman or child could not.

This necessary and constant borrowing of axes from older men by women and children was in accordance with regular patterns of kinship behavior. A woman would expect to use her husband's axe unless he himself was using it; if unmarried, or if her husband was absent, a woman would go first to her older brother or to her father. Only in extraordinary circumstances would she seek a stone axe from other male kin. A girl, a boy, or a young man would look to a father or an older brother to provide an axe for their use. Older men, too, would follow similar rules if they had to borrow an axe.

It will be noted that all of these social relationships in which the stone axe had a place are pair relationships and that the use of the axe helped to define and maintain their character and the roles of the two individual participants. Every active relationship among the Yir Yoront involved a definite and accepted status of superordination or subordination. A person could have no dealings with another on exactly equal terms. The nearest approach to equality was between brothers, although the older was always superordinate to the younger. Since the exchange of goods in a trading relationship involved a mutual reciprocity, trading partners usually stood in a brotherly type of relationship, although one was always classified as older than the other and would have some advantage in case of dispute. It can be seen that repeated and widespread conduct centering around the use of the axe helped to generalize and standardize these sex, age, and kinship roles both in their normal benevolent and exceptional malevolent aspects.

The status of any individual Yir Yoront was determined not only by sex, age, and extended kin relationships, but also by membership in one of two dozen patrilineal totemic clans into which the entire community was divided.[3] Each clan had literally hundreds of totems, from one or two of which the clan derived its name, and the clan members their personal names. These totems included natural species or phenomena such as the sun, stars, and daybreak, as well as cultural "species": imagined ghosts, rainbow serpents, heroic ancestors; such eternal cultural verities as fires, spears, huts; and

such human activities, conditions, or attributes as eating, vomiting, swimming, fighting, babies and corpses, milk and blood, lips and loins. While individual members of such totemic classes or species might disappear or be destroyed, the class itself was obviously ever-present and indestructible. The totems, therefore, lent permanence and stability to the clans, to the groupings of human individuals who generation after generation were each associated with a set of totems which distinguished one clan from another.

The stone axe was one of the most important of the many totems of the Sunlit Cloud Iguana clan. The names of many members of this clan referred to the axe itself, to activities in which the axe played a vital part, or to the clan's mythical ancestors with whom the axe was prominently associated. When it was necessary to represent the stone axe in totemic ceremonies, only men of this clan exhibited it or pantomimed its use. In secular life, the axe could be made by any man and used by all; but in the sacred realm of the totems it belonged exclusively to the Sunlit Cloud Iguana people.

Supporting those aspects of cultural behavior which we have called technology and conduct, is a third area of culture which includes ideas, sentiments, and values. These are most difficult to deal with, for they are latent and covert, and even unconscious, and must be deduced from overt actions and language or other communicating behavior. In this aspect of the culture lies the significance of the stone axe to the Yir Yoront and to their cultural way of life.

The stone axe was an important symbol of masculinity among the Yir Yoront (just as pants or pipes are to us). By a complicated set of ideas the axe was defined as "belonging" to males, and everyone in the society (except untrained infants) accepted these ideas. Similarly spears, spear throwers, and fire-making sticks were owned only

---

3. The best, although highly concentrated, summaries of totemism among the Yir Yoront and the other tribes of north Queensland will be found in R. Lauriston Sharp, "Tribes and Totemism in Northeast Australia," *Oceania*, Vol. 8, 1939, pp. 254–275 and 439–461 (especially pp. 268–275); also "Notes on Northeast Australian Totemism," in *Papers of the Peabody Museum of American/Archaeology and Ethnology*, Vol. 20, *Studies in the Anthropology of Oceania and Asia*, Cambridge, 1943, pp. 66–71.

by men and were also symbols of masculinity. But the masculine values represented by the stone axe were constantly being impressed on all members of society by the fact that females borrowed axes but not other masculine artifacts. Thus the axe stood for an important theme of Yir Yoront culture: the superiority and rightful dominance of the male, and the greater value of his concerns and of all things associated with him. As the axe also had to be borrowed by the younger people it represented the prestige of age, another important theme running through Yir Yoront behavior.

To understand the Yir Yoront culture it is necessary to be aware of a system of ideas which may be called their totemic ideology. A fundamental belief of the aboriginal divided time into two great epochs: (1) a distant and sacred period at the beginning of the world when the earth was peopled by mildly marvelous ancestral beings or culture heroes who are in a special sense the forebears of the clans; and (2) a period when the old was succeeded by a new order which includes the present. Originally there was no anticipation of another era supplanting the present. The future would simply be an eternal continuation and reproduction of the present which itself had remained unchanged since the epochal revolution of ancestral times.

The important thing to note is that the aboriginal believed that the present world, as a natural and cultural environment, was and should be simply a detailed reproduction of the world of the ancestors. He believed that the entire universe "is now as it was in the beginning" when it was established and left by the ancestors. The ordinary cultural life of the ancestors became the daily life of the Yir Yoront camps, and the extraordinary life of the ancestors remained extant in the recurring symbolic pantomimes and paraphernalia found only in the most sacred atmosphere of the totemic rites.

Such beliefs, accordingly, opened the way for ideas of what *should be* (because it supposedly *was*) to influence or help determine what actually *is*. A man called Dog-chases-iguana-up-a-tree-and-barks-at-him-all-night had that and other names because he believed his ancestral alter ego had also had them; he was a member of the Sunlit Cloud Iguana clan because his ancestor was; he was associated with particular countries and totems of this same ancestor; during an initiation he played the role of a dog and symbolically attacked and killed certain members of other clans because his ancestor (conveniently either anthropomorphic or kynomorphic) really did the same to the ancestral alter egos of these men; and he would avoid his mother-in-law, joke with a mother's distant brother, and make spears in a certain way because his and other people's ancestors did these things. His behavior in these specific ways was outlined, and to that extent determined for him, by a set of ideas concerning the past and the relation of the present to the past.

But when we are informed that Dog-chases-etc. had two wives from the Spear Black Duck clan and one from the Native Companion clan, one of them being blind, that he had four children with such and such names, that he had a broken wrist and was left handed, all because his ancestor had exactly these same attributes, then we know (though he apparently didn't) that the present has influenced the past, that the mythical world has been somewhat adjusted to meet the exigencies and accidents of the inescapably real present.

There was thus in Yir Yoront ideology a nice balance in which the mythical was adjusted in part to the real world, the real world in part to the ideal pre-existing mythical world, the adjustments occurring to maintain a fundamental tenet of native faith that the present must be a mirror of the past. Thus the stone axe in all its aspects, uses, and associations was integrated into the context of Yir Yoront technology and conduct because a myth, a set of ideas, had put it there.

IV: THE OUTCOME

The introduction of the steel axe indiscriminately and in large numbers into the Yir Yoront technology occurred simultaneously with many other changes. It is therefore impossible to separate all the results of this single innovation. Nevertheless, a number of specific effects of the change from stone to steel axes may be noted, and the steel axe may be used as an epitome of the increasing quantity of European goods and implements received by the aboriginals and of their general influence on the native culture. The use of the steel axe to illustrate such influences would seem to be justified. It was one of the first Europe artifacts to be adopted for regular use by the Yir Yoront, and whether made of stone or steel, the axe was clearly one of the most important items of cultural equipment they possessed.

The shift from stone to steel axes provided no major technological difficulties. While the aboriginals themselves could not manufacture steel axe heads, a steady supply from outside continued; broken wooden handles could easily be replaced from bush timbers with aboriginal tools. Among the Yir Yoront the new axe was never used to the extent it was on mission or cattle stations (for carpentry work, pounding tent pegs, as a hammer, and so on); indeed, it had so few more uses than the stone axe that its practical effect on the native standard of living was negligible. It did some jobs better, and could be used longer without breakage. These factors were sufficient to make it of value to the native. The white man believed that a shift from steel to stone axe on his part would be a definite regression. He was convinced that his axe was much more efficient, that its use would save time, and that it therefore represented technical "progress" towards goals which he had set up for the native. But this assumption was hardly born out in aboriginal practice. Any leisure time the Yir Yoront might gain by using steel axes or other western tools was not invested in "improving the conditions of life," nor, certainly, in developing aesthetic activities, but in sleep—an art they had mastered thoroughly.

Previously, a man in need of an axe would acquire a stone axe head through regular trading partners from whom he knew what to expect, and was then dependent solely upon a known and adequate natural environment, and his own skills or easily acquired techniques. A man wanting a steel axe, however, was in no such self-reliant position. If he attended a mission festival when steel axes were handed out as gifts, he might receive one either by chance or by happening to impress upon the mission staff that he was one of the "better" bush aboriginals (the missionaries' definition of "better" being quite different from that of his bush fellows). Or, again almost by pure chance, he might get some brief job in connection with the mission which would enable him to earn a steel axe. In either case, for older men a preference for the steel axe helped change the situation from one of self-reliance to one of dependence, and a shift in behavior from well-structured or defined situations in technology or conduct to ill-defined situations in conduct alone. Among the men, the older ones whose earlier experience or knowledge of the white man's harshness made them suspicious were particularly careful to avoid having relations with the mission, and thus excluded themselves from acquiring steel axes from that source.

In other aspects of conduct or social relations, the steel axe was even more significantly at the root of psychological stress among the Yir Yoront. This was the result of new factors which the missionary considered beneficial: the simple numerical increase in axes per capita as a result of mission distribution, and distribution directly to younger men, women, and even children. By winning the favor of the mission staff, a woman might be given a steel axe which was clearly intended to be hers, thus creating a situation quite different from the previous custom which necessitated her borrowing an axe from a male relative. As a result a woman would refer to the axe as "mine," a possessive form she was never able to use of the stone axe. In the same fashion, young men or even boys also obtained steel axes directly from the mission, with the result that older men no longer had a complete monopoly of all the axes in the bush community. All this led to a revolutionary confusion of sex, age, and kinship roles, with a major gain in independence and loss of subordination on the part of those who now owned steel axes when they had previously been unable to possess stone axes.

The trading partner relationship was also affected by the new situation. A Yir Yoront might have a trading partner in a tribe to the south whom he defined as a younger brother and over whom he would therefore have some authority. But if the partner were in contact with the mission or had other access to steel axes, his subordination obviously decreased. Among other things, this took some of the excitement away from the dry season fiesta-like tribal gatherings centering around initiations. These had traditionally been the climactic annual occasions for exchanges between trading partners, when a man might seek to acquire a whole year's supply of stone axe heads. Now he might find himself prostituting his wife to almost total strangers in return for steel axes or other white man's goods. With trading partnerships weakened, there was less reason to attend the ceremonies, and less fun for those who did.

Not only did an increase in steel axes and their distribution to women change the character of the relations between individuals (the paired relationships that have been noted), but a previously rare type of relationship was created in the Yir Yoront's conduct towards whites. In the aboriginal society there were few occasions outside of the immediate family when an individual would initiate action to several other people at once. In any average group, in accordance with the kinship system, while a person might be superordinate to several people to whom he could suggest or command action, he was also subordinate to several others with whom such behavior would be tabu. There was thus no overall chieftainship or authoritarian leadership of any kind. Such complicated operations as grass-burning animal drives or totemic ceremonies could be carried out smoothly because each person was aware of his role.

On both mission and cattle stations, however, the whites imposed their conception of leadership roles upon the aboriginals, consisting of one person in a controlling relationship with a subordinate group. Aboriginals called together to receive gifts, including axes, at a mission Christmas party found themselves facing one or two whites who sought to control their behavior for the occasion, who disregarded the age, sex, and kinship variables of which the aboriginals were so conscious, and who considered them all at one subordinate level. The white also sought to impose similar patterns on work par-

ties. (However, if he placed an aboriginal in charge of a mixed group of post-hole diggers, for example, half of the group, those subordinate to the "boss," would work while the other half, who were superordinate to him, would sleep.) For the aboriginal, the steel axe and other European goods came to symbolize this new and uncomfortable form of social organization, the leader-group relationship.

The most disturbing effects of the steel axe, operating in conjunction with other elements also being introduced from the white man's several subcultures, developed in the realm of traditional ideas, sentiments and values. These were undermined at a rapidly mounting rate, with no new conceptions being defined to replace them. The result was the erection of a mental and moral void which foreshadowed the collapse and destruction of all Yir Yoront culture, if not, indeed, the extinction of the biological group itself.

From what has been said it should be clear how changes in overt behavior, in technology and conduct, weakened the values inherent in a reliance on nature, in the prestige of masculinity and of age, and in the various kinship relations. A scene was set in which a wife, or a young son whose initiation may not yet have been completed, need no longer defer to the husband or father who, in turn, became confused and insecure as he was forced to borrow a steel axe from them. For the woman and boy the steel axe helped establish a new degree of freedom which they accepted readily as an escape from the unconscious stress of the old patterns—but they too, were left confused and insecure. Ownership became less well defined with the result that stealing and trespassing were introduced into technology and conduct. Some of the excitement surrounding the great ceremonies evaporated and they lost their previous gaiety and interest. Indeed, life itself became less interesting, although this did not lead the Yir Yoront to discover suicide, a concept foreign to them.

The whole process may be most specifically illustrated in terms of totemic system, which also illustrates the significant role played by a system of ideas, in this case a totemic ideology in the breakdown of a culture.

In the first place, under pre-European aboriginal conditions where the native culture has become adjusted to a relatively stable environment, few, if any, unheard of or catastrophic crises can occur. It is clear, therefore, that the totemic system serves very effectively in inhibiting radical cultural changes. The closed system of totemic ideas, explaining, and categorizing a well-known universe as it was fixed at the beginning of time, presents a considerable obstacle to the adoption of new or the dropping of old culture traits. The obstacle is not insurmountable and the system allows for the minor variations which occur in the norms of daily life. But the inception of major changes cannot easily take place.

Among the bush Yir Yoront the only means of water transport is a light wood log to which they cling in their constant swimming of rivers, salt creeks, and tidal inlets. These natives know that tribes 45 miles further north have a bark canoe. They know these northern tribes can thus fish from midstream or out at sea, instead of clinging to the river banks and beaches, that they can cross coastal waters infested with crocodiles, sharks, sting rays, and Portuguese men-of-war without danger. They know the materials of which the canoe is made exist in their own environment. But they also know, as they say, that they do not have canoes because their own mythical ancestors did not have them. They assume that the canoe was part of the ancestral universe of the northern tribes. For them, then, the adoption of the canoe would not be simply a matter of learning a number of new behavioral skills for its manufacture and use. The adoption would require a much more difficult procedure; the acceptance by the entire society of a myth, either locally developed or borrowed, to explain the presence of the canoe, to associate it with some one or more of the several hundred mythical ancestors (and how to decide which?), and thus establish it as an accepted totem of one of the clans ready to be used by the whole community. The Yir Yoront have not made this adjustment, and in this case we can only say that for the time being at least, ideas have won out over very real pressures for technological change. In the elaborateness and explicitness of the totemic ideologies we seem to

have one explanation for the notorious stability of Australian cultures under aboriginal conditions, an explanation which gives due weight to the importance of ideas in determining human behavior.

At a later stage of the contact situation, as has been indicated, phenomena unaccounted for by the totemic ideological system begin to appear with regularity and frequency and remain within the range of native experience. Accordingly, they cannot be ignored (as the "Battle of the Mitchell" was apparently ignored), and there is an attempt to assimilate them and account for them along the lines of principles inherent in the ideology. The bush Yir Yoront of the mid-thirties represent this stage of the acculturation process. Still trying to maintain their aboriginal definition of the situation, they accept European artifacts and behavior patterns, but fit them into their totemic system, assigning them to various clans on a par with original totems. There is an attempt to have the myth-making process keep up with these cultural changes so that the idea system can continue to support the rest of the culture. But analysis of overt behavior, of dreams, and of some of the new myths indicates that this arrangement is not entirely satisfactory, that the native clings to his totemic system with intellectual loyalty (lacking any substitute ideology), but that associated sentiments and values are weakened. His attitudes towards his own and towards European culture are found to be highly ambivalent.

All ghosts are totems of the Head-to-the-East Corpse clan, are thought of as white, and are of course closely associated with death. The white man, too, is closely associated with death, and he and all things pertaining to him are naturally assigned to the Corpse clan as totems. The steel axe, as a totem, was thus associated with the Corpse clan. But as an "axe," clearly linked with the stone axe, it is a totem of the Sunlit Cloud Iguana clan. Moreover, the steel axe, like most European goods, has no distinctive origin myth, nor are mythical ancestors associated with it. Can anyone, sitting in the shade of a *ti* tree one afternoon, create a myth to resolve this confusion? No one has, and the horrid suspicion arises as to the authenticity of the origin myths, which failed to take into account this vast new universe of the white man. The steel axe, shifting hopelessly between one clan and the other, is not only replacing the stone axe physically, but is hacking at the supports of the entire cultural system.

The aboriginals to the south of the Yir Yoront have clearly passed beyond this stage. They are engulfed by European culture, either by the mission or cattle station sub-cultures or, for some natives, by a baffling, paradoxical combination of both incongruent varieties. The totemic ideology can no longer support the inrushing mass of foreign culture traits, and the myth-making process in its native form breaks down completely. Both intellectually and emotionally a saturation point is reached so that the myriad new traits which can neither be ignored nor any longer assimilated simply force the aboriginal to abandon his totemic system. With the collapse of this system of ideas, which is so closely related to so many other aspects of the native culture, there follows an appallingly sudden and complete cultural disintegration, and a demoralization of the individual such as has seldom been recorded elsewhere. Without the support of a system of ideas well devised to provide cultural stability in a stable environment, but admittedly too rigid for the new realities pressing in from outside, native behavior and native sentiments and values are simply dead. Apathy reigns. The aboriginal has passed beyond the realm of any outsider who might wish to do him well or ill.

Returning from the broken natives huddled on cattle stations or on the fringes of frontier towns to the ambivalent but still lively aboriginals settled on the Mitchell River mission, we note one further devious result of the introduction of European artifacts. During a wet season stay at the mission, the anthropologist discovered that his supply of tooth paste was being depleted at an alarming rate. Investigation showed that it was being taken by old men for use in a new tooth paste cult. Old materials of magic having failed, new materials were being tried out in a malevolent magic directed towards the mission staff and some of the younger aboriginal men. Old males, largely ignored by the missionaries, were seeking to regain some of their lost power and prestige. This mild aggression proved hardly effective, but perhaps only because confidence in any kind of magic on the mission was by this time at a low ebb.

For the Yir Yoront still in the bush, a time could be predicted when personal deprivation and frustration in a confused culture would produce an overload of anxiety. The mythical past of the totemic ancestors would disappear as a guarantee of a present of which the future was supposed to be a stable continuation. Without the past, the present could be meaningless and the future unstructured and uncertain. Insecurities would be inevitable. Reaction to this stress might be some form of symbolic aggression, or withdrawal and apathy, or some more realistic approach. In such a situation the missionary with understanding of the processes going on about him would find his opportunity to introduce his forms of religion and to help create a new cultural universe.

DISCUSSION QUESTIONS

1. What role did the stone axes play in traditional (precontact) Yir Yoront culture?

2. Which aspects of Yir Yoront society were altered (and in what ways) with the introduction of the steel axes?

3. Why is the concept of *integrated cultures* so important in today's world?

 **RESOURCES ON THE
INTERNET**

 InfoTrac College Edition

infotrac-college.com

You can find further relevant readings by searching *InfoTrac College Edition*, an online library with access to thousands of scholarly and popular periodicals. Below are suggested search terms for this article:

- Stone Age
- totemism

**Anthropology Online: Wadsworth's
Anthropology Resource Center**

academic.cengage.com/anthropology

The Wadsworth Anthropology Resource Center contains a wealth of information and useful tools for students including information on careers in anthropology.

16

Globalization and Thomas Friedman

ANGELIQUE HAUGERUD

New York Times columnist Thomas Friedman, author of the Lexus and the Olive Tree, *and considered by many to be the 21st century guru on globalization, claims that the world is comprised of two types of people, modern people who are up to their eyeballs in open markets (represented by the Lexus) and traditional people (represented by the Olive Tree), who want to be left alone to tend to their subsistence garden plots. In this selection, Angelique Haugerud takes on Friedman's punditry head-on by suggesting that his conceptualization of globalization is naive at best and dangerous when applied to public policy.*

This selection appears in Catherine Besteman's and Hugh Gusterson's Why America's Top Pundits Are Wrong: Anthropologists Talk Back, *a 2005 publication that debunks the often sensible-sounding theories of such contemporary pundits as Samuel Huntington and Robert Kaplan, in addition to Thomas Friedman. All of these pundits have gained mass popularity not because their theories are based on the detailed presentation of all of the research facts, but rather because they have reasonable credentials, speak mostly to general audiences rather than to a wide spectrum of specialists, and develop large and bold theories that appear pragmatic, sensible, and easy to understand. Yet, when viewed from the "grass roots" perspective of the anthropological lens (that is, local populations) rather than from the perspective of elitist establishments (comprised of corporate leaders, government officials, and hedge-fund managers) these grand theories reveal their inherent weaknesses and can wind up being largely wrong.*

Haugerud argues convincingly—as do many of the other contributors to the Besteman and Gusterson collection—that anthropological data can make significant contributions to the description of such major world trends as globalization, and subsequently, to public policy designed to respond to these trends.

Who could possibly be against globalization? Only "a Noah's ark of flat-earth advocates, protectionist trade unions and yuppies looking for their 1960s fix," according to Thomas Friedman, foreign affairs columnist for the *New York Times.* "Senseless in Seattle" was his epithet for the thousands of protesters—many dressed as monarch butterflies and sea turtles—who disrupted the December 1999 World Trade Organization (WTO) meetings in Seattle. Unfortunately, Friedman utterly mistakes the protesters' agendas, starting with the antiglobalization label itself, which

SOURCE: Reprinted by permission of the publisher of "Globalization and Thomas Friedman" by Angelique Haugerud, published in Catherine Besteman and Hugh Gusterson (eds.), *Why America's Top Pundits Are Wrong.* Berkeley: University of California Press, 2005, pp. 102–120.

they reject as a media invention. The activists' real aims are global social justice and new forms of global democracy. But these goals are not Friedman's concern. Instead, in his best-selling book *The Lexus and the Olive Tree: Understanding Globalization*, Friedman praises globalization as an inexorable force that can solve many of the world's problems. Friedman's hype, however, is at variance with decades of anthropological research about the processes he describes. His globalization tale is, at best, wishful thinking, and potentially harmful if it shapes public policy.

Cultural and social anthropologists have long studied startling changes like those that excite Friedman and some of his readers. The anthropologist's quarry includes economic, political, cultural, legal, spiritual, and environmental transformations in locales that North Americans and Europeans consider remote, as well as those they find familiar. Careful ethnographic and historical research long ago led anthropologists to discard overwrought images of primordial "tribes" whose cultural differences supposedly cause them to kill one another. Also rejected are notions that any contemporary peoples are Stone Age homologues or tradition-bound exotics who stubbornly or irrationally resist change. Gone are yesterday's notions of boundaries as fixed, natural, or inevitable. Contemporary anthropology, however, appears to be unknown to Friedman, whose writings on globalization offer a caricature of a world torn between olive trees and Lexus luxury cars, between stasis and change.

Although Friedman's writing style is powerful and persuasive, its empirical underpinnings are deeply flawed. Influential policy makers and opinion shapers—even when they are journalists and not scholars—should be held to high evidential standards. This chapter shows why Friedman's approach, assumptions, and claims fare poorly under anthropological scrutiny. It begins by briefly outlining his tale of globalization as the key to understanding the post–cold war era, notes some limitations of his methods, and then identifies four fundamental flaws: an overly narrow observational frame, misunderstanding of tradition, misconception of ethnicity and culture, and failure to address the morality of economic neoliberalism. Next it

sketches anthropological alternatives to Friedman's misconceived olive groves and his narrow view of the 1999 WTO protests in Seattle. Contrary to what Friedman believes, globalizers include precisely those village societies he deprecates as rooted in olive groves, together with migrants to the industrialized North who sustain ties with their countries of origin and forge complex transnational networks. What villagers, migrants, shantytown dwellers, and protesters seek is global and local social justice, not isolated olive groves of tradition.

FRIEDMAN'S GLOBALIZATION WRITINGS

In this chapter, I use the term *globalization* to refer to accelerated flows or intensified connections—across national and other boundaries—of commodities, people, symbols, technology, images, information, and capital.

Friedman celebrates the recent emergence of a global market economy, driven largely by an "electronic herd" of global investors wielding such technology as the Internet, satellites, cell phones, and personal computers. He displays little patience with individuals or groups concerned about the increasing power of corporations that are not accountable to the public, or about declining living standards, curtailment of social expenditures in poor nations, harm to the natural environment, or growing global economic instability and inequality. The primary task of world leaders now, as he presents it, is to keep investors happy so that their corporations will not leave for other countries. For Friedman, a particular type of globalization known in much of the world as economic neoliberalism is an inevitable new world order worth applauding. Neoliberalism refers to supposedly free markets and minimal government direction of flows of goods, services, and finance—a set of policies Friedman terms the "golden straitjacket":

> The Golden Straitjacket is the defining political-economic garment of this globalization era.... If your country has not been

fitted for one, it will be soon. The Golden Straitjacket first began to be stitched together and popularized in 1979 by British Prime Minister Margaret Thatcher.... That Thatcherite coat was soon reinforced by Ronald Reagan.... It became a global fashion with the end of the Cold War.... Thatcher and Reagan combined to strip huge chunks of economic decision-making power from the state, from the advocates of the Great Society and from traditional Keynesian economics, and hand them over to the free market.

In poorer nations, the neoliberal golden straitjacket often means imperatives by the World Bank and International Monetary Fund (IMF) to reduce government subsidies for education and health care, privatize state-owned firms, liberalize trade, devalue currencies, emphasize production of primary goods for export, and deregulate financial and labor markets. The underlying logic is that market competition ensures efficient production of goods and services, and that market deregulation stimulates productive economic activity that benefits all in the long term. Friedman portrays those who do not celebrate this new economic order's competitive realities as "irrational backlashers" destined for Darwinian failure.

While urging everyone to jump on the globalization train, however, Friedman acknowledges that "both the booms and the busts will be coming faster," and he hopes that the entire system does not collapse (p. 462). Although he wishes he could slow this train down, "there's no one at the controls," and the system is "so new and so fast" that no one really "understands how it works and what happens when you pull a lever here or turn a dial there" (pp. 343, 459).

In addition to praising a system that, he concedes, risks catastrophic breakdown, Friedman argues that it is pointless to try to fight the powerful lobbies of American banks or to imagine a global central bank to regulate the global economy the way the U.S. Federal Reserve manages the American economy. Instead he finds hope in the market's capacity to discipline itself, noting that the 1998–1999 financial crises led to the ouster of chief executives of some of the world's largest banks and prompted many major banks to demand more transparency from those to whom they lend and to implement more serious risk management techniques. Such ad hoc approaches, he says, will have to suffice "until the day when some new global financial regulatory system can be erected" (460–61). In short, his advice is to let the market work as it will and not to be unrealistic about change.

Just as Friedman considers globalization to be an inevitable and positive force, he views resistance to it as an act of irrationality or ignorance. People either "get it," embrace globalization in its current guise, and join the "fast world," or they are ignorant "turtles" (his terms) left out of the race. There are two extremes in Friedman's world: that of the Lexus and that of the olive tree. Inspired by his visit to a Tokyo car factory where sixty-six human beings and 310 robots each day produce three hundred Lexus sedans, Friedman sees half the post–cold war world as "intent on building a better Lexus, dedicated to modernizing, streamlining and privatizing their economies in order to thrive in the system of globalization" (p. 31). The other half of the world is "still caught up in the fight over who owns which olive tree." Olive trees, he suggests, represent "everything that roots us, anchors us, identifies us, and locates us in this world—whether it be belonging to a family, a community, a tribe, a nation, a religion, or most of all, a place called home" (p. 31).

In Friedman's shorthand, then, the tale of globalization is a struggle between Lexus and olive tree, and the two must be kept in a "healthy balance." Yet in many respects, Friedman suggests, the outcome of the story is already known. Although olive trees should survive, and although the Lexus threatens the olive tree and so may provoke a "backlash" from the protectors of the tree, "sooner or later the Lexus always catches up with you" (p. 39).

His analytic vision thus circumscribed by the modern Lexus, on the one hand, and the ancient olive tree, on the other, Friedman ridicules those who dare to imagine more humane, environmentally safe, and democratic forms of globalization. In his view, those who protest the economic status quo are, at best, myopic denizens of olive groves. His descriptions of them are often much harsher.

Such language sells newspapers and books and has helped to make Friedman a visible television commentator on the Public Broadcasting System's *NewsHour, Washington Week in Review*, and elsewhere. Corporate leaders, financial analysts, and mainstream policy makers are likely to appreciate his arguments about the inevitability of the golden straitjacket, or neoliberal form of economic globalization, and his idea that globalization is the "one big thing" on which people should focus in order to understand the post–cold war world. Indeed most mainstream media representations of globalization are deferential toward big business and downplay the negative effects of neoliberal economic policies on education, health, and the environment; the reduction of labor's share in income; the astonishing rise in economic inequality; and the increasing power of corporations with little accountability to the public. Friedman has easy access to the powerful: in the acknowledgments to *The Lexus and the Olive Tree*, among those he particularly thanks are former treasury secretaries Lawrence Summers and Robert Rubin, the World Bank president James Wolfensohn, the vice chairman of Goldman Sachs, the chairs of Monsanto and Cisco Systems, members of the Davos World Economic Forum, and the Federal Reserve chairman, Alan Greenspan.

His stock is not so high with most academics. For example, political scientist Mark Rupert of Syracuse University; Rupert writes on his Website that "Friedman is frequently mistaken for an authority on globalization." Rupert notes Friedman's failure to engage the "vibrant scholarly literature on globalization" or to take seriously the alternatives to standard economic neoliberalism that are more democratic, sustainable, and egalitarian, put forward by an emerging global civil society of nongovernmental organizations, activist groups, and others.

Friedman sides with so-called realists who understand the status quo and the weighty forces that define the distribution of power and wealth, and who urge individuals to figure out how to profit from the system as it is. In belittling people who struggle to improve globalization by striving for better wages, labor rights, food-safety standards, and environmental safeguards, Friedman—whether intentionally or not—affirms the power and ostensible rationality of the elite architects of the status quo. Such a stance ignores a rich history of successful struggles against seemingly inexorable forces such as racism, sexism, environmental destruction, economic exploitation, and abuse of power.

Friedman describes himself as "a tourist with attitude," and he says he has the "best job in the world" as foreign affairs columnist for the *New York Times*. Is being a "tourist with attitude" enough to provide useful insight into issues of such profound importance? Admittedly anthropology, like journalism, has its touristic moments, but both anthropologists and journalists must do more than tell travel stories. They must work to understand and interpret other places and lives, try to balance objectivity and subjectivity, and acknowledge observer biases and effects as they record, describe, and analyze. Both anthropologists and journalists must make judgments about what is worth reporting, but anthropologists know that they should do so only after immersion in the social communities and networks they analyze. Moreover, anthropological research carries the professional imperative of systematic collection of information from individuals in a variety of situations, and careful attention to the kinds of biases that can accompany the selection of interviewees. An anthropologist's observations during extended field research offer opportunities to test inferences and conclusions and to complicate, enrich, and refine them. Without expecting journalists to become anthropologists, the former can learn from the work of the latter. So how might an anthropologist approach the task Friedman took on, that of making sense of globalization?

FRIEDMAN'S FLAWS

At first glance, Friedman's globetrotting approach might seem similar to that of modern anthropologists who have shed their discipline's earlier attachment to long-term field research, as both participant and observer, in a single, out-of-the-way locale. Today many anthropologists prefer multisite field research, which means that those studying economic development and social change in a Kenyan or Zambian village may now find it useful to interview not only African villagers but also migrants to New York and Lusaka, as well as project managers for the UN's Food and Agriculture Organization and the World Bank in Rome and Washington. Contemporary anthropology also values ethnographic writing that includes revelations about the author, as well as unstaged dialogues between the anthropologist and those being studied. Many anthropologists today are skeptical empiricists who find those authors who frankly express their own opinions or biases, and reveal their own effects on the data they collect, more credible than those scholars of human behavior who claim to be neutral, objective, or value-free observers. Friedman, too, pugnaciously declares what he thinks in a way many readers find engaging, and his prose is similarly enlivened by his reporting of such dialogue and self-revelations. Indeed, anthropologists may find Friedman annoying precisely because his work has some of the trappings of "a seductive, and thus extremely effective, form of the ethnography of globalization to which many of us vaguely aspire." Yet no serious anthropologist would recommend to students Friedman's approach. Seen through an anthropological lens, Friedman's work on globalization contains a number of fatal flaws.

Overly Narrow Observational Frame

Friedman's disposition to view the 1999 Seattle protesters as "crazy" and "ridiculous" prevents him from exploring their perspectives and aims; he simply overwhelms the reader with his own. Anthropologists, on the other hand, are judged by how deeply they penetrate or make sense of the motivations and behavior of others. Thus they are trained not to rely too heavily on a narrow segment of the population under study; rather they must observe and interview widely and record, describe, and analyze an event from multiple perspectives. The write-up should be a respectful portrait rather than a caricature.

Friedman fails anthropologists' test, then, by substituting ridicule for careful observation and analysis of others' understandings and aims. That error is compounded by his apparently heavy reliance on elite, mainstream sources in business and government and his failure to explore any but the most distant connections to other types of people. His book *The Lexus and the Olive Tree* depicts how the world's less fortunate peoples experience globalization through anecdotes and vignettes gleaned from Friedman's brief stays abroad, usually in luxury hotels in capital cities. (This globetrotting approach differs sharply from that of his earlier book, *From Beirut to Jerusalem*, which was based on many years in the Middle East.) Friedman's easy access to elites contrasts the way that the less privileged enter his global framework: through his casual conversations with street vendors, hotel clerks, room service waiters, shoe shiners, cooks, and other tourist service workers whose lives are profoundly affected by (and who also help to shape) the globalization processes he describes. Anthropologists too must deal with uneven access to different categories of people, but Friedman does not appear to have made much effort to overcome this bias in his sources. Moreover, what he does convey would be more persuasive if his own opinions did not obliterate those of so many other people who do cross his path.

Tradition Misunderstood

Friedman views tradition as an obstacle to progress, a romanticized domain to be protected, or a source of destructive backlash. Anthropologists, on the other hand, view tradition as a dynamic, adaptable, complex set of meanings and symbols manipulated to serve present interests and needs. Friedman appears captivated by misleading notions of an inevitable clash between a frozen "tradition," on the one hand (symbolized by the "olive tree"), and "modernity" (the Lexus), on the other. Missing the subtleties and complex capabilities of tradition (and culture), Friedman misrepresents resistance to some forms of economic globalization as simply a stark refusal of "modernity." Anthropologists, by contrast, recognize that resistance may very well signal rejection not of modernity per se but of the social injustices, environmental destruction, and brutal economic inequality that can accompany industrialization and economic neoliberalism. Viewing resistance simplistically as mere rejection of change or modernity leaves Friedman blind to profound historical processes and social movements that are redefining our era. He thus misses the main story.

Friedman simply fails to see the dynamism of societies that appear to him as static relics of an ancient past, such as when he gazes out his train window in Egypt and imagines that the "barefoot villagers" are contemporary survivors of the Egypt of 2000 B.C. (p. 339). In his perception, a dichotomy exists between two rigidly separate worlds: that of the constantly ringing cell phones in his train car full of forward-looking middle- and upper-class Egyptians, and that of the "barefoot Egyptian villagers...tilling their fields with the same tools and water buffalo that their ancestors used in Pharaoh's day." The latter image of what he takes to be a static "traditional" Egypt of course is utterly false: it is contradicted by Egypt's long history of agricultural innovation, production increases, economic growth, labor migration, and participation in farflung trading networks. The sharp dichotomy he imagines between two worlds—one traditional and the other on the globalization train—obscures the dense networks of social and economic relationships and reciprocities that actually bind these worlds together.

The force of such ties is illustrated, for example, in anguished questions put to him by educated Egyptians, such as a woman who asks, "Does globalization mean we just leave the poor to fend for themselves?" Or an Egyptian professor who wonders, "How do we privatize when we have no safety nets?" (p. 341). Friedman does not directly answer these questions, but instead tells us that such conversations led him to realize that "most Egyptians—understandably—were approaching globalization out of a combination of despair and necessity, not out of any sense of opportunity.... When you tell a traditional society it has to streamline, downsize, and

get with the Internet, it is a challenge that is devoid of any redemptive or inspirational force." Again, in Friedman's world, people either embrace contemporary (neoliberal) globalization and join the "fast world," or they are ignorant "turtles" left out of the race. If the government's social safety nets are shredded in the process, or if the capacity to create such safety nets is eliminated, or if ties to one's rural cousins must be broken, so be it.

Ethnicity and Culture Misconceived

Friedman sees ethnicity as cultural attachment to ancient identities (the olive trees again). Ethnicity, to him, is a potent natural and primordial source of conflict that must be contained. Contemporary anthropology, on the other hand, emphasizes the modern political and economic origins of conflicts often labeled as ethnic. Ethnic identities are not primordial, essential differences but—like any supposed traditions—manipulable symbols and dynamic understandings, myths, and narratives. Individuals may accentuate, efface, or disguise ethnicity: like any identity, it is situationally contingent. Friedman, however, clings to outdated stereotypes of ethnic conflict. Indeed, in his schema entire countries can be "olive trees," a characterization he attributes to Rwanda.

In briefly discussing genocide in Rwanda, Friedman invokes stereotypes of a country emerging from "an orgy of tribal warfare." He calls it a place where "Tutsi and Hutu tribesmen [have] tak[en] turns downsizing each other to grab more resources for themselves." He does not mention the ways modern political party competition, regional (not just ethnic) oppositions within Rwanda, patronage politics, hate radio, and governmental structures all helped to fuel the 1994 genocide which was carried out by well-organized extremist militias using lists of targeted individuals drawn up years before. The genocide was made possible by the capacities of a strong state that had received substantial external support when it adopted precisely the kinds of neoliberal economic policies Friedman praises. In short, far from being an atavistic resurgence of "ancient tribal hatreds," the genocide emerged from very modern political and economic forces. Those contemporary political and economic complexities, however, seem to have escaped Friedman, who instead lazily invokes familiar stereotypes of perennial conflict in a "tribal" Africa. He ignores the many careful, scholarly accounts of the Rwanda genocide produced by anthropologists, historians, and political scientists as well as Friedman's fellow journalist, Philip Gourevitch. To reduce the modern political complexities of Africa—or any region—to "ancient animosities" or simplistic tribal or ethnic conflicts is not only misleading but also dangerous when they inform U.S. foreign policy or become an official pretext for inaction.

The Ethical Bankruptcy of Blind Faith in Markets

Friedman asserts that "countries basically get the economic outcomes they deserve" (pp. 455–56). This position makes no allowance for the unequal starting positions of countries, classes, or individuals in today's race to globalize. Does he believe that a child born into poverty in Ethiopia or Haiti or Peru gets the outcome she or he "deserves?" The ethical bankruptcy of that argument is obscured by Friedman's portrayal of the economic system as "rational" (notwithstanding his concession that it risks spinning out of control and leaving casualties in its wake).

Friedman does acknowledge that globalization impoverishes as well as enriches, and it disempowers as well as empowers. He insists nonetheless that free trade and globalization offer the poor the "best ladder out of misery," and does so with a fine disregard for what scholars term *structural violence*— widespread hunger, disease, and unemployment— caused or exacerbated by economic neoliberalism.

Moreover, it is simplistic to talk as if markets are entirely "free," unfettered, or unshaped by government laws. An anthropologist might inquire instead, Who benefits from the rules that define market competition? Who has the power to define the rules? Government intervention in the market is an everyday practice; without it we would lack many of the services, goods, and protections many of us take for granted, such as relatively safe food,

water, and workplaces. But, the anthropologist might ask, What political dynamics encourage vilification of poor recipients of welfare benefits while winking at government assistance for wealthy corporations? Why do most free market cheerleaders not condemn tax breaks or subsidies for developers of a sports stadium or government bailouts of failing airlines? Economic neoliberalism as both theoretical edifice and societal vision deserves careful scrutiny rather than enshrinement. Even that iconic champion of the market, Adam Smith, cautioned against low wages, too sudden removal of protectionist tariffs, and the runaway greed of the powerful.

By treating a particular form of economic globalization as if it were natural and inevitable, and then hyping it, Friedman also rationalizes the growing poverty of much of the world's population, as well as environmental destruction, human rights and labor abuses, and denial of basic freedoms to people who inconvenience the large corporations, the focus of nearly all his deferential attention. His view seems to be that nothing should stand in the way of corporatism—a powerful partnership of transnational corporations, global regulatory and financial institutions, and the state (which offers corporations contracts for weapons, antibiotics, prison management, and security services). Friedman's world citizens in turn are reduced to consumers or brand boycotters who can protest only with their wallets—assuming they have anything in them.

Friedman weaves symbols such as the Lexus and the olive tree into seductive tales based on false pictures of "free" markets and about the Other: the region, country, or individual that differs from "us." His picture of the olive tree is particularly distorted: into the olive grove, he dumps an improbable array of phenomena, including the politics of conservation, consumer protection, welfarism, labor, human rights, culture, nationalism, and ethnicity. Although, astonishingly, he makes them all expressions of something he labels "tradition," they are—to the contrary—profoundly important forces of change.

Anthropologists have, in fact, for several decades analyzed how those who resist or challenge status quo inequalities of race, class, and gender may contribute to change that is ultimately progressive. There is no reason, and Friedman does not offer one, to assume along with Friedman that resistance to the golden straitjacket is necessarily ignorant, regressive, irrational, or foolish.

Friedman romanticizes and demonizes the olive grove and treats it as a repository of all that is irrational, but he never analyzes it with attentiveness or insight. His narrow observational framework, his misconceptions of culture and tradition, and his refusal to take a morally grounded point of view all produce a globalization narrative that is more panegyric than analysis, more fiction than truth, more arrogance than understanding. For Friedman, there is nothing to be done about globalization except to proclaim it to be inevitable and desirable and then celebrate.

But the term *globalization* need not be limited to international financial markets, capital flows, and Disney-fication; instead, it could also signify an increasing capacity for political alliances and declarations that transcend the nation-state. Imagine that we identify as "globalizers" precisely those village societies that Friedman deprecates for being rooted like olive groves, together with the new transnations they constitute with migrants in the industrialized North and the complex traffic in culture, social ties, and cash remittances that connects them. How then might we reread Friedman, drawing on anthropological evidence and approaches?

THE LEXUS AND THE . . .
MIGRANT? SHANTYTOWN?
SWEATSHOP?

First, let us replace Friedman's imaginary notion of who inhabits olive groves with some real people: for example, rural and urban East Africans (Kenyans), among whom I have carried out field research at various times during the past two decades. Even rural Kenyans do not fit Friedman's binary between modernity and isolated olive groves of tradition. Many Kenyans are on the move

between town and countryside, office job and farm, small business and outdoor market, constantly adjusting to rapid economic and political shifts and careful to diversify their economic activities. Small-scale farmers in central Kenya keep an eye on world coffee prices and frosts in Brazil that might signal higher prices for their exports. Many sustain relationships with relatives and friends abroad, some of whom have used the Internet to create international networks and discussion groups. Rural-urban migration patterns once thought to be one-way, from countryside to city, no longer are seen to be so, as urban economic decline sends migrants back to rural areas, and as growing numbers of urban civil servants who have retired or lost their jobs (often as a result of retrenchment mandated by the IMF and World Bank) decide to move back to the countryside.

Familial, social, and economic relations underwrite networks of reciprocity linking rich and poor, educated and uneducated, city dweller and farmer. Such relations of sociality, reciprocity, and clientage often are strengthened rather than attenuated by agrarian commercialization, industrialization, and globalization (the opposite of what earlier evolutionary models of social and economic change predicted). Rural land rights, even if one possesses an official title deed, often are not more secure or predictable than urban employment or business or other income. Thus, urban workers attempt to maintain rights in rural land, which entails material and social exchanges with rural kin and acquaintances. Uncertain economies, institutions, and politics place a premium on flexibility and encourage people to multiply social relationships and networks in order to acquire and safeguard access to markets, credit, and laborers. It is advantageous to spread one's risks by cultivating access to a range of people, resources, and income-earning opportunities.

Many educated urban Kenyans whom Friedman might characterize as having joined the "fast world" do not embrace globalization in its current neoliberal guise. Rather, they worry about deteriorating infrastructure (such as roads in disrepair or unreliable phone and electrical services), growing poverty and economic inequality, and declining access to health care and education following reductions in government spending and imposition of user fees for social services. These Kenyans who oppose standard neoliberal policies do not fit easily into Friedman's categories: neither ignorant "turtles" nor sentimental denizens of isolated olive groves, they are informed citizens who resent their government's diminished control over its own economic policies due to IMF and World Bank intervention.

Looking beyond Kenya, we can find others who are not part of the Lexus class but who do not sit under the olive tree either. A recent survey of popular attitudes to markets in four African countries—Ghana, Malawi, Nigeria, and Zimbabwe—found that substantial majorities were dissatisfied with their government's structural adjustment programs mandated by the IMF and World Bank, and that they disagreed with the statement that government policies in the era of structural adjustment have helped most people. Some distinguished economists share that opinion, including former supporters of neoliberal economic policies. Joseph Stiglitz, a Nobel Prize–winning economist and former chief economist at the World Bank, has criticized the economic consequences of standard IMF policies in Asia and elsewhere. Jeffrey Sachs, a former supporter of structural adjustment programs, has become a prominent advocate of the Jubilee 2000 debt cancellation movement.

Today nearly half the world's population lives on less than two dollars per capita per day. By the mid-1990s, the wealth of the world's 447 billionaires was valued at $1.1 trillion, which was equivalent to the total income of the poorest half of the world's population. By 1998 the combined assets of the world's wealthiest three billionaires exceeded the total gross national product of all the least developed countries and their 600 million citizens. The wealthiest fifth of the world's people receives over four-fifths of the world's income. The poorest 60 percent receives only 6 percent of the world's income. The golden straitjacket Friedman touts not only has failed to offer a solution to growing poverty and rising economic inequality but also does not even recognize them as problems.

Instead it grants extraordinary freedom to corporations accountable only to their most powerful shareholders.

This sketch only hints at the complexities of globalization, such as the capacities for reform as well as violence of a postcolonial state controlled by historically advantaged elite classes, and the viability of nationalisms that envision strong states capable of resisting or reshaping IMF and World Bank conditions. Those who protest the status quo sometimes have contradictory agendas, and these too require careful study rather than Friedman-style ridicule or dismissal.

Friedman's misleading caricature of opposition between the Lexus and the olive tree, or between one kind of "modernity" and a supposedly static tradition, should be replaced with more accurate symbols. Friedman's binary vision obscures vital struggles under way—not over the protection of isolated olive groves of tradition but over social justice and economic opportunity on global as well as local scales. Perhaps he—or we—should be looking at the Lexus and the migrant, the shantytown, or the sweatshop.

REFORMING THE GLOBAL MARKET?

Now let us imagine anthropological alternatives to Friedman's narrow observational frame in looking at the 1999 WTO protests in Seattle. Instead of simply dismissing the protesters as lunatics, an anthropologist would ask questions: How does the WTO work and why do some favor reforming it or abolishing it? How and with what consequences does the WTO exercise its power to overturn a country's laws protecting environmental or health standards in the name of international free trade? What political inequalities are embedded in the sorts of trade negotiations that provoke growing criticism from poorer nations that would, for example, like to see an end to some European and North American farm subsidies?

An anthropologist also would want to know what modes of organization characterized the 1999 Seattle protesters. In Seattle in 1999, broad coalitions of labor, environmental, farm, and human rights groups called for a less secretive and more democratic WTO; some demonstrators wanted to abolish the WTO, others to reform it. What alternative visions of globalization inspired thousands of protesters from around the world to march through the streets of Seattle? Why did the anti-WTO demonstrations draw together such unlikely allies as the United Steelworkers of America and the Rainforest Action Network? Here was a chance to examine both the obstacles and the possibilities facing such movements. An anthropologist would explore the political networks and organizational modes that produced the street theater in Seattle as well-organized and peaceful "turtle" marchers formed an improbable alliance with teamsters, with shouts of "turtles love Teamsters!" and "Teamsters love turtles!"

Friedman, however, shunned such knowledge or inquiry. His first critical column on the Seattle protests, for example, does not address at all the issues raised by the protestors concerning WTO secrecy and lack of democratic accountability. Friedman dismisses the Seattle protesters' concerns about the broad impact of WTO rulings. He mentions just one example of the type of ruling protesters find problematic, and terms it a "narrow case": namely, the WTO ruling that the U.S. prohibition on catching tuna in nets that also trap dolphins was an illegal barrier to trade. He suggests that it is "nonsense" to conclude from such rulings that the WTO "is going to become a Big Brother and tell us how to live generally."

Friedman suggests that, rather than targeting the WTO and urging it to set different rules, the protesters should recognize that the global market itself encourages reform. Here he cites Microsoft's application of pressure on Sri Lanka by refusing to sell its products there until the latter passed stronger intellectual property laws. He also points to reforms achieved through the "hard work of coalition-building with companies and consumers," by, for example, showing corporations how they can be "both green and profitable." Thus he notes that DuPont and Victoria's Secret modified their practices in response to pressures from activist groups who mobilize consumers and who publicize environmental damage or harsh child labor or sweatshop conditions on the World Wide Web. Friedman contrasts such Web-based tactics with the Seattle protesters' "1960s tactics," accusing them of the "fool's errand" of "blocking trade, choking globalization or getting the WTO to put up more walls." In reality, however, many of the activist groups represented in the Seattle protests exercise precisely the kinds of consumer mobilization and Web-based tactics Friedman praises, and many of their battles have yielded the kinds of reforms and democratically enacted laws that the WTO has the power to overturn. Friedman presents contradictory arguments about when activism is appropriate and what it should look like.

A week after his "Senseless in Seattle" column on the WTO protests, Friedman returned with "Senseless in Seattle II," in which he reported that he had checked every can of tuna in his local supermarket and found that they were all labeled "dolphin safe" notwithstanding the WTO ruling that the law requiring this was an illegal barrier to free trade. The dolphin-safe tuna he credits to "smart activists" who ignored the international trade body's ruling and mobilized consumers to put economic pressure on the tuna companies. Mexican fishermen, not wishing to lose customers, responded to these pressures by using dolphin-safe nets.

When the save-the-dolphins-from-tuna-nets activists first mobilized a couple of decades ago, however, one could expect from his other writing that Friedman would have dismissed them as hopeless idealists. The activists' success in this instance (assuming—possibly a stretch—that the tuna labels are true) may have depended in part on the affection American consumers already had for dolphins. If securing more humane, healthy, and environmentally friendly forms of globalization depends on intangibles such as which mammals Americans find charismatic, then the reform tactics favored by Friedman will often fail. Reforming globalization demands diverse tactics and forms of struggle; these deserve to be documented and analyzed.

By mid-2001, Friedman began to suggest that the "serious protesters" (those concerned with how we globalize) had made their point, and he, urged them to "design solutions in partnership with big businesses and governments." Such a formulation has unfortunate affinities with the "constructive engagement" posture of apartheid apologists some years ago, and today it might simply be called "corporatism": the assumption that huge corporations, states, trade unions, and consumer groups can reconcile their competing (never contradictory) interests in a manner that will improve the welfare and prosperity of everyone. Corporate scandals in the United States, such as Enron's meltdown and public revelations about top executives of other firms who prospered during their company's decline or collapse, as thousands of employees lost their livelihoods or retirement funds, suggest a much darker view of the potential Friedman sees in ordinary citizens' partnerships with big business.

In 2003, global trade dilemmas that derailed the 1999 WTO meeting in Seattle again surfaced spectacularly as world trade talks collapsed in Cancun. Representatives of many poor countries were elated at their success in banding together

this time and standing up to the rich countries that refused to eliminate their farm export subsidies. Others warned that poor countries would suffer most from the failed negotiating round in Cancun. Yet even *The Economist* termed rich countries' farm subsidies "grotesque" and noted that "America's unwillingness to curb its cotton subsidies—which have an especially severe effect on poor-country producers—is unforgivable. So too is Japan's unyielding defence of its own swaddled rice farmers." Nongovernmental organizations such as Oxfam helped to shine a spotlight on the crushing effects of rich-country cotton subsidies on poor cotton farmers in West Africa. In short, global markets are far from free and open, and the challenges of constructing a fair multilateral trade system remain enormous. In addition to the subsidy hypocrisies and corporate scandals, the costs of globalization in its present form are starkly apparent in the colossal and continuing loss of U.S. jobs to countries where labor is much cheaper and where environmental and worker protections are weaker. These challenges demand attention to more humane forms of globalization (not alternatives to globalization). Far from meriting Friedman's ridicule or smug dismissal, activists in the global movement for social justice deserve praise for sounding an alarm about a careening economic globalization train.

DISCUSSION QUESTIONS

1. How would you define the term "globalization"? How does your definition differ from that of Angelique Haugerud and Thomas Friedman?

2. In what ways do peasants in Kenya differ from Friedman's notion of the "olive tree" people?

3. Summarize three of Angelique Haugerud's criticisms of Friedman's conceptualization of "globalization."

RESOURCES ON THE INTERNET

InfoTrac College Edition

infotrac-college.com

You can find further relevant readings by searching *InfoTrac College Edition*, an online library with access to thousands of scholarly and popular periodicals. Below are suggested search terms for this article:

- globalization
- deregulation
- privatization
- International Monetary Fund (IMF)

Anthropology Online: Wadsworth's Anthropology Resource Center

academic.cengage.com/anthropology

The Wadsworth Anthropology Resource Center contains a wealth of information and useful tools for students including information on careers in anthropology.